MW00476571

The Tainted Muse

THE TAINTED MUSE

Prejudice and Presumption
in Shakespeare and His Time

ROBERT BRUSTEIN

Yale University Press   New Haven and London

Published with assistance from the foundation established in memory
of Philip Hamilton McMillan of the Class of 1894, Yale College.

Set in Electra Roman types by Tseng Information Systems, Inc.
Durham, North Carolina.
Printed in the United States of America by Sheridan Books,
Ann Arbor, Michigan.

Library of Congress Cataloging-in-Publication Data
Brustein, Robert Sanford, 1927–
The tainted muse : prejudice and presumption in Shakespeare
and his time / Robert Brustein.
p.   cm.
Includes bibliographical references and index.
ISBN 978-0-300-11576-5 (cloth : alk. paper) 1. Shakespeare, William,
1564–1616—Characters. 2. Prejudices in literature. 3. Misogyny in
literature. 4. Stereotypes (Social psychology) in literature. 5. Characters
and characteristics in literature. I. Title. II. Title: Prejudice and
presumption in Shakespeare and his time.
PR2989.B78 2009
822.3'3—dc22
2008046997

A catalogue record for this book is available from the British Library.

This paper meets the requirements of ANSI/NISO z39.48–1992
(Permanence of Paper). It contains 30 percent postconsumer waste
(PCW) and is certified by the Forest Stewardship Council (FSC).

10   9   8   7   6   5   4   3   2   1

For the students who helped me explore Shakespeare; for the scholars who helped me understand him; for the actors who helped me love him And always for Doreen.

CONTENTS

Introduction

In Hamlet, act IV, scene iv, the Danish Prince reflects on a seemingly purposeless adventure by saying, "This is th' imposthume of much wealth and peace,/That inward breaks, and shows no cause without/Why the man dies." I have always been taken by that physiological and metaphorical image of an imposthume—a canker or tumor—that can deeply affect one's health without showing any outward sign or apparent cause.

Indeed, it may be a way to describe the workings of Shakespeare's plays, where an inner pain results in an outer burst of creation, and where certain prejudices, predispositions, and obsessions find their way into the souls of his characters. Hitherto we have identified such qualities with Shakespeare's plays, but rarely with Shakespeare himself. When Hamlet, pretending madness, warns Polonius against the danger of Ophelia's conceiving out of wedlock, and her father replies, "Still harping on my daughter," it is obvious that Hamlet is obsessed, just as it is later obvious that Othello and Leontes are obsessed, with the infidelity of womankind. But are these fixations solely the characteristics of fictional dramatic characters, or do they reveal a condition of their author?

Normally, we think of Shakespeare as standing apart, detached and aloof, paring his nails—the classic example of the detached observer. Yet certain prejudices and obsessions sometimes leap out of his plays and enter the realm of social and moral discourse, springing, as it were, from the root of a hidden imposthume. For example, many postmodernists think the antifemale attitudes of some Shakespeare characters often come perilously close to prejudice, which one dictionary defines as "a preformed opinion, usually an unfavorable one, based on insufficient knowledge, irrational feelings, or inaccurate stereotypes." Stereotyping races and nationalities is a tendency just one step short of bigotry, defined as "intolerance toward people who hold different views, especially on matters of politics, religion, or ethnicity." Shakespeare certainly wrote about such intolerant people, but did he share their narrow views? Was he as anti-Semitic as Antonio in *The Merchant of Venice,* as racist as Bassianus in *Titus Andronicus,* as imperialist as Prospero in *The Tempest*? One might accuse Marlowe of such narrowness, and possibly Ben Jonson, but Shakespeare? For if obsession could be construed as an imposthume of character (or nature), a quality that separates you from your contemporaries, prejudice is more an imposthume of the environment (or nurture), a canker that you share with your time.

There is no doubt that Shakespeare occasionally created characters who reflect the assumptions of a prejudiced age — Shylock the Jew comes to mind, and Aaron the Moor in *Titus Andronicus.* But Shylock and Aaron are ethnic villains derived from Marlowe's caricatured Jew and cartoon Moor, Barabas and Ithamore in *The Jew of Malta,* and however derivative they may be, each of Shakespeare's characters reveals more humanity than his supremely evil prototype. Moreover, one has only to measure the satanic Aaron in *Titus,* for example, against the engaging Prince of Aragon in *Merchant* or the big-hearted Othello in order to note that Shakespeare held many different attitudes toward dark-skinned people. Characters like Shylock and Aaron are products of a commonly shared prejudice rather than individual bigotry, insofar as the Elizabethan period was almost routinely anti-Semitic and racist, and Shakespeare was hardly a rebel against the beliefs of his day.

In short, while these characters may seem politically incorrect to us, they are surely historically correct in Shakespeare's time. Theodore Dalrymple, in his *In Praise of Prejudice,* correctly observes that "to overturn a prejudice isn't to destroy prejudice as such. It is rather to inculcate another prejudice." Dalrymple's vigorous defense of preconceived ideas is a challenge to our habit of patronizing the beliefs of our ancestors, where too often we criticize the values of another age in order to prove the superiority of our own. On the other hand, while Shakespeare's predispositions and prejudices are clearly the products of his time, this book will occasionally propose, admittedly without conclusive proof, that they may be a result of his personal convictions and experiences as well.

Bardolaters would say that *prejudice* is too harsh a word with which to describe such a generous, large-hearted artist. It certainly seems odd to charge William Shakespeare with "insufficient knowledge" or "irrational feelings," or to accuse such a master of character of creating "inaccurate stereotypes" or making narrow, inflexible generalizations about other human beings. To believe so is to risk making narrow, inflexible generalizations about Shakespeare himself. Certainly, every time one tries to capture this subtle poet, he escapes the categorical net, eluding our poor efforts to define or confine him. Without doubt, there is danger in speculating about the personal convictions of a dramatist so various and universal that he seems not one but rather hundreds of men, all of them already thoroughly analyzed and investigated. At the end of a long book called *Shakespeare the Thinker,* A. D. Nuttall makes the poignant admission, "We do not know what he thought, finally, about anything."

Of course, we know what his characters thought, and one must resist the temptation to attribute to Shakespeare the opinions of his fictional creations. Still, despite this acknowledged danger, a number of recent biographies and critical studies have been devoted to just this kind of speculation about Shakespeare's own beliefs. After Nuttall's *Shakespeare the Thinker in 2007*, the year 2008 produced Philip Davis's *Shakespeare Thinking* and Barry Edelstein's *Thinking Shakespeare*. All of a sudden, everybody seemed to be exploring the contents of Shakespeare's mind. This examination, along with new information and new insights into his life by historicist scholars, has encouraged me to stake out my own claims. With the help of these studies, I believe it is now possible to excavate some of Shakespeare's ongoing emotional and intellectual obsessions, convictions, yes, and prejudices, that "hidden imposthume" that motivates those feelings, whether central or marginal to the plays themselves.

I fully realize the dangers of such an endeavor. Chief among them is the literary sin of the intentional fallacy. How often have we been warned to separate the dancer from the dance (or the creator from his creation), to distinguish between what a dramatist believes and what a dramatic character says? For decades, Classical critics have been trying to correct the Romantic notion that artists wrote out of subjective states of mind. T. S. Eliot, preeminently, insisted that "the more perfect the artist, the more completely separate in him will be the man who suffers and the mind which creates," offering the improbable example of Henry James, who had "a mind so fine that no mere idea could ever penetrate it."[1]

Eliot had considerable respect for such "impersonal" Stuart dramatists as Thomas Middleton, and professed to admire the same dispassionate qualities in Shakespeare. And it may be that impersonality is a crucial characteristic of artists who compose in dialogue, a shorthand way by which to distinguish the dramatist, who always writes of others, from the lyric poet, who usually writes of the self, or from the epic poet, who generally writes about the self in relation to others. Still, I believe one can find a sufficient number of instances in Shakespeare's plays when he seems to be scratching at a particular sore, when an extreme statement, supported neither by the plot nor by the character, breaks through the skin of the dramatic action, when the man who suffers seems at one with the man who creates.

Actors call this the "emotional subtext," a buried motive that indicates what a character feels rather than what a character says. *Hamlet,* for example, is so dominated by subtext, which is to say by unrepressed subjectivity (or obsessions), that Eliot called the play "most certainly an artistic failure." He famously rejected it for lacking an "objective correlative," thereby dismissing, as being insufficiently impersonal, the very qualities that make the work so tantalizing and powerful. But *Hamlet* is not alone in combining such tensions. The presence of a subjective subtext colliding with, and sometimes undermining, an objective design can be found often enough in Shakespeare to suggest that this most elusive and evasive playwright did indeed suffer from a hidden imposthume.

Was this occasionally a form of prejudice? I think it was, keeping in mind the fact that prejudices are received ideas that have not yet been subjected to rational or scientific examination. In a notable essay, Lionel Trilling defined "The Meaning of a Literary Idea" as "what comes into being when two contradictory emotions are made to confront each other and are required to have a relationship with each other."[2] The confrontation between the dramatic and the extradramatic, between the public demands of the play and the private obsessions of the playwright, between the objective design of the plot and the subjective pull of the subtext, are the tensions I hope to examine in this book.

This collision of emotions issuing in an obsession is clearly what James Joyce had in mind when he constructed a whole chapter of *Ulysses* ("Scylla and Charybdis," also called "the Library sequence") out of the theory that Shakespeare's plays are driven by a highly personal agenda. Joyce's surrogate hero, Stephen Dedalus, pursues a thread of sexual betrayal from play to play, concluding that Shakespeare's "unremitting intellect is the hornmad Iago ceaselessly willing that the Moor in him shall suffer." Some of these speculations are highly fanciful. When asked whether he believes his own theories, Stephen blithely answers "No." Still, much of what he says is extremely revealing about the artist's relationship to his work. In trying to cast Shakespeare in his own image, Joyce, a highly autobiographical writer, contributes what I consider to be some of the deepest insights into Shakespeare's process.

One of Joyce's fancies is that the cuckolding of William Shakespeare (like that of Joyce's hero, Leopold Bloom) had a profound effect on his life and work. Certainly, Shakespeare's recurrent harping on female duplicity, and its consequence in the creation of male sex nausea, is a common theme of his plays, and it is one of the hidden imposthumes that I examine in this book. Shakespeare's sex hatred is a theme that, however unacceptable or repellent to our own age, is rampant in the Elizabethan-Jacobean period, almost its common currency. That is another reason to suspect that Stephen Dedalus was preternaturally astute, and that Shakespeare experienced it as well.

In what was perhaps Shakespeare's most famous epitaph, Ben Jonson, an admiring if often competitive rival, wrote that "He was not of an age, but for all time." Jonson was right — and he was wrong. Shakespeare's art is undeniably "for all time," which is to say eternal. But in the sense that his work is set in a historical moment, it is unquestionably contemporary ("of an age") as well. Many of Shakespeare's obsessions and prejudices are shared by his fellow dramatists, poets, and satirists, who document and echo them, often using similar language. Indeed, the uniqueness of Shakespeare can be partly attributed to the fact that his work proceeds along two parallel lines, the ageless and the immediate. Most Shakespeare criticism understandably emphasizes the first equation. In this book I shall concentrate more on the second, maintaining that this great dramatist is notable not just for powerful actions, memorable characters, and luminous verse but for opinions or convictions that continually mirror the moral, political, sexual, and metaphysical issues of his own period.

That he sometimes comes down on what most postmodern scholars would consider the wrong side of this equation should not prevent us from pursuing the examination. Rather than repelling us, an understanding of Shakespeare's historical prejudices will allow us to better understand his intentions. This act of understanding is becoming more and more necessary now that so many English Departments have transformed into Departments of Cultural Studies, one result being that Shakespeare, along with many other major writers, has fallen into decline in the academy. Despite his continued popularity on stage and in publishing houses, Shakespeare, according to a recent report, is no longer a requirement in fifty-five out of seventy leading American universities, where English majors can earn a bachelor of arts degree without having been required to read *Hamlet*.

Such neglect is one of the casualties of our postliterate age, but I suspect it is also a spoken or unspoken reaction to Shakespeare's historical obsessions, which is all the more reason to examine them. But there is also reason to proceed with caution, since any conclusions that might be formed about Shakespeare's beliefs can often be contradicted by evidence in his other plays—indeed, sometimes in the same play. I have noted that if Shakespeare tends to identify black Africans with devils, for example, as he does in *Titus Andronicus* and elsewhere, he is perfectly capable of imagining noble black men as well. A similar case could be made regarding his prejudices toward mannish females, democratic politics, and Jews, though I do not think he is as flexible about faithless women (almost always objects of revulsion), or effeminate courtiers (almost always objects of scorn), or plain-dealing soldiers (almost always objects of admiration). As for his attitudes toward religion, these are the most diverse and evolving ideas in his work. The important thing to recognize is that although Shakespeare may have transcended his time, he also reflected it, just as he reflected and occasionally transcended the age's prejudices and his own predispositions.

So what criteria have I used to define an obsession? To take the faithlessness of women as an example, first and foremost I note the *frequency* with which it is expressed, as in the recurrent outbursts against women by so many Shakespeare characters; second, the *vehemence* with which it is expressed, especially when the feelings break free from some private mooring or are confirmed in Shakespeare's more personal writing (such as the sonnets); and third, the *urgency* with which it is expressed, as in the case, say, of *Hamlet,* where the hero's brutal treatment of Ophelia far exceeds any justification for it in the plot.

To trace an obsession or a prejudice, I have examined not only its presence in individual plays but its progress from play to play. This sometimes has us looking at Shakespeare's work less as a body of individual works of art than as one long dramatic sequence where a variety of characters share similar or developing attitudes. My purpose is to examine how a prejudiced idea, or a obsessed character, evolves through various stages in the playwright's career, how or whether the fixation develops, and most important, how it is resolved, for Shakespeare's attitudes do not always remain entirely consistent throughout his career. With a subjective writer such as Strindberg, it is common procedure to examine his plays as a continuum, a kind of dramatic autobiography rooted in actual happenings. Although we know too little about Shakespeare to match his life with his art, I have tried wherever possible to draw a psychic biography of the man, examining how the obsessions of his characters and himself may have changed over the course of his career. I recognize this as a precarious endeavor. The reader will tell me how well or badly I have succeeded.

In the six chapters of this book, therefore, I examine what I perceive to be six central obsessions in Shakespeare's plays, as seen through his characters, themes, and actions. In the first, investigating Shakespeare's complicated attitudes toward the female sex ("Misogyny"), I take a look at the nature of some of his heroines and how they are often mistreated by his male characters. In the second, an analysis of Shakespeare's dislike of womanish men ("Effemiphobia"), I explore Shakespeare's ambivalence toward male love, and toward the flattering, circumlocutory, and always menacing upstart courtier. In my third chapter, regarding Shakespeare's notions of manliness ("Machismo"), I examine the playwright's affinity for the honest, blunt, straight-talking plain-dealer, usually a military man, showing how Shakespeare's plain-dealers evolve into the misanthropes and malcontents featured in such plays as *King Lear*, *Troilus and Cressida*, and most notably *Timon of Athens*.

In the fourth chapter, focusing on Shakespeare's political beliefs ("The Elite and Mobocracy"), I explore another of his ambiguous themes, his reverence toward monarchy and his suspicion of populism and democracy. In the fifth chapter ("Racialism") I deal with Shakespeare's attitudes toward blacks, Jews, and subjugated people. And in the final chapter ("Intelligent Design") I deal with Shakespeare's metaphysical and religious convictions, examining the evolving attitude of this playwright, probably born a Catholic and possibly still a recusant, toward ghosts and gods and the natural universe.

It may be noted that many of the terms in my chapter headings (*misogyny, effemiphobia, machismo, racialism, intelligent design,* and the like) are borrowed from the vocabulary of contemporary academic discourse rather than from any Elizabethan lexicon. My decision to use such postmodern language in an essentially historical study is deliberate—and somewhat mischievous. The terms serve two purposes. First, they emphasize how Shakespeare is being imported, willy-nilly, into our current scholastic debates. And second, they suggest how anachronistic it is to impose modern concepts onto the belief structure of a previous historical period.

I believe we must try to steer a path between the school of academics that embraces Shakespeare as a postmodern pioneer, doing battle with contemporary racial, gender, and class issues, and the not unrelated school that rejects him for being insufficiently liberal or progressive, and therefore out of touch with today's politics. Since Shakespeare is firmly fixed in his own more conservative time, it is disheartening to see him inducted into a politically correct army, or expelled from the academic pantheon (along with Thomas Jefferson, say, or Sigmund Freud) as an irrelevant patriarchal white man who fails to meet certain ideological standards. This is further evidence of how we substitute our own contemporary prejudices for his Elizabethan ones.

For although Shakespeare's characters, plots, and themes will always be universal, his obsessions and prejudices will continue to make him a creature of his own age, with the potential to trouble our minds and ruffle our spirits. George Bernard Shaw once half-humorously declared himself to be artistically superior to Shakespeare because he possessed a higher intelligence and more modern ideas. He was right about his intellect. He was wrong about his artistic superiority because, regardless of Shaw's powerful mind, considerable wit, and encyclopedic knowledge, Shakespeare possessed the greater imagination, and the deeper understanding of human motive. If in one area— his freedom from Elizabethan prejudice—Shaw was indeed superior to Shakespeare, he certainly compensated with enough prejudices of his own (his early admiration for Mussolini and Hitler, for example, or his rejection of inoculation). Each reader must decide whether acknowledging the prejudices of a great artist diminishes one's respect for his work, or whether the recognition of such differences can improve our understanding of his world, even enhance our appreciation of his art.

I

Misogyny

THE HAMLET OBSESSION

But to the girdle do the gods inherit;
Beneath is all the fiends'.
—*King Lear, IV.vi.123–24*

The quotation belongs to a British king, but the words could
have come from the mouth of a Danish prince. Nowhere is
Shakespearean sex hatred expressed more openly than in the
play he called *Hamlet,* and nowhere more forcefully than in the
colloquy between Hamlet and Ophelia in act III, scene i.

In this scene, Ophelia has been enjoined by Polonius and
Claudius to encounter Hamlet, while they secretly look on, in
order to discover the root cause of his mysterious melancholy.
The torrent of abuse Hamlet subsequently pours on this hapless
woman, and not just on her but on her entire sex, is shocking
in view of their past relationship, though it would hardly have
shocked many of Shakespeare's misogynistic contemporaries.
Let us look at this peculiar outburst, first in the context of the
play, and later in its historical context.

I have seen any number of brilliant actors undertake the scene:
John Gielgud singing it, Leslie Howard purring it, Laurence
Olivier shouting it, Richard Burton barking it, Nicol Wil-
liamson nasalizing it, Mark Rylance (in pajamas) sleepwalking
through it, Simon Russell Beale camping it—none can soften
its unbridled cruelty. After denying the truth of an obvious fact,
that he had ever given her gifts, Hamlet assails Ophelia with
repeated negations of any links between beauty and honesty, or

for that matter between women and chastity—"for the power of beauty will sooner transform honesty from what it is to a bawd than the force of honesty can translate beauty into his likeness. This was sometime a paradox, but now the time gives it proof" (III.i.113–16). What was a paradox in the Golden Age has now been proven truth, and not just truth but, even more poignantly, truism, undermining all traditional Platonic links regarding inward and outward beauty. Claiming that he never loved Ophelia, exhorting her to breed no more sinners like himself, Hamlet urges her to enter a nunnery. Only in a cell sheltered against unchaste behavior can beauty be cloistered from corruption.

Some critics have suggested that Hamlet is using *nunnery* here in its colloquial Elizabethan meaning, as a whorehouse, but that makes nonsense of the scene. He is clearly warning Ophelia either to find refuge in the celibate life or risk falling victim to the "paradox" of the time, the contamination of a fair outside by inward lust and lechery. Can beauty ever coexist with purity? The answer is moot. Beauty by its very nature invites abuse. The plague Hamlet gives Ophelia "as a dowry" is that no matter how "pure" she may be, she will not escape "calumny." Ironically, Hamlet himself has become her chief calumniator. If women are to be slandered and defamed, it will be by the likes of him.

Hamlet completes his dowry of plagues by showering insults upon Ophelia, indeed upon her entire sex, for "painting" or using makeup, dancing, behaving seductively, and (in a curious anticlimax) nicknaming God's creatures. These "vices" he identifies as the cause not only of his despair but also of his weakened mental state—"Go to, I'll no more on't. It hath made me mad" (III.i.145–46). He concludes by calling for a moratorium on future marriages. All but one already wedded couple "shall live. The rest shall keep as they are" (147–48). The exception to this universal divorce, of course, is Claudius and Gertrude, who will not be "allowed to live" as husband and wife, or, in the case of Claudius, as a mortal being. Again exhorting Ophelia to withdraw to a nunnery, he makes his exit, leaving the girl shaken and in tears. How to explain this peculiar outburst by a man thought to be in the very "ecstasy" of love?

The most common explanation is Freudian. Hamlet, having interpreted Gertrude's "o'er hasty marriage" as a form of infidelity dishonoring not only her husband but her son, generalizes it into a common failing of every woman, including Ophelia herself. It has also been suggested (and enacted in Olivier's film version) that Hamlet knows that Ophelia has been functioning as a stalking horse for Claudius and reacts as if to a personal betrayal. But if this were true, Shakespeare, who is never hesitant to indicate when conversations are being overheard (as, for example, when Othello eavesdrops on Cassio and Iago), would surely have suggested as much. No, the verbal assault on Ophelia can best be interpreted as another expression of Hamlet's belief in the undependability of womankind, motivated in turn by his anguish over his mother's adulterous behavior. His obscene exchanges with Ophelia during the play-within-the-play, when he is lying with "my head upon your lap," punning about what lies between "maids' legs" (III.ii.103, 107), constitute yet another instance of his denigration of the female sex in general and Ophelia in particular, with Gertrude's hasty marriage as the motive: "For look you how cheerfully my mother looks, and my father died within's two hours" (114–15).

Is Ophelia a virgin? Hamlet says she is, but addresses her as he would his whore. At least one version of the play (the Kenneth Branagh film) includes a flashback showing the two of them making love. Whatever happened in the past, however, Ophelia now evokes only Hamlet's anger and sex nausea. When she remarks on his comments regarding "The Murder of

Gonzago"—"You are as good as a chorus"—he responds with coarse innuendo: "I could interpret between you and your love, if I could see the puppets dallying." When she remarks on his keen wit, he responds with obscene sneers: "It would cost you a groaning to take off mine edge" (III.ii.224-26, 228). Hamlet naturally assumes that—like his mother—Ophelia will have multiple husbands.

When Hamlet, bypassing Claudius at his prayers, goes to Gertrude's closet to rebuke his mother for adultery and lust, his generalizing instinct at last has found a more appropriate target. He offers to set up a glass where she will see her "inmost part," not a self-regarding mirror reflecting cosmetic surfaces but the face of reality itself. He is so intent on showing her the spiritual reflection of her tainted soul that even his rash and inadvertent murder of Polonius fails to interrupt his moral hectoring. For him, at the peak of his fury, a murder is less deplorable than an adultery, for the adultery is incomprehensible. He will not call it love, for "at your age the heyday in the blood is tame, it's humble" (III.iv.67-68), and it is not reason either, for sense would reserve some quality of choice. Eager to endorse his culture's identification of women and demonic spirits, Hamlet charges that only the devil could allow Gertrude to live

> In the rank sweat of an enseamèd bed,
> Stewed in corruption, honeying, and making love
> Over the nasty sty. (82-84)

The closet scene contains some of the nastiest examples of sex nausea in the language, among them images of mildew, blisters, ulcers, infection, rankness, and contagion. This is a man for whom sexuality no longer holds a hint of pleasure or love or healthy human connection.

When Ophelia goes mad, "divided from herself and her fair judgment" (IV.v.81), she becomes as sex-obsessed as Hamlet.

Indeed, in Ingmar Bergman's 1988 production, the whole court is sex-obsessed. Claudius takes Gertrude from behind in full view of the court, and in the prayer scene is seen cavorting with a besotted hag who turns out to be the Player Queen, her lipstick-smeared face fixed in a grotesque drunken grin. As for Bergman's Ophelia, she falls into a degenerative psychosis—mutilating her hair with a dangerous pair of shears and distributing heavy iron nails in place of flowers. Ophelia's elegies for her father alternate with bawdy songs riddled with sexual puns and phallic allusions ("Young men will do't if they come to't,/By cock, they are to blame" [59–60]). The songs also acknowledge that premarital sex can invalidate marriage vows:

> Quoth she, "Before you tumbled me,
> You promised me to wed,"
> "So would I 'a done by yonder sun,
> An thou hadst not come to my bed." (61–64)

No such obstacle prevented the marriage of Shakespeare himself, who tumbled Anne Hathaway and then fulfilled his wedding promise when she was three months pregnant. But the Valentine maid of the song enters as a virgin at her lover's door and leaves as a castaway, discarded in the same way that Hamlet rejects Ophelia.

At her funeral ceremony, Hamlet publicly swears he loved Ophelia, but he has shown little sign of that in the play. After killing Polonius, in the mistaken belief that he is killing Claudius, he calls the father of his former love "a foolish prating knave" (III.iv.189), demeans his corpse as "guts" to be "lug[ged]" into the neighboring room, and fails to apologize for, or even mention, the murder to his grief-stricken daughter. Except for that odd early moment Ophelia describes in act II, when Hamlet comes to her, "doublet all unbraced . . . pale as his shirt" (II.i.79–82), as if mourning his lost passion, she functions mainly as a conduit for his hatred of her sex. Bergman's Peter Stormare caught this quality exactly, playing Hamlet as an edgy, agitated, entirely unpleasant brute, who mauls and almost rapes Ophelia in the play scene. Claudius is correct to reject the spurned-lover motive for Hamlet's madness: "Love? His affections do not that way tend" (III.i.161).

Indeed, there is a real question whether Hamlet's melancholy state of mind permits him to have erotic feelings at all. At her graveside, he expresses hyperbolic grief. And leaping into her grave after Laertes, he shouts,

> I loved Ophelia. Forty thousand brothers
> Could not, with all their quantity of love,
> Make up my sum. (V.i.254–56)

He goes on to enumerate all the extreme things he would do to prove his love, including burying himself alive with her corpse. Yet when the scene is over, he does not appear to give Ophelia another thought, being more concerned with informing Horatio about the deaths of Rosencrantz and Guildenstern. Nor does he drop a tear either for these old, albeit treacherous, school chums, showing as little remorse over their executions as he did over Polonius after stabbing him through the arras— much less over the death of the one woman he claims to have loved, and drove to a watery grave.

Commentators have given this play a very special place in Shakespeare's works, regarding Hamlet as a particular kind of sex-obsessed melancholiac. But although Hamlet's motiveless brutalizing of Ophelia is the clearest expression of misogyny in Shakespeare's works, it is far from the only example. From this point on, there is hardly a single play that does not contain some expression of animus against women. And although the charges are more often baseless than not, and the woman is innocent, they echo Hamlet's obsession in intensifying form.

No doubt, these sentiments belong first and foremost to the characters Shakespeare created. But let us acknowledge that they have also been inhaled from the cultural air, and, if we are to credit the biographical nature of the sonnets, that they may have been disturbing the peace of the playwright himself. That such feelings are expressed so nakedly in the sonnets, the most autobiographical of his writings, where (in his persona as "Will") Shakespeare inveighs against the faithless woman commonly known as the Dark Lady, would suggest that Shakespeare's misogyny had a personal as well as a literary stimulus.

Of course, it would be absurd to suggest that all of Shakespeare's women are objects of suspicion, or that all of his sexual relationships are tainted. Only the *faithless* female characters — or those assumed to be faithless, however wrongly — arouse the scorn of their husbands or lovers and stimulate their misogyny. "'Tis brief, my lord," says Ophelia, referring to an actor's prologue (III.ii.137–38). "As woman's love," replies Hamlet, referring to a woman's inconstancy ("Frailty, thy name is woman" [I.ii.146]). But when a woman's love is steady and honest — when, like Viola, she is willing to wait for her lover "like patience on a monument" — Shakespeare will regard her as an almost holy vessel.

Being examples of spotless women, falsely accused, such characters as Desdemona and Ophelia run the risk of displaying a cloistered virtue, lacking a strong feminine dynamic. But there are few more appealing women in literature than Shakespeare's heroines, Desdemona and Ophelia included, and rarely because they are demure or feminine. Shakespeare obviously admired (indeed, he may have invented) the literary type that Bernard Shaw would centuries later call "the unwomanly woman" — that witty, independent, spirited heroine personified by Rosalind in *As You Like It,* Beatrice in *Much Ado About Nothing,* Portia in *The Merchant of Venice,* Helena in *All's Well That End's Well,* and preeminently perhaps by Cleopatra, Queen of the Nile, in *Antony and Cleopatra*—whose chief quality is her refusal to be defined by male concepts of virtue and domesticity. And he often endorsed, though not without a touch of irony, the conventions of Petrarchan courtly love, along with its idealized bucolic variant, pastoral romance.

At the same time, an astonishing number of his male characters continue to express a powerful anti-Petrarchan revulsion against any woman who deviates from the strict prevailing views of female virtue, while the sexual love he dramatizes as taking place at court is usually identified with adultery.[1] (As for Shakespeare's pastoral lovers, they sometimes seem like the "country copulatives" dismissively described by Touchstone in *As You Like It* (V.iv.53). Shakespeare's more misogynistic passages, framed in language as extreme as any in the time, are stimulated not only by such "lustful" creatures as Gertrude in *Hamlet* and Cressida in *Troilus and Cressida*. They touch such supremely chaste women as Desdemona (*Othello*), Imogen (*Cymbeline*), and Hermione (*The Winter's Tale*), and, of course, Ophelia. The accusations against the particular woman, however mistaken, almost always become attacks upon the entire sex. Thus while a misogynistic character, such as Othello or Leontes, may ultimately be disabused of his libels on his innocent woman victim, his more general accusations continue to linger in the tainted air.

But this chapter is not about the extraordinary appeal of Shakespeare's heroines, which has been sufficiently celebrated elsewhere; rather, it is an account of his numerous sexist assaults on their imagined (and sometimes real) departures from virtue. This fixation, which I have called The Hamlet Obsession, appears most often in Shakespeare's later career, though even in an early romantic tragedy such as *Romeo and Juliet* a character like Mercutio will ironically deprecate some of the very women the playwright would later celebrate, along with the whole convention of courtly love: "Now is [Romeo] for the numbers that Petrarch flowed in. Laura, to his lady [Rosaline] was a kitchen wench . . . Dido a dowdy, Cleopatra a gypsy, Helen and Hero hildings and harlots, Thisbe a grey eye or so, but not to the purpose" (II.iii.35–38).

This is spoken in jest, but the trace of misogynistic blood in Mercutio's veins colors those fractious outbursts against the real or assumed infidelity of women we find throughout Shakespeare. Shakespeare was hardly alone in expressing this attitude. He was echoing a prejudice of his age. Male suspicion of female virtue, particularly toward ladies of the court, was almost pandemic in the last years of Elizabeth's rule and increased exponentially during the reign of her successor, James I. Even some of the age's favorite theatrical conventions gave some playwrights extradramatic opportunities for antifemale expression.

Take the issue of women in male disguise, a common enough convention of the time, partly dictated, and considerably complicated, by the fact that all the younger female roles in this period were invariably played by boys. Shakespeare himself seemed to have no trouble with the convention. Some of his most charming and intelligent heroines—Viola, Rosalind, Imogen, Helena—take off their gowns and put on doublet and hose (or, in Portia's case, a lawyer's robe), often in order to follow their male lovers into foreign or forbidden territories. Their cross-dressing was chosen primarily to avoid the perils that women faced abroad in dangerous times, but their male disguise sometimes led to human encounters of considerable sexual ambiguity, most notably in Olivia's scenes with Viola in *Twelfth Night,* where the countess, mistaking Viola for a man, seeks to claim her for her husband. (Orsino's feelings for the disguised Viola reflect a similar ambiguity.)

Such treatments of the disguise convention have encouraged

some feminist commentators, most notably Marjorie Garber in *Vested Interests* and elsewhere, to regard the sexual confusion implicit in cross-dressing as a precocious early model of liberal gender politics.[2] This is one of the ways that postmodern critics confirm their belief that Shakespeare was "not of an age but for all time." "All time," of course, usually means *our* time, as every generation attempts to claim Shakespeare as its own social bellwether. Further pressing her belief in Shakespeare's contemporary relevance, diversity, and postmodernity, Garber, in her often valuable book *Shakespeare After All,* goes on to declare Shakespeare "strikingly 'modern'" in regard to "race, class, and gender," praising his "uncanny timeliness," which she describes as "a capacity to speak to circumstances the playwright could not have contemplated or foreseen."[3]

Few would wish to deny Shakespeare his prophetic powers, and Garber reinforces the important point that there is not one single Shakespeare, that his views, if he actually held personal views, are everywhere. Nevertheless, let us beware lest Shakespeare lose his historical identity in feminist and neocolonial interpretations, or that his characters become distorted by being viewed through a special postmodernist lens.

There is no question that not a few of Shakespeare's heroines, notably Katherina in *The Taming of the Shrew,* Beatrice in *Much Ado About Nothing,* and Helena in *All's Well That Ends Well,* display the liberated qualities associated with modern women, even when not wearing doublets and hose. And there is no question that the dramatist deeply admires the female capacity to challenge men in intellectual matters—*vide* the witty exchanges between Rosaline and Biron in *Love's Labour's Lost,* not to mention those between Benedick and Beatrice in *Much Ado About Nothing* and Hotspur and Lady Percy in *1 Henry IV.*

But how do we explain those poisonous explosions of sex nausea and anger toward woman's unfaithfulness that often permeate the poems and saturate the plays? Reflections of contemporary attitudes? Examples of personal prejudice? Garber says no. Insisting that it is wrong to interpret Shakespeare's recurrent misogynistic eruptions as stemming from "sex horror," she rejects the popular hunch that these may have been inspired by "his ambivalent relationship to his wife." Rather, Garber prefers to interpret such passages as the insights of "a keen analyst of power and gender," the accomplishments of a man who writes plays that are extremely "modern" in regard to "race, class, and gender."[4]

We have no way of knowing what Shakespeare actually thought of Anne Hathaway, or whether he intended any insult when bequeathing her his second-best bed. In her recent book *Shakespeare's Wife*, Germaine Greer affirms that Hathaway was a perfectly normal Stratford housewife, and that critics who suggest any strain in their relationship may be sexists and misogynists themselves. Perhaps. But there is no doubt that Shakespeare's characters express "sex horror" frequently and passionately enough to make us suspect that Shakespeare may have experienced such feelings firsthand. Unquestionably, Shakespeare is sufficiently various to support any point of view about him. But one makes the case that he shares our modern attitudes toward race, class, and sexual disposition—that his use of the convention of cross-dressing belongs to "a keen analyst of power and gender"—only by pulling him out of history and yanking him out of time.

Cross-dressing was a crucial Elizabethan theatrical convention, especially in a theatre forbidden by law to put woman actors on the stage. And had Shakespeare been prevented from fitting his women into the Elizabethan version of trousers, we would have been deprived of some of his greatest plots and characters. But this popular dramatic convention was hardly endorsed by everybody; indeed, it was strongly repudiated by the more hard-nosed evangelicals of the time as expressly contrary to the laws cited in Deuteronomy 22:5, "A woman shall not wear man's clothing, nor shall a man put on a woman's clothing; for whoever does these things is an abomination to the Lord your God." Such proscriptions, in fact, constituted a central tenet in the Puritan condemnation of the stage. And if contemporary Puritans were outraged by the idea of boys dressing up as girls in order to play female parts, they were even more aroused over the gender confusion created when women put on doublets and hose, for whatever reason.

"Mannish" women—namely, those who wore male clothing or imitated male behavior—were a source of extreme concern not only for Puritans but for many contemporary moralists and satirists, not to mention a large number of Shakespeare's fellow playwrights. The impact of Puritan extremism on Elizabethan and Jacobean literature has yet to be properly analyzed. The Puritan suspicion of womankind influenced even Shakespeare at times, though, at least in his earlier plays, he does not often inveigh against masculine women. The militant Joan La Pucelle in *1 Henry VI* is the one exception who forfeits any claim to female virtue because she dresses as a man. Perhaps because she is considered a foreign enemy, a "foul fiend of France," a whore who consorts with "lustful paramours" (III.v.12–13), but also for the sin of wearing the clothes (not to mention the armor) of the opposite sex, is she burned at the stake. (Garber seems to concede as much when she calls her "the cross-dressed martial Joan.")[5]

Those women who wore the figurative pants in the family were not really treated more sympathetically. The Frenchwoman Margaret in *3 Henry VI* is identified as a "tiger's heart wrapped in a woman's hide" (I.iv.138) because of her dominating role in the court of her husband, the innocent King Henry.[6] And the shrewish Kate of Padua comes off, at least in the early scenes of *The Taming of the Shrew*, as a repellent virago by virtue of her masculine aggressiveness, until she is transformed, through a process of indoctrination just a few procedures short of water-boarding, into an entirely compliant heroine at the end. Nor is there much doubt about how Shakespeare felt toward those masculinized women whom Garber calls "the unisex witches" in *Macbeth*.[7]

Theatrical costumes aside, women who assumed the garments of men, in the uncertain sexual dynamic of this time, were thought by many moralists to be assuming the prerogatives of men as well, not just rule over the realm or the home, but the masculine rights of sexual and marital freedom. These are the panic-filled issues that James Joyce cites in *Ulysses*, in the famous Library or "Scylla and Charybdis" section, as haunting Shakespeare's conscious and unconscious mind. Joyce, through his fictional alter ego, Stephen Dedalus, joins those commentators who believe the origins of Shakespeare's sex nausea to have been biographical. Calling the Elizabethan period "an age of exhausted whoredom groping for its god," Stephen ascribes this strain to Shakespeare's unwilling entrapment into marriage with a pregnant woman eight years his senior, and even invents a fanciful plot in which Anne Hathaway ("a slack dishonoured body") commits adultery with one or more of Shakespeare's brothers while her husband is earning a living in London.

This scenario unequivocally casts Shakespeare as the "the spurned lover in the sonnets," cuckolded by the Dark Lady and "the fair youth," prodded by "a goad of the flesh [which drives] him into a new passion." Most of this highly imaginative stuff is also highly imaginary. But it is not necessary to reconstruct Shakespeare's unrecorded private life in order to recognize that his occasional expressions of misogyny, if not wedged in his nature, are indigenous to his age, embedded in the culture of his time and repeated in the theatre of his contemporaries.

It is curious, however, that apart from recurrent criticism of shrews, present as early as the fourteenth century in such plays as the Wakefield *Noah*, one does not find attacks on women, either on middle-class wives or on ladies of the court, to any noticeable extent in the drama until 1599, though the expression of male misogyny is common enough in other forms of literature. 1599 was a notable date in Shakespeare's career regarding the kind of plays he began to write, as well as an important date in the history of the theatre.[8] It was the year when the literary satire being practiced by Marston, Jonson, Nashe, and others was banned from publication by a bishop's edict because of its extremely personal and scurrilous nature, and thereupon found its way into the less regulated medium of drama.

As O. J. Campbell has noted, in *Comicall Satyre and Shakespeare's Troilus and Cressida,* the transfer of tragical satire and comical satire from the backrooms of publishing houses to the forefront of the English theatre in 1599 and after made criticism of the court lady, if not of women in general, a commonplace. This may explain why misogyny thereupon enters the stage in a form more virulent than at any time in English theatre history. First Elizabethan, and subsequently Jacobean, dramatists assume the role of medieval troubadours with a crucial change in subject. They begin to sing now not of love but of lust.

Shakespeare's contemporaries, and even Shakespeare himself upon occasion before 1599 (*vide* Tamora in *Titus Andronicus*), depict the court lady as a sink of evils, a stews, a loathsome pit of rottenness, a painted image, a gilded pill, a decked idol of May-tide, a skin-full of lust, a school of uncleanness. But after 1599 (*vide* Gertrude in *Hamlet*), the indictment intensifies. Her painted good looks are a snare for the innocent, her lascivious fashions an invitation to lechery, her wanton eye a bait for adultery. Because of her total lack of moral stamina, man's appetite is quickened. He can either submit to the sinful pleasures she easily tenders—in which case he is damned—or take refuge in sex hatred and give way to sex nausea. Only by contemplating beauty in decay can man counteract the power of this beauty. The worms are his most effectual allies against his uncontrollable desires.[9] Christianity from its beginnings had included a semimisogynistic strain—the identification of women with the temptations of the flesh was virtually a mantra of Saint Paul. One medieval canard in particular, perpetuated by Saint John Chrysostom, Robert Manning, Bernard of Clairvaux, and Robert Rypon, regarded women as evil temptresses bent on accomplishing man's destruction by luring him from his preferred celibate path. In images that recall Hamlet's remarks to the skull of Yorick regarding women who paint ("to this favour she must come" V.i.179), Chrysostom wrote: "Take her skin from her face and thou shalt see all the loathsomeness under it."[10] Cosmetics and costumes are only superficial coverings for the rot below.

Contemporary Puritans intensified the attacks on premarital sexuality. But they were equally disapproving of mannish females, a critique intimately related to Puritan disapproval of female government. Even in the hands of the nominally beloved Queen Elizabeth, female rule represented woman's continuing effort to dominate men, which is why the queen was often compared invidiously with an Amazon. John Calvin ranked female government with original sin in that it was "a deviation from the original and proper order of nature." And in his *The First Blast of the Trumpet Against the Monstrous Regiment of Women* (1588), Calvin's Scottish follower John Knox delivered a not very subtle attack on the new queen ("To promote a Woman to beare rule, superiorite, dominion, or empire above any Realme, Nation, or Citie, is repugnant to Nature") that he later amended but never retracted even under church rebuke.

A monstrous regiment, armed and dangerous. As this suggests, the central Puritan criticism of woman was that she was in rebellion against male domination, being herself masculine, in the sense that by exercising control over her husband and her household, she was usurping the proper functions of the male. In a series of anonymous seventeenth-century pamphlets that regurgitated all the sixteenth-century fulminations against the type, this mannish woman was in 1620 to receive a generic name—*Hic-Mulier* (The masculine woman). Here is a typical passage:

> Since the daies of *Adam* women were never so Masculine, Masculine in their genders and whole generation, from the Mother, to the youngest daughter; Masculine in their number, from one to multitudes; Masculine in Moode, from bold speech, to impudent action; Masculine in Tense: for (without redresse) they were, are, and will be still most Masculine, most man-kinde, and most monstrous.

The use of the Latin masculine pronoun (*hic*) with the feminine noun (*mulier*) was a semantic demonstration of the sexual topsy-turvydom the Puritans were perceiving to be roiling England.

One of the few sympathetic portraits of masculine women was that drawn by Thomas Middleton and by Thomas Dekker in *The Roaring Girl* (before 1611), where Moll Cutpurse puts on pants, and curses and roars with the best of her male companions. But elsewhere that self-same Dekker, in *The Batchelars Banquet* (1603), calls it "a generall imperfection of women . . . to strive for the breeches," while his collaborator, Middleton, in *A Mad World My Masters* (1608), creates a male character who disguises himself as a woman only from the waist down because in this "Amazonian time" "we're all male to th' middle; mankind from the beaver to th' bum" (III.iii).

It is significant that none of these writers charge, except in the most indistinct way, that these mannish women are homosexual. If one woman conceives a passion for another, as Olivia does for the disguised Viola in *Twelfth Night,* this is usually a matter of misapprehension rather than of true attraction ("Fortune forbid my outside have not charmed her," says the puzzled Viola, "Disguise I see thou art a wickedness" [II.ii.16, 25]). The criticism is less a question of sexual persuasion than of sartorial style, more a focus on fashion than on sexual choice, though it is related to shrewish behavior. Most often in misogynist satire and religious tracts, women are likened to beasts because of their basically animal nature. For just as animals were assumed to have no rational soul, so the female sex was thought to have negligible quantities of rationality as well. Woman permitted her appetites to dominate her reason, her rational soul to be undermined by her concupiscible soul (or affections). The two souls were always in conflict, a theological metaphor for the struggle between vice and virtue. More frequently than not, virtue was the loser. When a woman went mad, for example, she was thought to be totally at the mercy of sexual desire, her reason having been conquered by her reigning affections. This accounts for the raw sexual obsessions of such literary madwomen as Ophelia in *Hamlet,* not to mention her kissing cousin, the Jailer's Daughter in Fletcher and Shakespeare's *The Two Noble Kinsmen.* When her guard is down, the female behaves no better than an animal in heat. Women's beauty and her lust are man's prime obstacles because, having lost her own battle with restraint, the temptress woman, like Eve, enjoins the male to lose his as well.

Woman could effect man's fall passively, by arousing lust through her beauty, or actively, by laying snares for his soul. The latter was the elective course of the prostitute.[11] How much worse the fate and behavior of the court lady, a prey not only to her own appetites but also to the various allurements of her environment? No writer better described this condition than John Marston in *The Malcontent,* where his hero, Malevole, asserts he would rather leave his lady in a whorehouse than have her subjected to the wicked temptations of the court:

> When in an Italian lascivious palace, a lady
>   gardianlesse,
> Left to the push of all allurement,
> The strongest incitements to immodestie,
> To have her bound, incensed with wanton sweetes,
> Her veines fild hie with heating delicates,
> Soft rest, sweete Musick, amorous Masquerers,
> Lascivious banquets, sinne it selfe gilt o'er,
> Strong phantasie tricking up strange delights,
> Presenting it dressed pleasingly to sence, sence leading it unto the soule, confirmed with potent example, impudent custome inticed by that great bawd opportunities, thus being prepar'd, clap to her easie eare, youth in good clothes, well shapt, rich, faire-spoken, promising noble, ardent bloud-full, witie, flattering:
> *Ulisses* absent, O *Ithacan,* chastest *Penelope,* hold
>   out. (III.ii.190–207)

Marston doubts whether even the chaste Penelope can "hold out" under such conditions, for, like many of his contemporaries, he was convinced that no woman's virtue could withstand the irresistible seductions of the court and "that great bawd opportunitie." This may be the explanation for a much-disputed scene between King Richard and Lady Anne in Shakespeare's *Richard III,* where the very hog who murdered her husband and her father-in-law, a man who obviously inspires in her unspeakable loathing, wins the woman as his wife in just over two hundred lines of unctuous dialogue. With Ulysses absent (in this case dead), chaste Penelope finds it impossible to hold out.

Shakespeare's Richard woos his "Penelope" with a pretense of piety and penitence. Other writers believed that Penelope was more active in her own seduction. In Dekker's *The Honest Whore* (1604) the hero links women with devils (a recurrent association) because of their part in the fall of man: "You should be mans blisse, but you prove their rods./Were there no women, men might live like gods" (III.1). Of course, were there no women, men would not exist at all, but this biological fact did not prevent moralists from associating the female sex with every species of evil. One of these was illness, since women as carriers of venereal diseases had the power to damn men in a physical sense as well.[12] Only by removing woman completely from the source of corruption—to the country, say, or, as Hamlet suggests, to a nunnery—could one be certain of her soundness and chastity. "It is so rare a thing to be honest amongst you," says a character in Beaumont and Fletcher's *The Woman Hater* (1606), "that some one man in an age, may perhaps suspect two women to be honest, but never believe it verily" (I.3)—an obvious exaggeration of Hamlet's already morosely exaggerated estimate: "To be honest, as this world goes, is to be one man picked out of ten thousand" (II.ii.179–80).[13]

Few writers took the woman's side of this argument, although Aemilia Lanyer (a leading candidate for the Dark Lady of the sonnets) tried to defend the female sex against such slander in her *Salve Deus Rex Judaeorum*.[14] John Donne was a notable male exception, offering in his *Paradoxes and Problems* (c. 1600) a "Defense of Women for their Inconstancy & Their Paintings." But even that defense was an ironic form of criticism: "That Women are *Inconstant,* I with any man confesse, but that *Inconstancy* is a bad quality, I against any man will maintaine." Donne goes on to make the playful suggestion that the name of *inconstancy* should be changed to *variety*, which he calls "the most delightfull thing in this world."

Not many Englishmen, however (not even Donne himself, consistently) displayed such sophistication and tolerance toward woman's alleged promiscuity, because few, if any, were willing to grant the good of pleasure. The Page in George Chapman's *All Fools* (1604), for example, like Donne an ironic defender of women against slander, makes the point that the female is unchaste because she is basically unstable: "Is she not a woman? Did she not suck [unchastity] from her mother's breast? And will you condemn that as her fault which is her nature?" (III.i)

But if wives and spinsters were easily seduced, the inconstancy of widows, for whom the marriage act had become habitual, was even more inevitable. That is why Saint Paul urged widows to remarry to avoid the risk of eternal damnation. Elizabethan moralists, by contrast, were more stony hearted in their disapproval of second marriages. At best, taking multiple husbands was considered a form of legal adultery, at worst, a reflection of the widow's lustfulness. Duke Ferdinand tells his sister in John Webster's *The Duchess of Malfi* (1613): "Marry? They are most luxurious/Will wed twice" (I.ii). For Hamlet, the taking of a second husband "makes marriage vows as false as dicers' oaths" (III.iv.43–44), constituting an especially lubricious decision in middle age when "the heyday in the blood is tame":

> Rebellious hell
> If thou canst mutine in a matron's bones,
> To flaming youth let virtue be as wax . . .
> Since frost itself as actively doth burn. (68, 72–77)

In Hamlet's portrait of Gertrude as an adulterous wife, who marries her second husband within four months after the death of her first, who nestles in "a couch for luxury and damnèd incest" (I.v.83), is she not a quintessential example of the faithless court lady as seen through the lens of contemporary satire?[15]

At the same time that the aristocratic Platonists at court were emphasizing the harmony between inner and outer beauty, the middle-class satirists were expressing extreme skepticism about the ability of attractive women to remain chaste. John Donne's "Song" in his *Collected Poems* dourly concludes that "No where / Lives a woman true and faire." There are echoes here of the most famous example of this debate, the dialogue between Hamlet and Ophelia in act III, scene i:

> Hamlet: Ha, ha? Are you honest?
> Ophelia: My lord!
> Hamlet: Are you fair?
> Ophelia: What means your lordship?
> Hamlet: That if you be honest and fair, your honesty should admit no discourse to your beauty.
> Ophelia: Could beauty, my lord, have better commerce than with honesty?
> Hamlet: Ay, truly, for the power of beauty will sooner transform honesty from what it is to a bawd, than the force of honesty can translate beauty into his likeness. This was sometime a paradox, but now the time gives it proof. (105–16)

Ophelia, ignorant of the "paradox" of the age, upholds the Platonic view of beauty as the handmaiden of a virtuous spirit, while Hamlet, a disenchanted Petrarchan lover like the satirists he echoes, finds this Platonic theory invalidated by his mother's adulterous example.

Consider the pejorative similes and analogies Hamlet uses in his soliloquies and dialogues. When he wishes to express self-loathing, he compares himself to the most abject species of women—a "bawd," a "drab," a "scullion," a "harlot," a "strumpet," a "whore" who unpacks herself with words. These are women who paint the lily through makeup and dress, but so, in Hamlet's mind, do those wives who make "monsters" (which is to say cuckolds) of men through the application of synthetic enhancements.[16]

Although misogynists like Hamlet could hardly blame women for their natural beauty, the artificial improvement of that beauty by means of cosmetics and sumptuous attire was another thing entirely. Such treatments were considered the proper province of prostitutes. Indeed, the whores in Middleton's *Father Hubbard's Tales* (1604) turn out to be "discontented and unfortunate gentlewomen"—more inclined to "venture a maidenhead than a head-tire"—who have sold their bodies to pay for the trinkets they so admire. ("She that hath given kisses to have her hayre shorn," writes the anonymous author of *Hic-Mulier,* "will give her honestie to have her upper parts put into a French doublet").

Of course, women had been decking themselves out in finery ever since the silkworm first started spinning silk, but court fashions in this time seem to have been particularly extravagant. Upstart imitations had reached a new high as well. The majority of Englishwomen were proving the literal truth of Ben Jonson's assertion about the court in *Cynthia's Revels* (1601): "In thee, the whole kingdom dresseth it selfe, and is ambitious to use thee as her glasse." Perhaps to preserve her distance from her middle-class sister, the English court lady was changing her fashions as quickly as they were copied, and making her gowns as costly as possible.[17] There is little doubt that the queen's love of finery was equal to, if not greater than, that of her waiting women. At her death, the queen's wardrobe was said to number two thousand gowns.

Some of these articles of dress were extremely daring, even

by the standards of our own more liberated age. Although wives and widows were still required to cover themselves to the neck, a doublet had been designed for single women that exposed the breasts almost entirely. Puritans were quick to observe that only courtesans had hitherto exposed their breasts in the street, and left their readers to make the obvious inferences.[18] If there is any doubt that this fashion was modish at court, we have only to remember that, by appearing before him with her breasts exposed, Queen Elizabeth once forced a visiting French diplomat to keep his eyes focused on the floor during the entire interview.[19]

But the form of artificiality that undoubtedly caused the most violent revulsion among English moralists was the practice of painting. John Lyly in 1580 had absolved English court ladies of this assumedly Italian practice, and foreign travelers like Samuel Kiechel, writing in 1595, confirmed that English women "do not falsify, paint or bedaub themselves as in Italy or other places." But if the cosmetic art was limited to Italy in the early period of Elizabeth's reign, it clearly spread through the English court in subsequent years. Thomas Nashe in 1593 wrote: "Gorgeous ladies of the Court, never was I so admitted so neere any of you, as to see how you torture poore old Time by spunging, pynning, and punsing." Elizabeth, by using cosmetics herself, seems to have given her ladies tacit sanction for the practice. In her old age, particularly, the queen was prone to extreme expressions of vanity. Ben Jonson once told Drummond of Hawthornden that "Queen Elizabeth never saw her self after she became old in a true Glas. They painted her & sometimes would vermilion her nose." By the time of James and his queen, Anne of Denmark, the practice of painting had become even more widespread in the court.

The court lady's artificial complexion, along with her habit of dyeing her hair, inspired not only the Puritan moralists but also the Elizabethan-Jacobean satirists to accuse her of tampering with the handiwork of God. The next step, inevitably, was to link the use of cosmetic aids with immorality. As Thomas Nashe asked in 1593, "If not to tempt and to be thought worthy to be tempted, why dye they & diet they theyre faces with so many drugges as they doe, as it were to correct Gods workmanship?" This assumption is later echoed by Hamlet in the course of insulting Ophelia: "I have heard of your paintings too well enough. God hath given you one face, and you make yourselves another" (III.i.142–43). Rather than reflecting spiritual harmony, the use of cosmetics invariably was thought to cover spiritual corruption. William Burton, in his dedicatory epistle to a translation of Tatius's *Clitophon and Leucippe* (it is addressed to Shakespeare's bisexual patron the earl of Southampton), identified women's painting and perfuming as good reasons for preferring boys: "The beauty of boys is not besmeared with the counterfeit of painting, neither sponged up with borrowed perfumes; the very sweat of the brows of a boy, doth excel all the sweet savors of musk and civet about a woman . . . the very image and picture of their kisses are so sweet and pleasant, that you might very well think, that heavenly nectar to be between your lips." Christopher Marlowe was to frame Burton's Socratic admiration of young male purity more tersely: "All they who love not tobacco and boys are fools."

As a result of their loathing for paint, playwrights passed on from one to the other a simile that compared women to a gilded tomb or temple, handsome without, within full of rottenness, corruption, and disease. In a few cases, the gilding even causes the disease. Barnabe Barnes, for example, in *The Devil's Charter* (1607) kills his heroine, Lucretia Borgia, after a prolonged session in front of her mirror, by poisoning her with her own cosmetics ("Who painted my faire face with these foule spots,/You see them in my soule deformed blots" [IV.iii]). Vindice's remarks to the skull of his dead mistress in Cyril Tourneur's (or Thomas Middleton's) *The Revenger's Tragedy* (1607), a woman he presumably loved, are among the most brutal in the brutal language of misogyny: "See Ladies, with false formes you deceive men, but cannot deceive wormes" (III.v). Vindice's words are clearly influenced by Hamlet's harrowing remarks to the skull of Yorick regarding the kinship between vanity and death: "Now get you to my lady's chamber, and tell her, let her paint an inch thick, to this favour she must come" (V.i.178–79). The literature was full of morbid X-rays of the skull beneath the skin.

Thus at the same time that Shakespeare's heroines are proving to be among the most engaging in literature, his male characters are continuing to rant about female corruption, often with no reason to do so. Let us look more carefully at the act IV, scene vi speech from *King Lear* that serves as epigraph to this chapter:

> Behold yond simpering dame,
> Whose face between her forks presages snow;
> That minces virtue, and does shake the head
> To hear of pleasure's name;
> The fitchew, nor the soilèd horse, goes to't
> With a more riotous appetite.
> Down from the waist they are Centaurs,
> Though women all above:
> But to the girdle do the gods inherit;
> Beneath is all the fiends'. (115–24)

What happens in the play to make Lear cast this libel on the female sex? Surely, one important motive is Goneril and Regan's mistreatment of the old king, and the way they discard their husbands in order to compete with each other for Edmund. Lear's awful curse on Goneril—

> Into her womb convey sterility!
> Dry up in her the organs of increase;
> And from her derogate body never spring
> A babe to honor her (I.iv.255–58)

—is one of the most awful imprecations in the language. Cordelia is said to redeem nature "from the general fault," a hint that only she is exempt from the "riotous appetite" of women like her sisters (IV.vi.120). Lear had earlier uttered inflammatory woman hatred. But in act IV, it is not the proud and foolish Lear speaking, it is Lear the madman touched with a visionary gleam. Lear's remarks about women, that they are virtuous only above the waist, shows him to be another victim of the Hamlet Obsession. For both these misogynists, women have become a nation of whores and adulterers.

The origins of this *ad feminem* argument go back to Shakespeare's early poems. Not *The Rape of Lucrece,* of course, which chronicles the violation of a virtuous woman by a sadistic rapist, but more likely *Venus and Adonis,* where a ripening goddess lusting after a younger mortal has been likened to another seductress, Anne Hathaway, pursuing the eighteen-year-old Will (Adonis is also sometimes identified with the earl of Southampton). The misogyny in this poem is admittedly debatable, but in his sonnet sequence Shakespeare's Hamlet Obsession is openly exposed. There is a drama hidden in the sonnets, taking the form of a love triangle between a poet (Will) who is attracted both to the Lord for whom he writes his poems and to a Dark Lady who beguiles him from his conjugal bed.

In sonnet 40 we first learn that his patron has deceived him with his mistress, and in the deception poems that follow, he gnaws on this theme like a hungry mastiff on a bone. Much as he senses vice and betrayal in his male friend, it is the woman who bears the brunt of his rage and disappointment. Although he has broken his marriage vows with her ("Robb'd other beds revenues of their rents" [sonnet 42]), he has received only dishonor in return. In sonnet 144, the Dark Lady is depicted as a "worser spirit . . . a woman colour'd ill" who has stolen away his "better angel from my side, / And would corrupt my saint to be a devil." That corruption the Poet has already condemned (in sonnet 129), famously calling it "th'expense of spirit in a waste of shame," a form of "lust in action." In an age when the devil was thought to be black, the Poet dwells on the dark complexion of his mistress as a sign of her sullied nature. Reversing Petrarchan conventions, he compares his mistress's hair to wires and her breasts to dun, in a prescient forecast of a famous illustration of 1654 that literalized the beloved mistress as her woebegone servant often metaphorically described her—a ferociously ugly creature with a Cupid sitting on her forehead, hearts sticking from her head, roses plastered on her cheeks, bows glued to her eyebrows, hemispheres for breasts, suns for eyes, and pearls for teeth.

Three other virtuous Shakespearean heroines are treated as no better than whores by jealous men (in each case, their husbands)—namely, Desdemona, Hermione, and Imogen. Desdemona is calumniated not by a clinical depressive, as Ophelia is by Hamlet, but rather by a gullible general in the grip of a guileful, malevolent subaltern. Iago is a master of deception—a Machiavellian villain masquerading as an honest soldier—but on certain issues, namely female inconstancy, he speaks without equivocation. He believes, without much evidence, that his wife Emilia has been unfaithful with Cassio and Othello. And this suspicion turns him into the most cutting and incisive satirist of courtly love in all of Shakespeare.

A powerful example of this satire is Iago's extended dialogue about women in act II, scene i, when he, Desdemona, and Emilia are awaiting Othello's arrival. Admitting that he is "nothing, if not critical" (II.i.122), Iago caustically describes the qualities of females fair and dark, foolish and witty, in diction indistinguishable from that of any courtly cynic. In his lively exchanges with Desdemona he elaborates on the theme, defaming women as

> Bells in your parlours; wildcats in your kitchens,
> Saints in your injuries, devils being offended,
> Players in your housewifery, and hussies in your
>   beds. (113–15)

Throughout the play, in fact, he is the cynical satirist, Othello and Cassio and Roderigo the idealizing lovers. At times Iago speaks like a traditional Shakespearean wit, in the style of Benedick in *Much Ado* or Biron in *Love's Labour's Lost*. He is clearly the most intelligent character in the play, and needs to be performed by a particularly intelligent actor. (Christopher Plummer captured this superior intellect perfectly in 1981, playing Iago to James Earl Jones's Othello.)

In a scene with Roderigo soon after, Iago reveals his animalistic views of love (which he calls "a lust of the blood and a permission of the will" [I.iii.329]). In contrast to Roderigo's puppy-dog infatuation, Iago characterizes Desdemona as insatiable, continually in need of new lovers to feed her "fresh appetite." What Roderigo calls "courtesy," Iago calls lechery. Watching her hold hands with Othello, he translates that into lewd paddling — "an index and obscure prologue to the history of lust and foul thoughts" (II.i.248–49).[20] Roderigo thinks Desdemona "full of most blessed condition." "Blessed fig's end," snarls Iago. "The wine she drinks is made of grapes" (242–43). Woman, like wine, for Iago, are merely the sum of their chemical components.[21]

Soon after, in Iago's debate with Cassio over Desdemona's qualities, Shakespeare provides perhaps the most brilliant contrast in literature between the Petrarchan lover and the cynical Naturalist on the subject of womankind:

> Cassio: She's a most exquisite lady.
> Iago: And I'll warrant her full of game.
> Cassio: Indeed, she's a most fresh and delicate crea-
>   ture.
> Iago: What an eye she has! Methinks it sounds a
>   parley to provocation.
> Cassio: An inviting eye, and yet, methinks, right
>   modest.
> Iago: Well, happiness to their sheets. (II.iii.17–25)

Every time Cassio glorifies Desdemona's spiritual beauty, Iago translates his innocent phrases into carnal imagery, as if sexual congress reduced men and women to animals, what he called earlier "the beast with two backs" (I.i.118). In their opposing views of love as a sacred ideal (Cassio) and a bodily function (Iago), the two men might be speaking different languages, though Cassio is far from the perfect courtier himself in the way he comports himself with the courtesan, Bianca, whom he treats less as a mistress than as a convenience.

Although Iago's suspicions of his wife are probably without any basis in fact, Emilia is one of the few woman characters in Shakespeare allowed to contemplate infidelity without being blistered for it. Consider this wonderful exchange after Desdemona has disingenuously asked her maid whether women are ever unfaithful to their husbands.

> Emilia: There be some such, no question.
> Desdemona: Would'st thou do such a deed for all
>   the world?
> Emilia: Why, would not you?
> Desdemona: No, by this heavenly light.

> Emilia: Nor I neither, by this heavenly light; I
> might do't as well i' th' dark. (IV.iii.62–68)

Emilia jokes that "all the world" is "a great price for a small vice," but goes on to say, her teasing tone laced with resentment, that it is the husband's fault if wives "do fall": "The ills we do, their ills instruct us so" (101). Desdemona's shocked response reflects the strict morality with which she was raised, but Emilia's argument strikes the modern ear with absolute correctness. It is the kind of reasoning one rarely hears in Shakespeare, that what is sauce for the goose is sauce for the gander. Coleridge commented about this scene that Emilia wears her virtue loosely, without casting it off. His point is arguable. She would cast it off in a minute were she to find her husband betraying her with another.

But Iago is too busy undermining the love lives of others to have one of his own. He is determined to poison Othello's benign view of womankind and convert him to Hamlet's obsession. And through brilliant theatrics, sly insinuations, and masterful cunning, he succeeds magnificently in persuading the general that his love is a whore. Othello's feelings for Desdemona are passionate, undeviating, almost apocalyptic:

> Perdition catch my soul,
> But I do love thee; and when I love thee not,
> Chaos is come again. (III.iii.91–93)

But his insecurities about his race ("Haply, for I am black"), his manners ("[I] have not those soft parts of conversation / That chamberers have"), and his age ("or for I am declined / Into the vale of years" [267–70]) make him highly vulnerable to Iago's insinuations regarding his wife's fidelity: "Her honour is an essence that's not seen. / They have it very oft that have it not" (IV.i.17–18).

Under that malignant influence, Othello misperceives a perfectly innocent physical manifestation, such as a warm hand, as a sign of sexual liberality ("hot, hot, and moist" [III.iv.37]). And it is not long before he, too, begins to regard women exclusively in terms of their lusts and functions:

> O curse of marriage,
> That we can call these delicate creatures ours,
> And not their appetites. (III.iii.272–74)

Once Othello accepts Iago's refusal of transcendence, once he acknowledges that the wine a woman drinks is made of grapes, he is quickly converted from a doting husband into a paranoid misogynist.

Othello's vocabulary of sexist abuse henceforth will be as ripe and charged as Iago's: Emilia is a "simple bawd" and "subtle whore," Desdemona an "impudent strumpet," "a cistern for foul toads to knot and gender in" (IV.ii.21–22, 63–64). But even at the moment of her death, Othello is still torn between his veneration for Desdemona as the "cunning'st pattern of excelling nature" (V.ii.11) and his impression of her as "the cunning whore of Venice" (IV.ii.93). (Surely there are Iago-influenced puns hidden in Othello's use of "cunning'st" and "cunning.") Only after Iago has been exposed as a treacherous villain is Othello able to reinstate his Platonic regard for his wife as a "heavenly sight" (V.ii.285), the worthy object of his unworthy love.

The Iago figure in *Cymbeline* has a similar name, Iachimo, and works on Posthumus Leonatus, the Othello of the play, in a similar manner. Like Othello, Posthumus swears eternal fealty to Imogen, even when she urges him to remarry following her death. But he regards her more as a trophy wife when he boasts that Imogen is "more fair, virtuous, wise, chaste, constant, qualified, and less attemptable, than any the rarest of our ladies in France" (I.iv.51–52). That she is not "attemptable" inevitably obliges Iachimo to "attempt" her, wagering his estate of ten thousand ducats against the braggart husband's diamond ring. And Posthumus is vain enough to accept the offer.

Iachimo wins his wager through trickery, by hiding in a trunk, stealing Imogen's bracelet, and ogling the cinque-spotted mole on her breast. It is enough evidence to convince Posthumus that his wife is a whore, and to launch him into a Hamlet-like tirade on the subject of female inconstancy:

> The vows of women
> Of no more bondage be to where they are made
> Than they are to their virtues. (II.iv.110–12)

He is prepared "to tear her limb-meal" (147), just as Othello was ready to chop Desdemona "into messes" (IV.i.190), and takes the occasion to question the paternity of himself and every man ("We are bastards all" II.v.2). He visualizes not goats and monkeys, like Othello, but "a full-acorned boar, a German one" who "cried O!, and mounted" (16–17):

> For there's no motion
> That tends to vice in man, but I affirm
> It is the woman's part; be it lying, note it,
> The woman's; flattering, hers; deceiving, hers;
> Lust and rank thoughts, hers, hers; revenges, hers;
> Ambitions, covetings, change of prides, disdain,
> Nice longing, slanders, mutability,
> All faults that man can name, nay, that hell
>   knows,
> Why hers, in part or all; but rather all. . . .
> The very devils cannot plague them better. (20–35)

And this from the man who earlier claimed his wife to be the most virtuous woman in the world.

Leontes in *The Winter's Tale* is much like Othello and Posthumus in his jealousy, but his Iago (or Iachimo) lurks within, hidden and internalized. Seeing his wife, Hermione, give her hand to the Bohemian King Polixenes, he is seized with a jealousy so sudden and violent that it seems pathological, even though it was he who encouraged her to persuade his close friend to remain at the Sicilian court. Images of lust similar to those that poison the minds of Hamlet and Othello and Posthumus begin to shake his imagination, not goats and monkeys or German boars but hot hands, paddling palms and pinching fingers:

> Too hot, too hot:
> To mingle friendship farre is mingling bloods,
> I have *tremor cordis* on me. (I.ii.110-12)[22]

Because of this harmless touching of hands (Leontes does not overhear his wife questioning her husband's and Polixenes' early sexual experience), Leontes immediately doubts the paternity of his son, Mamillius. He acknowledges how people say that he and his child look exactly alike—but it is "women say so,/That will say anything" (132-33). He believes his wife has been "sluiced" in his absence, that his pond has been "fished by his next neighbor" (195-96). He imagines Hermione and Polixenes "kissing with inside lip" and "meeting noses" (287-88), images worthy of the sex-hating Iago. On this "bawdy planet," one-tenth of mankind have unfaithful wives, and his own, Hermione, is a "hobby-horse," who "deserves a name/As rank as any flax-wench" (228-29).

Astonishingly, Leontes is stirred into generalizations on the subject of faithless women by a single handshake between Polixenes and Hermione. Like Hamlet, who abuses Ophelia as a result of his mother's adultery, Leontes becomes an instant paranoid (his counselor, Camillo, begs him "to be cured/Of this diseased opinion" [298-99]). But in Leontes' mind, his only affliction is a pair of cuckold's horns, and "many thousand on's / Have the disease, and feel't not" (207–8). Even the Delphic Oracle cannot shake his conviction that his wife is false and his children bastards, and for the better part of three acts, he rails against Hermione and the entire female sex. *The Winter's Tale* is not a tragedy but rather a tragicomedy in the fashion of Beaumont and Fletcher, which is why Hermione, unlike Desdemona, survives her husband's jealousy. But the king's subsequent actions bring his wife very close to death, and actually result in the death of his son. Leontes characteristically interprets Mamillius's mortal illness as being caused not by his own fault but by "the dishonour of his mother" (II.iii.13).[23]

Following the appearance of Time as a chorus announcing the passage of sixteen years, we come upon a vastly changed Leontes. Paulina, Hermione's waiting woman, whom he earlier rated as a bawd, as Othello did Emilia, he now thinks "grave and good" (V.iii.1). Cured of his Hamlet Obsession, he is eager to see the statue of his supposedly dead wife. One might say, as the Doctor says of Lear, that "the great rage . . . is killed in him" (IV.vii.79–80), and now he wishes only to repent. When Hermione's "statue" comes to "life" at the very end of the play, her reconciliation with Leontes is perfunctory indeed. Leontes asks pardon for his "ill suspicion" (V.iii.150), but the play ends before Hermione gets around to granting it.[24] It is one of the most abrupt and puzzling final scenes in all of Shakespeare, as if the playwright had lost interest in anything but the quick resolution of the plot. But when the play is over, what we most vividly remember is not the romance of Florizel and Perdita, not the rascally behavior of Autolycus, not even the startling resurrection of Hermione, but the Hamlet Obsession of the pathologically hornmad Leontes.

Troilus and Cressida and *Antony and Cleopatra*, two plays set in classical times, each contain a heroine who, through her sexual infidelity, excites misogynistic feelings in her lover. Garber calls Cressida the "anti-Juliet" and "anti-Desdemona," and nicely captures the sour nature of the play when she says it might almost have been written by Hamlet. Actually, it could also have been written by Marston, who first transferred into drama the scurrilous attitudes of comical and tragical satire.

Through the good offices of Pandarus, Cressida shares Troilus's bed for a brief moment before being delivered to the Greeks as what Ulysses calls one of the "sluttish spoils of opportunity / And daughters of the game" (IV.vi.63–64). Troilus has neither the language nor the wit to describe his disillusionment with Cressida. He is a fatuous courtly lover, still living, like his fellow Trojans, in a bygone world of chivalry and honor.

Othello had said of Desdemona,

> I had been happy, if the general camp,
> Pioners and all, had tasted her sweet body,
> So I had nothing known. (III.iii.350–52)

It is Cressida who actually has her body tasted by the general camp, pioneers and all, with Troilus forced to look on helplessly. One by one, each of the Greeks gets to kiss Cressida and trade bawdry with her, until Diomedes takes her off to be his mistress. This liaison between a Greek warrior and a Trojan woman mirrors the love affair between the Greek woman and the Trojan warrior (Helen and Paris) that started this ill-fated war. In the act of bedding Cressida, Diomedes gets to express his revulsion toward Helen in the strongest terms:

> For every false drop in her bawdy veins
> A Grecian life hath sunk; for every scruple
> Of her contaminated carrion weight,
> A Trojan hath been slain. (V.i.71–74)

Ulysses holds the same opinion of Cressida, concluding that "her wanton spirits look out / At every joint and motive of her body" (IV.vi.57–58).

Are we thereby meant, like Hamlet, to see this wantonness as a universal female failing? Frailty, thy name is woman? Cressida certainly seems to think so when she remarks, "Ah, poor our sex! This fault in us I find, / The error of our eye directs our mind" (V.ii.109–10). It is true that Troilus resists such generalizations:

> Let it not be believed for womanhood!
> Think, we had mothers; do not give advantage
> To stubborn critics, apt, without a theme,
> For depravation, to square the general sex
> By Cressid's rule. (129–33)

On the other hand, Ulysses' famous speech about the disarrangement of "degree" suggests that Helen's "bawdy veins" and Cressida's "wanton spirits" are not individual failings but rather the consequence of a universal breakdown:

> Then everything includes itself in power,
> Power into will, will into appetite;
> And appetite, an universal wolf,
> So doubly seconded with will and power,
> Must make perforce an universal prey,
> And last eat up himself. (I.iii.119–24)

An universal wolf pursuing an universal prey! Indeed, the entire Trojan War, beginning with Paris's abduction of Helen, is, as Thersites suggests, the consequence of indiscriminate lust and ravenous appetite: "Lechery, lechery, still wars and lechery! Nothing else holds fashion. A burning devil take them" (V.ii.193–94).

Antony and Cleopatra is one of the greatest of Shakespeare's love plays, but unlike *Romeo and Juliet,* where the lovers concentrate only on their passion and its consummation, the older figures in this play have more important matters at hand. As in *Troilus and Cressida,* love and warfare are inextricably connected. Romeo notes that Juliet's beauty "hath made me effeminate" (III.i.109). The same thing holds true of Antony. His passion for Cleopatra has robbed him of his sword, and caused Hercules, the manly demigod he loves, to abandon him. Unlike the virgin Juliet, Cleopatra is an aging veteran of the amorous wars. "You were half blasted ere I knew you" (III.xiii.105), Antony tells her, after he finds her flirting with Octavius's messenger. She was Julius Caesar's mistress as a girl and, according to Antony, spent a little time with Pompey, a memory that sets him musing Othello-like upon her erotic history:

> I found you as a morsel cold upon
> Dead Caesar's trencher; nay, you were a fragment
> Of Gnaeus Pompey's, besides what hotter hours,
> Unregistered in vulgar fame you have
> Luxuriously picked out. (117–21)

Luxury and *luxuriousness* are among Shakespeare's most noxious erotic nouns. In his book *Shakespeare on Love and Lust,* Maurice Charney notes the repeated sexual imagery in the play; even Cleopatra's death is described in erotic terms. But this is also the play where love and lust are entwined in the most complicated fashion, where the two lovers have the most developed relationship. *Antony and Cleopatra* is the maturest of Shakespeare's meditations on the erotic nature of womankind, for it is, in a sense, the most forgiving. Unlike Hamlet, unlike Othello, unlike Leontes, unlike Troilus, and unlike Shakespeare in his sonnets, Antony can contemplate his lover's sexual history without wallowing in a sea of sex hatred. His love for Cleopatra outlives his recriminations, and perhaps resolves them as well.

Antony is the great Might-Have-Been of Shakespeare's heroes, a kind of early sketch for Jamie Tyrone Senior in O'Neill's *Long Day's Journey into Night*. A brilliant orator and clever general, he has too great a weakness for drink and women (for "luxurious wassails") to realize his political potential. In the very opening lines of the play, he is called "The triple pillar of the world transformed / Into a strumpet's fool" (I.i.12–13). But the "strumpet" in this play is Cleopatra, and the way Shakespeare characterizes her suggests that very few men—apart from cold-blooded Puritans like Octavius—could have resisted her magnetic appeal. It is ironic that the man who best describes her "infinite variety" (II.ii.241), her resistance to the aging process, her ability to stimulate the male sexual appetite, is another person who remains impervious to her charms—the soldier Enobarbus. (He is also Antony's most severe critic for yielding to those charms.)

Cleopatra, the personification of the womanly woman, is an unwomanly woman as well, just as the masculine Antony is often a feminized man. To me, the most persuasive example of Garber's theory of trans-sexuality in Shakespeare is her description, in *Shakespeare After All*, of "the exchange of gender roles and adornments" in this play. Octavius contemptuously observes that Antony is "not more manlike than Cleopatra" and Cleopatra is not "more womanly than he." Cleopatra boasts that she once outdrank her lover and dressed him in her woman's clothes while wearing his sword Philippan. The arc of the play, as Garber remarks, is described in the process of masculinizing Cleopatra and feminizing Antony until he has become another of the queen's eunuchs.

It is because of these reversals of sexual roles that "the god

Hercules, whom Antony loved,/Now leaves him" (IV.iii.13–14). Hercules abandons Antony because Antony has chosen Venus instead of Mars. The servant who refuses to kill Antony is named Eros, after a Greek god of love, and when Eros kills himself instead, Antony remarks, "Thy master dies thy scholar" (IV.xv.102). Is Antony's scholarship a study in courageous self-sacrifice or in erotic self-indulgence? The demigod Hercules himself, as the playwrights of this period often like to note, was once forced to do women's tasks by another overbearing Eastern queen, Omphale.[25]

After Antony dies, Cleopatra monopolizes the entire fifth act for the purpose of reflecting on their love, enacting a much more brilliant death scene than Antony's botched suicide. At last, Shakespeare seems to be endorsing the *Hic-Mulier* character that previously he scorned and feared: Cleopatra enters myth as a masculine spirit even more heroic than her military lover. Like Lady Macbeth, she has managed to unsex herself:

> I have nothing
> Of woman in me. Now from head to foot
> I am marble-constant. (V.ii.234–36)

It is the male hero that remains womanized, as Shakespeare shakes off his distrust of the mannish woman for a moment to celebrate a heroine of substance and of strength.

And in his late romances, Shakespeare seems much more absorbed with pardon and reconciliation than with blame and disapproval, despite the occasional antifemale eruptions in *The Winter's Tale* and *Cymbeline*. One finds those forgiving qualities particularly in relations between fathers and their daughters. Leontes and Perdita, Prospero and Miranda, Pericles and Marina, and, most poignantly and tragically, Lear and Cordelia represent the resolution of old tensions and anxieties through powerful parental bonding. Do these relationships mirror the strong attachment between Shakespeare and his surviving children, Susanna and Judith, to whom he left the bulk of his fortune, excluding his second-best bed? There is no way to know. But such feelings more than compensate for any lingering misogyny in the plays. The Hamlet Obsession with faithless women has finally evaporated into tender fatherly love. Shakespeare will prove much less forgiving of feminized men.

2

Effemiphobia

THE OSRIC COURTIER

He made me mad
To see him shine so brisk, and smell so sweet
And talk so like a waiting gentlewoman
Of guns, and drums, and wounds, God save the mark!
— (1 Henry IV I.iii.52–55)

By the end of the century, satirists had divided the courtier into two categories, the soldier and the carpet knight, admiring the one and resenting the other. Perhaps the most telling example of this division can be found in the scene from which this chapter's epigraph is taken, in the contrast between the battle-weary Hotspur and the perfumed, snuff-taking lord who interrupts his well-earned respite from combat with his foppish behavior and fastidious manners. Shakespeare makes this courtier into a creature as awkward on the field of arms as Hotspur would have been at a court masque. Which is the reason Hotspur expresses so much contempt for him:

> But I remember when the fight was done,
> When I was dry with rage, and extreme toil,
> Breathless and faint, leaning upon my sword,
> Came there a certain lord, neat and trimly dressed,
> Fresh as a bridegroom; and his chin, new-reaped
> Showed like a stubble land at harvest home.
> He was perfumèd like a milliner,
> And 'twixt his finger and his thumb he held

A pouncet-box, which ever and anon
He gave his nose. . . .
And as the soldiers bore dead bodies by,
He called them untaught knaves, unmannerly,
To bring a slovenly unhandsome corpse,
Betwixt the wind and his nobility.
With many holiday and lady terms
He questioned me. (I.iii.29–46)

Here, in Hotspur's heated account, are listed all the deficiencies of the carpet knight: his pretentiousness, his ignorance about war, his battlefield-inappropriate costume and barbering, his affected verbosity, his disrespect for soldiering, and, above all, his effeminate "waiting-gentlewoman" behavior and appearance as displayed in his "chin new-reaped" beardlessness. This "certain lord" will rematerialize a few years later as Osric in *Hamlet*.

Indeed, it may be Osric who best represents Shakespeare's idea of the flowery and effeminate upstart courtier (though his near namesake Oswald, Goneril's steward in *King Lear,* runs him a close second). With his fancy apparel, his sinister intentions, his newly rich status, his flattering tongue, and, above all, his chop-logic vocabulary, Osric is the very personification of Hotspur's "certain lord." (Peter Cushing in Olivier's *Hamlet* caught these qualities exactly with his ostentatious bowing and scraping, and fulsome flourishes of his bonnet.) Nor does Hamlet find Osric untypical. This "water-fly" is merely one of many that "the drossy age dotes on" (V.ii.141–42).

Hamlet calls Osric a "water-fly," the same expletive Thersites will later use to describe Patroclus, partly because he is "a diminutive of nature," but also because he is bait for Claudius's hook. Osric "hath much land, and fertile" (87), having acquired a substantial parcel of real estate and thus found a place at the royal table.[1] In a court that values goods over goodness, even a beast can "stand at the king's mess" if that particular animal owns his own herds. Osric is a courtier who can go either way, in every sense of the phrase, but particularly regarding the manner in which he flatters and equivocates. When Hamlet says the climate is "very sultry and hot for my complexion," then Osric must confirm his forecast: "It is very sultry, as 'twere" (97–98). When Hamlet, changing his weather report, says that it is cold, then Osric is perfectly willing to contradict himself as well: "It is indifferent cold" (96). At court, an upstart does not argue with power, and truth sits in the shade.[2]

In *Hamlet*, Osric is an instrument of Claudius's Machiavellian policy. It is he who stage-manages Hamlet's duel with Laertes, and in a number of modern productions, including the Olivier movie, it is he who prepares the poison for the cup that Claudius intends for Hamlet, and envenoms Laertes' unbated sword. One certain proof of his villainy, relatively harmless as it might seem to a later age, is the quality that most exquisitely exemplifies his style, the tangled skein of his verbosity. Hamlet's verbal exchanges with Osric are clearly intended to ridicule the kind of flowery neologisms and circumlocutory language then in fashion at court.[3] It is typical of this thick-skinned fop that he is never aware of being satirized or mocked:

> Osric: Sir here is newly come to court Laertes, believe me, an absolute gentleman, full of most excellent differences, of very soft society and great showing. Indeed, to speak feelingly of him, he is the card and calendar of gentry, for you shall find in him the continent of what part a gentleman would see.
>
> Hamlet: Sir, his defilement suffers no perdition in you, though I know to divide him inventorially would dizzy th'arithmetic of memory, and yet

but yaw neither in respect of his quick sail. But
in the verity of extolment, I take him to be a soul
of great article, and his infusion of such dearth
and rareness as, to make true diction of him, his
semblable is his mirror, and who else would trace
him his umbrage, nothing more.

Osric: Your lordship speaks most infallibly of him.
(V.ii.102–15)

Hamlet may speak infallibly, but far from lucidly. He has found
the perfect metaphor-bloated vocabulary with which to mock
Osric's unintelligible chop-logic.

As Osric is to Hamlet, so Oswald is to Kent, though Kent,
being more unmannerly than Hamlet, makes no effort to hide
his contempt or mask his insults. When Oswald asks, "What
dost thou know me for?" Kent lets loose a torrent of invective
designed to leave the man in ruins:

A knave; a rascal; an eater of broken meats; a base,
proud, shallow, beggarly, three-suited, hundred-
pound, filthy, worsted-stocking knave; a lily-livered,
action-taking knave, a whoreson, glass-glazing,
super-serviceable, finical rogue; one trunk-inheriting
slave; one that wouldst be a bawd in way of good
service. . . . (II.ii.12–17)

And so on for another hundred words or so. Although Kent
concentrates less on Oswald's affected speech than on his
ostentatious dress and sinister service, Osric and Oswald are
peas in a pod, both agents of evil as well as of pretentiousness,
each having to deal with an honest plain-dealer who mocks his
affectations.

What generated Shakespeare's distaste for the effeminate
upstart courtier? Perhaps the same mind set that animated his

attacks on the faithless woman. If it is true, to quote a popular scientific maxim, that ontogeny recapitulates phylogeny, it is equally true that misogyny recapitulates androgyny: Fear and hatred of the female sex can often be accompanied by confusion about male identity. Questions regarding Shakespeare's sexuality have been the subject of much discussion lately, the speculation largely driven by the passion he expresses in the sonnets toward a young man, probably his patron, Henry Wriothesley, third Earl of Southampton, who was famously bisexual. (One of Southampton's soldiers testified that he saw the earl "clip and hug" a corporal general in his army "and play wantonly with him.") The question is whether Shakespeare was bisexual himself and how that might have influenced his work.

One finds a few examples of open same-sex love exchanges in Shakespeare plays around the same period as the sonnets, the most transparent of them in *The Two Noble Kinsmen,* where Emilia praises "the true love between maid and maid" (I.iii.81) and where Arcite tells Palamon, "We are one another's wife" (II.ii.80).[4] Shakespeare, however, wrote this work in collaboration with John Fletcher, who might have been responsible for some of the more explicit passages, and such references could simply be metaphors for passionate friendship.

But there are other examples. The merchant Antonio, for example, is so attached to his heterosexual young friend Bassanio in *The Merchant of Venice* that he seems to have gone into a clinical depression, and the same sort of passion is expressed by his namesake, the sea captain Antonio, toward Sebastian in *Twelfth Night.* Such love between males, similar to that expressed in the sonnets, falls short of physical consummation, though some productions have made such relationships more explicit. (Andrei Serban's version of *Twelfth Night* at the American Repertory Theatre in 1989, for example, playfully located the first scene between Antonio and Sebastian in a gay bar, with Shakespeare sitting at a nearby table, writing down the dialogue.) Other commentators have been more cautious about such interpretations. Maurice Charney in *Shakespeare on Love and Lust,* for example, is persuaded that in spite of intermittent glances of this sort in Shakespeare's poems and plays, "contemporary terms such as 'homosexuality,' 'lesbianism,' and 'bisexuality' have no direct references to the sexual ideologies of the late sixteenth and early seventeenth centuries."

Whatever they were called, such practices were publicly condemned. A 1553 statute made "the detestable and abominable vice of buggery committed on mankind or beast" to be a felony punishable by death. And although there are no known cases of execution in England at this time because of homosexual acts, "sodomy" continued to be a source of extreme fear and loathing, especially in Puritan circles. Shakespeare only hints at such sexual predilections. Openly gay writers like Christopher Marlowe were clearly exceptions in their willingness to celebrate a passion for boys, though there is a legend that Shakespeare's brother, Edmund, followed him to London to act upon the stage and had a gay relationship with the boy actor Samuel Guilpin.[5] The distinction most often found in Shakespeare is not so much between heterosexuality and homosexuality as between talk and action, between the rhetoric of same-sex love and its physical expression.

In Shakespeare one often finds males admitting love for males, but almost always as an expression of Platonic friendship. Sexual congress is an activity normally conducted only among men and women. The sonnets include punning hints that "Will," as the poet calls himself, is erotically aroused by a "fair youth" whom he unblushingly identifies as the "master-mistress of my passion" (sonnet 20). Will even rhapsodizes about his sexual appeal:

> Flesh stays no father reason,
> But rising at thy name doth point out thee,
> As his triumphant prize. (sonnet 151)

But the poet also makes it clear, in an oft-quoted passage, that despite his rising flesh and strong feelings, he cannot contemplate having sexual relations with this young man:

> And for a woman wert thou first created,
> Till Nature as she wrought thee fell a-doting,
> And by addition me of thee defeated,
> By adding one thing to my purpose nothing.
>> But since she pricked thee out for women's pleasure,
>> Mine be thy love, and thy love's use their treasure. (sonnet 20)

He can love the male, but not the male organ—that "one thing" is reserved for womankind. Honest enough to confess his sexual attraction to a man, he cannot make the leap into a gay relationship with him.

Shakespeare may not be homophobic, but he is certainly effemiphobic. Whatever ambiguities one finds in his works about same-sex love, there are none whatsoever about effeminate men. He fully shares the prejudices of his age regarding the slightest hint of unmanly conduct. Some of this prejudice washes off on Lady Macbeth when she expresses doubts about her Lord's manly resolve regarding the killing of Duncan:

> When you durst do it, then you were a man;
> And to be more than what you were you would
> Be so much more the man. (I.vii.49–51)

Goneril expresses a similar kind of feeling when she (unfairly) characterizes Albany as womanish and "milk-livered" because he refuses to endorse her murderous behavior ("Marry your manhood! mew!" IV.ii.69). In these rare exchanges, the insinuations of unmanliness reflect more discredit on the accuser than on the accused.

The best illustration of Shakespeare's not always consistent distinction between unmanliness and homosexuality can be found in the relationship between the only openly gay lovers in his plays, Patroclus and Achilles (*Troilus and Cressida*). Achilles may prefer men to women, but he is the most admired warrior in the Greek camp. He is called effeminate only when, sulking in his tent, he refuses to do battle with the Trojans. Indeed, it is Patroclus himself, scurrilously characterized by Thersites as Achilles' "male varlet . . . [and] masculine whore" (V.i.14, 16), who identifies the masculine deficiencies of himself and his gay lover:

> A woman impudent and mannish grown,
> Is not more loathed than an effeminate man
> In time of action. (III.iii.210–12)

Note that Patroclus does not consider himself or Achilles effeminate because of their sexual relationship or because they fail to perform with women. It is because they fail to engage with men—on the battlefield—that he finds such lovers wanting in manhood. Note also that Patroclus couples effeminate men and mannish women as twin sources of "loathing." Those two apparent deviations were always closely joined in contemporary Puritan and satirical writings. If the pamphlet known as *Hic-Mulier* (or The mannish woman) was an attack on women who wore pants, the companion piece it inspired—*Haec-Vir* (or The womanish man)—was equally disapproving of sexual confusion in the male gender.[6]

For Shakespeare and his contemporaries, effeminate males are almost invariably courtiers, endowed with inverted social as well as sexual characteristics. In addition to being womanish in war, this courtier is very frequently identified as an upstart or "carpet knight," who may have bought his way into the aristocracy (a subject of particular concern after James I ascended the throne in 1603 and began selling off knighthoods for a hundred pounds apiece). Most important, he is an *Italianate* courtier, which is to say one influenced by the politics, manners, behavior, and literature of the Italian city-states.

Allow me to digress at this point about this powerful foreign influence—the fascination of the English court with Italy during the sixteenth century. The closest parallel is the impact of French culture on the Russian aristocracy in the eighteenth and nineteenth centuries. English courtiers, conscious of their deficiencies in manners and good breeding, looked to Italy for guidance and education, either through travel or through reading. Italian-style clothes were imported into England, among them perfumed gloves for the men, and masks, busks, muffs, fans, periwigs, and bodkins for the women. The method of address known as "courtly complement" became increasingly elaborated through Italian example, and Italian became the language of diplomatic address. Furthermore, the Italian pastoral ideal found its way into the novels of Greene and Lodge and thence into the romantic comedies of Greene, Lyly, and, of course, Shakespeare. Influenced by the writings of Ariosto, Tasso, Guarini, and others, those in courtly circles looked to Italy for good manners, chivalrous behavior, and romantic guidance.

The reaction against this was equally strong. To the English moralists and satirists, and most of the English dramatists (including Shakespeare), Italy was also a breeding ground for poison, revenge, dissimulation, affectation, "and beastly Sodomy," as it was often called, a place where honest men feared for their lives and honest women (the handful who remained) feared for their virtue. Unlike virtually every one of his later contemporaries—among them Marston, Webster, Tourneur, Middleton, Ford, Jonson, Barnabe Barnes, and Beaumont and Fletcher— Shakespeare never wrote a play that was actually situated in the murderous precincts of the Italianate court, despite the number of plots he set in Italy. (A technical exception is the mini-Italianate court play-within-a-play in *Hamlet* called "The Murder of Gonzago" about a king who is poisoned by his Machiavellian brother for his queen and his crown.) But there is no question that he employed all the Italianate court conventions, most particularly the character of the lecherous court lady, the dissembling Machiavellian villain, and the effeminate flattering courtier, whether he set his tragedies in Denmark, Scotland, or ancient Britain.

And Shakespeare was perfectly aware of the malignant influence Italy was said to be having on the English court. When York speaks, in *Richard II*, of the

> fashions in proud Italy,
> Whose manners still our tardy-apish nation
> Limps after in base imitation (II.i.21–23),

he is speaking not as a fourteenth-century noble so much as a sixteenth-century English moralist deploring a Tudor rather than a Plantagenet condition. As Thomas Nashe wrote in *The Unfortunate Traveller* (1593): "The onely probable good thing [Italy has] to keep us from utterly condemning it is that it maketh a man an excellent Courtier, a curious carpet knight; which is, by interpretation, a fine close leacher, a glorious hypocrite. It is nowe a privie note amongst the better sort of men, when they would set a singular marke or brand on a notorious villaine, to say, he hath beene in *Italy*."

These strictures were partially motivated by the fact that Italy was the seat of Romanism, and most Englishmen (though the jury is still out on Shakespeare) had a violent hatred of anything

Papist. But the two major Italian influences on the English court were not religious but literary ones — namely, the political writings of Machiavelli and the courtesy books of Castiglione. Machiavelli determined the English courtier's attitude toward practical policy; Castiglione influenced his behavior at the dining table and in polite society.

The Machiavelli associated with the name of Italy in the English mind, however, was not the subtle political theorist of *Il Principe* and the *Discorsi* but the diabolical scoundrel misrepresented and libeled in Innocent Gentillet's *Contre-Machiavel* (1576). According to this French Huguenot's distorted account, Machiavelli was an advocate of ruthlessness, deceit, sodomy, flattery, acquisitiveness, impiety, and murder by poison — qualities that were "spotting" England through his example.[7] In actuality, Machiavelli was as critical of the presumed vices of his Italian countrymen as were the English, but it is Gentillet's caricature of Machiavelli that finds its way into English theatre, not just informing villains like Iago and Richard III (who puts "the murderous Machiavel to school" [III.ii.193]), but emerging as a dramatic character in his own right — notably, as the Prologue to Marlowe's *Jew of Malta*, where he functions as the inspiration for a tale of murder, poisoning, and treachery, the guiding spirit of the villainous Barabas.

A remark by Roger Ascham — "Englese Italianato e un diabolo incarnato" ("An Italianate Englishman is a devil incarnate") — was to become an axiom of the time. In the popular view, Italianated English courtiers were particularly vulnerable to Machiavelli's diabolical doctrines, which included advice about how to acquire and enjoy power through treachery and poison. On the other hand, if courtiers wanted counsel about how to behave themselves in the royal presence, how to hold a fork, or how to woo a lady, they had only to consult the writings of Baldassare Castiglione.

Castiglione's *Il Cortegiano* or *The Book of the Courtier,* first published in 1528, had a dominating influence on English court circles from the time of Thomas Hoby's translation in 1561 until the end of the century. From it, Elizabeth's courtiers learned the value of table manners, Platonic love, courtly conversation, grace, humility, and *sprezzatura* (detachment and modesty). Men like Raleigh, Essex, and Sidney (who reputedly carried Castiglione's book in his pocket whenever he went abroad) successfully balanced the qualities of soldier, scholar, and courtier admired in *Il Cortegiano*. (This Castiglione trinity is affirmed by Ophelia when she praises Hamlet as "the courtier's, soldier's, scholar's eye, tongue, sword" [III.i.150].) Furthermore, the court of "Gloriana" modeled itself to a large extent on Castiglione's ideal court of Urbino.[8]

Castiglione had been scornful of the carpet knight, but through some curious misunderstanding of his doctrine he became known, among many English, as the carpet knight's patron saint. When King James in the early seventeenth century began his indiscriminate selling of baronetcies, the works of Castiglione became, for a newly rich arriviste, the best access to information concerning court manners. The "fustian phrases" and "sugred words" that Joseph Hall said courtiers employed "to creep into men's bosoms" came directly from his courtesy books: "Balthazar affords/Fountaines of holy and rose-water words," wrote Edward Gilpin, calling him the "Dictionary of complements,/The Barber's mouth of new-scrapt eloquence." Indeed, the very names Balthazar and Castilio in satire and drama (derived, of course, from Baldassare Castiglione) would henceforth be applied to the most affected and Italianated upstarts.[9]

Robert Greene, in *A Quip for an Upstart Courtier* (1592), also took off after Castiglione, satirizing the presumptuous "Velvet

Breeches" as "an upstart out of Italy," where presumably he has learned from the Italians to imitate his betters, and to study the art of "self-love, sodomy, and strange poisonings."

Greene was Shakespeare's nemesis, the man who, in his *Groatsworth of Wit,* had charged him with beautifying himself with the feathers of his fellow playwrights. But Greene certainly seemed to speak for many of his fellow playwrights, Shakespeare included, in the way he satirized the upstart's speech and his use of "inkhorn" locutions. Shakespeare often expressed the same kind of distaste, not only toward Osric and Oswald but even earlier in *Love's Labour's Lost* when Biron abjures

> Taffeta phrases, silken terms precise,
> Three-piled hyperboles, spruce affectation,
> Figures pedantical,

vowing to speak henceforth in "russet yeas and honest kersey noes" (V.ii.406–13). Indeed, when Hamlet observes that "the age is grown so picked, that the toe of the peasant comes so near the heel of the courtier he galls his kibe" (V.i.128–30), he is actually describing the social confusion for which the upstart had become responsible, where one must "speak by the card or equivocation will undo us" (126–27).

Is it possible that the long-winded Polonius, who also has trouble making himself understood, may have been conceived as an aged, doddering version of the Italianate courtier? The notion that the wise counselor may be the stupidest man in the room is hardly a radical thought in our own age. Like Osric, Polonius often speaks in a language that is loquacious and obscure, stimulating Gertrude's demand that he use "More matter with less art" (II.ii.96).[10] ("Madame, I swear I use no art at all," he responds, more wisely than he knows [97].) He gets gummed up in his own logic like a spider spinning itself inside its own web. And like Osric, he is perfectly willing to participate in the entrapment of Hamlet by Claudius.

It a similar type of courtier who arouses Mercutio's ire in *Romeo and Juliet* when he describes Tybalt as a "courageous captain of compliments," one of those "antic, lisping, affecting phantasms," those "new tuners of accent" (II.iv.25–26) who were currently butchering the plain, unadorned English tongue. Even John Lyly, himself responsible for a lot of contemporary verbal mannerisms, was known to complain (in *Euphues and His England*) about the affectation of English speech ("In tymes past they used to wooe in playne tearmes, now in piked sentences . . . every one following the newest waye, which is not even the nearest way"). It is this old-fashioned use of "playne tearmes" that Biron endorses in *Love's Labour's Lost* when he resolves to speak in "russet yeas and honest kersey noes" (V.ii.416). It is this brand of directness that Hotspur prompts of his wife, Kate, in *1 Henry IV,* when he asks her for a "good mouth-filling oath" in place of "protest of pepper-gingerbread" (III.i.250–51). And it is this kind of wooing that Henry rehearses with Catherine of France in *Henry V,* when he claims he has "neither words nor measure," being a "plain king" without access to or interest in courtesy books: "I have no cunning in protestation," he protests, "only downright oaths, which I never use till urged, nor never break for urging" (V.ii.141–43). As we shall see in the next chapter, these are the men who represent the plain-dealing soldiers Shakespeare most admired, and used as a counterweight to the verbose Italianate courtier.[11]

The new speech was roundly condemned not just because it was artificial but also because it was considered an instrument of seduction and sycophancy. "Nay, do not think I flatter," says Hamlet, assuring Horatio that the vocabulary of compliment is not in his lexicon. But it is surely in the lexicon of the courtiers attending on King Claudius, as Hamlet goes on to emphasize:

No, let the candied tongue lick absurd pomp
And crook the pregnant hinges of the knee
Where thrift may follow feigning. (III.ii.53–55)

Flattering and fawning are the currency not of true noblemen but of licking spaniels and buzzing waterflies like Osric, as well as of timeservers like Rosencrantz and Guildenstern, who would ascend the ladder of power on bended knees.

Since the Middle Ages, satirists had considered flattery one of the prime vices of the courtier, but circumstances at court in Shakespeare's time certainly aggravated the traditional satiric animus. Elizabeth in her declining years had grown considerably more vulnerable to the blandishments of younger men (the very convention that acclaimed her a demure and beautiful virgin was steeped in insincerity), while the court of James became notorious for the king's insistence on compliments.[12]

A more political reason for the satirist's hatred of flattery was that it had come to be linked with Machiavellian dissimulation, another evil quality employed in the climb to power. The dissembler, like the flatterer, concealed his real intentions behind a false smiling front.[13] The "Flattering Lords" of *Timon of Athens* are typical of the way forked tongues take precedence in court over straight speech, a condition that eventually plunges the hero into misanthropy. These are the same sort of flatterers who once crowded around Lear ("They told me I was every thing. / 'Tis a lie, I am not ague-proof" [IV.vi.102–3]). Hamlet may claim "I know not 'seems,'" but the Machiavellian courtier knows nothing else. Like all Shakespearean villains, he prefers appearance to reality, art to nature, seeming to being. Uneasiness with these issues stimulated the congenital Elizabethan questioning of such abstractions as honor, loyalty, love, and fidelity. Were these mere words or intrinsic truths, breaths or realities? It is a question that permeates *Hamlet, King Lear,* and especially *Othello,* whose central character makes the cardinal error of thinking "men honest, that but seem to be so" (I.iii.382).

Satire on speech, idleness, flattery, and dissimulation occupied much of the criticism leveled against the Italianate courtier in Shakespeare's time. A large section of the broadside was also directed against his outerwear. The abuse of fashion had become particularly flagrant in the Elizabethan-Jacobean period, and largely because of foreign influences. As Lyly noted in *Euphues,* "The attire they use is rather ledde by the imitation of others, then their owne invention, so that there is nothing in Englande more constant, then the inconstancie of attire."[14] It is worth repeating that, when Shakespeare's duke of York chides his nation for imitating Italy, he is referring specifically to Italy's fashions in dress.

Although *Richard II* is a historical play, York's remark is contemporary. The courtiers of the "tardy-apish nation" called Albion were no doubt forced to compete with each other in finery in order to catch the eye of the aging queen. But by the end of the century, the upstart's passion for "ordinate excess in apparel" had become so extreme that even Elizabeth was offended, reviving an old clothing statute that determined exactly what dress was appropriate for each class. A proclamation was issued in 1599 to check the prevalent excess in apparel, and Bishop Pilkington took advantage of the occasion to reprove "fine-fingered rufflers, with their sables about their necks, corked slippers, trimmed buskins, and warm mittens . . . never content with enough, but always devising new fashions and strange."

Keeping in the latest fashion was later to become an almost certain method of attracting the attention of King James, with his weakness for well-dressed young men. In fact, James even encouraged his courtiers to maintain a large wardrobe. Writing to Sir John Harington, Thomas Howard noted ruefully: "You are not young, you are not handsome, you are not finely suited; and yet will you come to Court and think to be well favoured?" Hamlet wears black because he is in mourning, but also perhaps as a counterweight to Osric's colorful bonnet and other items of flamboyant court attire. The French philosopher Michel de Montaigne, in his essay "Of the Use of Apparell," called clothes superfluous, arguing that if nature had intended a man to wear them "she would have grown them on his back." Montaigne, like Hamlet, preferred to dress in black as a solemn correction to the excesses of his day. Thomas Dekker, writing in *The Gull's Horn Book* (1609), observed: "For Adams holyday hose and doublet were of no better stuffe then plaine fig-leaves, and Eves best gowne of the same peece. There was then neither the *Spanish* slop, nor the Skippers galligaskins: the *Switzers* blistred Codpiece, nor the *Danish* sleeve sagging down like a Welch wallet, the *Italian* close strosser, nor the French standing coller. . . . Fashions then was counted a disease, and horses died of it."

"Thou owest the worm no silk, the beast no hide, the sheep no wool, the cat no perfume," says Lear to poor Tom, for him the embodiment of "unaccommodated man." In contrast to the "sophisticated" figures in the court, Tom o' Bedlam is "the thing itself . . . a poor, bare, forked animal" (III.iv.96–100). His clothes, like his wits, are but lendings, always subject to being repossessed by their owner, Nature. Just as Lear is rudely, inexorably stripped of his "accommodations"—namely his retinue of one hundred knights—so unaccommodated man will be divested of all his proud transient possessions, reduced to "the thing itself." Paradoxically, however, this process of stripping and divesting represents some kind of progress toward normalcy. Philosophers like Montaigne believed that nakedness was the most natural state, everything else being vanity, and so did John Donne, one of the few Englishmen in the age (if we are to believe his Elegie 20, "Going to Bed") willing to celebrate the pleasures of sex:

> Full nakedness! All joyes are due to thee,
> As souls unbodied, bodies uncloth'd must be
> To taste whole joyes.[15]

Donne's love of pleasure is hardly typical of his time. Most often, the courtier's sense of excess was identified not only with his clothes and manners and speech but also with his indulgent sexual activity. We have noted that charges of unmanliness were sometimes, not always, related to that primary Italianate vice: homosexuality.[16] Many of Shakespeare's contemporaries make insinuations about the inverted sexuality of courtiers, but John Marston is one of the few satiric writers outspoken enough (or nasty enough) to make these hints fully explicit. In *The Scourge of Villainy* (1599), Marston unequivocally announces to his readers that the gaily dressed Italianate courtier is a sodomite, and his page a catamite:

> Seest thou yon gallant in sumptuous clothes,
> How brisk, how spruce, how gorgeously he shows?
> Note his French herring-bones: but note no more,
> Unless thou spy his fair appendant whore,
> That lackies him. Mark nothing but his clothes,
> His new-stamp'd compliment, his cannon oaths;
> Mark those: for naught but such lewd viciousness
> E'er graced him, save Sodom beastliness.
> Is this a man? Nay an incarnate devil,
> That struts in vice and glorieth in evil.

He sounds curiously like Hotspur's "certain lord."

Among the homosexual characters that appear in English drama, Marlowe's Edward II is the most sympathetically treated, a king who suffers a horrible death as a result of his fondness for such favorites as Gaveston. And Shakespeare's Marlovian cousin, King Richard II, while never identified as gay, also seems at times to be as attracted to sycophantic courtiers and "caterpillars of the commonwealth" (Bushy, Bagot, and Greene) as he is to his own queen, which is one of the reasons he is later drowned in a butt of malmsey. (In Robert Woodruff's American Repertory Theatre production, Richard was played as a flaming queen, applying makeup in his dressing room before making an entrance sweeping down a staircase like Norma Desmond in *Sunset Boulevard.*) Marlowe's Jupiter, in *Dido, Queen of Carthage,* enjoys a moment on stage in which he fondles Ganymede, the young page he adores (Achilles' relationship to Patroclus in *Troilus* may be modeled on this scene). And Oberon's obsession with the changeling Indian boy in *A Midsummer Night's Dream* has sometimes been construed as motivated by more than paternal affection, just as Titania's feelings for the child's mother might be considered something other than sisterly.[17]

But in the Elizabethan mind, courtiers demonstrated their effeminacy not so much by same-sex activity as by engaging, excessively, in heterosexual forms of courtly love. If the word *effeminate* in this age meant being afflicted with the weakness of a woman, then the most conspicuous way to display this weakness was through excessive sexual intercourse. Sex was assumed to have a particularly emasculating effect on the courtier, for by becoming the "servant" of his idealized mistress the courtier was thought to have surrendered his manhood to her and absorbed her feminine qualities. Sir John Davies (1598) ridiculed the conventions of chivalric love whereby the courtier gets drunk toasting the health of his mistress and hangs dirty favors on his hat, calling the amorist a "servile Asse" and a "sworn pesant to a female smock." Marston, always displaying more sex nausea than his contemporaries, was as disgusted with the slavish lover as with the active lecher, comparing his "*Inamorato, Curio*" to that habitual butt of macho writers, the emasculated Hercules under the rule of Omphale.[18]

Like Achilles, Antony invited comparison with Hercules by choosing Cleopatra's "weak'ning bed" over the battlefield, just as that same demigod Hercules, whom Antony loved, was himself once enslaved and feminized by working at Omphale's distaff.[19] Hamlet ascribes this kind of passive male weakness to "the imposthume of much wealth and peace" (IV.iv.9.17). Gloucester in *Richard III* observes that "Grim-visaged war," having ceased all martial activities, "capers nimbly in a lady's chamber / To the lascivious pleasing of a lute" (I.i.12–13). And it is said of Bertram, in *All's Well That End's Well,* that he will not spend his "manly marrow" (II.iii.265) in the marriage bed, but rather on the battlefield.[20]

If a courtier was idle, his thoughts turned toward sensuality and riot; if he was engaged in manly pursuits, he had no time for such effeminate recreations. "Make love, not war" was the primary motto of protesters against the Vietnam conflict. Elizabethans would have reversed this axiom, for moral reasons of course, but also for physical ones—making war, not love, was believed to improve one's health. Contemporary physiological studies affirmed that the rich meats and wines consumed at court tables, along with insufficient vigorous exercise, swelled the veins, a painful condition alleviated only by the discharge of semen through sexual intercourse (in humours theory, semen was thought to be dried-up blood). As Robert Burton wrote in *The Anatomy of Melancholy* (1621): "Diet alone is able to cause [amorousness]: a rare thing to see a young man or woman that lives idly, and fares well, of what condition soever, not to be in love." And copulation, according to many sources, was thought to weaken a man, dim his eyesight, impair his hearing, weaken his joints, consume the moisture of his skin, shrivel his face, dull his spirits, and induce old age and baldness—pretty much the way masturbation in the more benighted areas of the United States is still believed to cause blindness in the young.[21]

That may be why many people no longer supposed the court to be highly populated with scholars or military men, though it was teeming with amorous courtiers. In place of learning and valor, in the popular mind, the court was afflicted with the degenerative cancer of too much "wealth and peace," and the carbuncles of dissimulation, treachery, poisoning, adultery, and drunkenness. "They clepe us drunkards," says Hamlet of the Danish court, "and with swinish phrase / Soil our addition." (I.iv.18.3–4). Hamlet is speaking here of the notorious drinking habits of his fellow Danes, but Shakespeare is no doubt thinking of his English countrymen as well. (Iago also makes this identification when he praises the Englishman's superior capacities for absorbing alcohol: "He drinks you with facility your Dane dead drunk" [II.iii.71].)[22]

All of these vices and sins at court, according to the satirists and moralists, were leading inexorably to the feminizing of England. Looking at the world around him, and finding the masculine part of man to have been eaten away by "beastly appetite," Marston in *The Scourge of Villainy* paraphrased Richard III calling for a horse, by writing "A man, a man, a kingdom for a man." The poet Joseph Hall looked back nostalgically to a golden age of chastity and manliness: "Then men were men, but now the greater part / Beastes are in life, and women are in heart," while Barnabe Rich in his 1606 broadside *Faultes, Faultes, and Nothing Else But Faultes,* called the courtly amorist "the staine of manhood" and urged him to "go learne with Sardanapalus to spinne."[23]

To recapitulate, out of these satiric views of love and lovers emerges a clear characterization of the effeminate courtier. He is compelled by everything Italian: pride, poison, gaudy clothes, courtly complement, and courtly love. Instructed by Italian courtesy books, his manners have become extremely artificial. He is persistently idle, fond of banquets, riot, and drinking. He is a parasite on the body politic, constantly maneuvering for a place with the prince or the prince's favorite; he will use any means at hand to work himself into power and preferment. He is frequently an upstart and always a carpet knight, fearful or contemptuous of war or scholarship.

In place of manly activities, he has taken to soft and effeminate recreations like the tourney, music, dancing, and erotic poetry. He pays too much attention to the beauty of his person, setting, powdering, and arranging his hair, and perfuming his clothes. His costumes are gaudily colored, imported from foreign countries, and frequently changed; they give him a feminine appearance. He speaks with an affected lisp and is frequently guilty of circumlocution and flattery. Conscious that the court is more attracted to show than to plain and honest simplicity, he lays much stress on appearances himself. He is cruel, ambitious, lustful, cowardly, predatory, untrustworthy, effeminate, and vain. At best, he is a foolish fop; at worst, a Machiavellian politician, with no hint of conscience about poisoning his rivals. He woos his lady with sonnets and oily blandishments, idealizes her, and hopes by serving as a slave to entrap her into adulterous sex. He is not above homosexual relations with his page.

This describes a number of Shakespeare's characters, of course, but how does it explain his famously erotic Ovidian sequence, *Venus and Adonis,* and his often amorous, occasionally adulterous sonnets and plays? Clearly, that elusive shadow named Shakespeare resides somewhere in the middle, as usual. He is both the subject of satiric disapproval and a disapproving satirist himself, depending on the context, various as always, never easy to catalogue. In *Love's Labour's Lost, Two Gentlemen of Verona, As You Like It, Twelfth Night,* and *Much Ado About Nothing,* Shakespeare provides us with demonstrations of courtly love as practiced by amorous courtiers and witty court ladies. Indeed, Romeo's feelings for Rosaline, before he learns true love for Juliet, are expressed in the almost stilted language of the conventional Petrarchan wooer. In some of the sonnets, and in such plays as *Troilus and Cressida* and *Hamlet,* and even to some extent in *As You Like It,* on the other hand, he exposes a much more complicated underside of the courtier, similar to that being scourged by his satiric contemporaries. It is that effemiphobic prejudice that I find generally overlooked.

In *Love's Labour's Lost* (c. 1596), for example, what would seem to be a harmless Euphuistic love comedy still manages to evoke overtones of anticourt feeling. King Ferdinand of Navarre has decided to establish a scholarly academy with three of his courtiers, Dumaine, Longuevile, and Biron, that would not only exclude women but also avoid all contact with the female sex. To achieve "fame" as true scholars (that is, to be manly) they will war against their own carnal desires, sleep but three hours a night, and never nod during the day. Biron, the most sensual of the three, rebels against these monastic imperatives. Ferdinand's penalties for any violations of his prohibitions are actually quite cruel and even sexist—the errant man shall lose his fame, but his mistress shall lose her tongue.

The verbose, flattering courtier in this lot is not any of the duke's close followers but the pompous Spaniard Don Adriano de Armado, whose very name in a play written ten years after the Spanish Armada suggests his alien nature. Yet even this preposterous clown concedes that "it is base for a soldier to love" (I.ii.53–54). ("Cupid's butt-shaft," he remarks in a pun suggestive of homoeroticism, "is too hard for Hercules' club" [156–57]). When the Princess of France inquires after the quality of these courtiers, she is informed about their wit but also about their glory in arms. And it is significant that the very first encounter between Ferdinand and the princess is a quarrel over land and money owed as a result of a recent war.

Almost instantly, the men fall for the women and the play becomes a love comedy—in the case of Biron and Rosaline, a wit comedy. Yet once again, the language is in excess of the situation, for in talking about a desirable wife, Biron seems to be describing a whore:

> A whitely wanton with a velvet brow,
> With two pitchballs stuck in her face for eyes,
> Ay, and by heaven, one that will do the deed
> Though Argus were her eunuch and her guard.
>   (III.i.181–84)

This is not a lover speaking but another of Shakespeare's misogynists, recalling Shakespeare's own description of a woman's charms in the sonnets ("If snow be white, why then her breasts are dun; / If hair be wires, black wires grow on her head" [sonnet 130]).

I do not wish to make too much of verbal asides in what is obviously intended as a romantic comedy, except to repeat that, in parallel with his theatrical conventions, Shakespeare often introduces, subtextually, both his own personal prejudices and those he shared with his age. Before too long, responding to the demands of the plot, all four of the men at Navarre are sighing, groaning, and composing love poetry. And before too long, women are being praised as the very fount of knowledge and of learning. Biron's Rosaline, let it be noted, is also dark, like Will's mistress in the sonnets. The king observes, "By heaven, thy love is black as ebony," to which Biron responds, "No face is fair that is not full so black" (IV.iii.243, 249), which is an interesting remark from a poet who, in the sonnets, was usually not so admiring of dark ladies.

In short, the men are smitten, but Shakespeare still remembers to chide, if only gently, the courtier's weakness for lovemaking. Biron's characterization of the "honeytongued" Boyet, for example—

> This gallant pins the wenches on his sleeve
> Had he been Adam he had tempted Eve;
> 'A can carve, too, and lisp, why this is he
> That kissed his hand away in courtesy.
> This is the ape of form, Monsieur the nice
> (V.ii.321-25),

etc.—makes him sound like a rough sketch for Osric, which is to say, for a traditional satiric portrait of the effeminate Italianate courtier. When Biron starts to woo Rosaline in earnest, he forswears conventional courtly lovemaking altogether—

> Taffeta phrases, silken terms precise,
> Three-piled hyperboles, spruce affectation,
> Figures pedantical

—rejecting these devices as "summer flies" (V.ii.406-8).

What he and his companions substitute is an edgy wit, not meant to flatter and subdue a woman so much as emphasize her equality with her lover. Following a long and somewhat tedious masque, news comes of the death of the princess's father, and instead of the conventional tying up of knots, all lovemaking is postponed for the period of a year. Not marital bliss but "Frosts and fasts, hard lodging and thin weeds" (783) will be the lot of the four lords (in the case of Biron, this will include social work at local hospitals). Thus in this early play Shakespeare appears to want it both ways, to celebrate the courtly rituals and satirize them, too. And as if to mock his own artificial handiwork, Shakespeare ends the play with two of his most simple country songs, both woven out of homespun realism—one of them returning to his recurrent theme of how married men are made into cuckolds.

As You Like It is one of Shakespeare's warmest and most engaging love comedies, but even here his prejudice against the effeminate courtier occasionally sneaks through the charming pastoral exterior and scratches at the romance. When Rosalind takes on male disguise to flee the court for the Forest of Arden, she assumes the name of "Jove's own page" (I.iii.118), Ganymede. Familiar with classical mythology, and certainly with Marlowe's play *Dido, Queen of Carthage,* Shakespeare undoubtedly knew that Ganymede and Jove were same-sex lovers. Indeed, the Greek name Ganymede had already metamorphosed into the Latin-derived word *catamite,* meaning a boy or youth who engages in homosexual activities.

The good Duke Senior, sitting around an outdoor fire with his fellow exiles, speaks of the "painted pomp" of the court, which he is happy to have forsaken.[24] The duke prefers the pleasures of pastoral existence:

> Even till I shrink with cold, I smile and say
> "This is no flattery. These are counselors
> That feelingly persuade me what I am." (II.i.9–11)

Honest counselors rather than flatterers, kersey language rather than taffeta phrases, the country life is continually being held up, in this play, as a rebuke to the court, with the simple shepherd proposed as superior in his virtue and honesty to the courtly sycophant. In Shakespeare, the privileged Fool is customarily a character licensed to speak the truth to his sovereign. Touchstone may be the one exception, because, unlike most court jesters (Feste in *Twelfth Night,* say, or the Fool in *Lear*), and despite his sharp wit, he is deeply implicated in the general romancing that constitutes the main action of the play. A former lover of Jane Smile, he is now preoccupied with courting the sluttish "unclean dish" Audrey.

Touchstone is a lover because (unlike any other jester in Shakespeare), he "hath been a courtier," as Jaques reminds us, displaying all the repellent courtlike qualities of the breed. "I have trod a measure," says Touchstone; "I have flattered a lady; I have been politic with my friend; smooth with mine enemy; I have undone three tailors; I have had four quarrels, and like to have fought one" (V.iv.41, 43–46). Flattery, frippery, dissembling, seduction, and cowardice, all the marks of the Italianate courtier—and to these qualities, as evidenced in his discourse with the simple countryman Corin (III.ii.35–36), add the stigma of the social snob ("Why, if thou never wast at court, thou never sawest good manners").

Jaques himself hath been a courtier and also, we are told, a libertine, but it is interesting that in his "Seven Ages of Man" speech the one stage of life he omits is that of the courtier. Jaques, however, does not ignore the scholar, the soldier, or the lover, "sighing like furnace." Indeed, it is Orlando's sincere feeling for Rosalind, and hers for him, that drive the play. The dispossessed Orlando has been brought up unmannerly, and the action of *As You Like It* follows his progress from an uncouth swain to a lover trained in courtly manners. Although hardly a courtier, and despite his clumsy verses, he is not entirely without wit either, as he demonstrates in his colloquy with Jaques (III.ii), who tells him "The worst fault you have is to be in love" (257).

It is Rosalind disguised as Ganymede who will teach Orlando not how to love (he is already "love-shaked" [331]) but rather how to behave in love. She doubts his authenticity as an amorist because he does not wear the proper garments—ungartered hose, unbanded bonnet, unbuttoned sleeve, etc.—the stock desolated look that Ophelia will later ascribe to the (presumably) love-sick Hamlet:

> his doublet all unbraced,
> No hat upon his head, his stockings fouled;
> Pale as his shirt, his knees knocking each other.
> (II.i.79–82)

In *As You Like It*, on the other hand, virtually everyone is lovesick, some in a unwashed version of pastoral love (Silvius swooning over Phebe), some in a priapic version of romantic love (Touchstone lusting after Audrey), some in a muddled variant of same-sex love (Phoebe panting over Rosalind), some in a fairy-tale version of love-at-first-sight (Oliver's worship of Celia), and some (like Rosalind and Orlando) in a forthright expression of passionate love. Rosalind says her feelings for Orlando are past her capacity to say "how many fathom deep I am in love"; yet she remains a love skeptic, doubting that anyone has ever expired in a "love-cause" (IV.i.83): "Man have died from time to time," she tells Orlando, "and worms have eaten them, but not for love" (91–92). (This from the man who wrote *Romeo and Juliet*.)

Stage-managing the entire love menagerie, Rosalind makes it possible for virtually everyone to marry his or her chosen partner—even Touchstone, who presses in "among the rest of the country copulatives" with Audrey in tow. The "bad" Duke Frederick, having been converted by a religious man in the forest, abandons his usurped dukedom and throws "into neglect the pompous court." Only Jaques remains single, the one figure who consistently refuses the court's appeals, remaining an outcast and a loner like Malvolio in *Twelfth Night* and Shylock in *The Merchant of Venice*. Steadfast love, in this play, has prevailed over the adulterous variety prevailing among the aristocracy, partly because of the demands of the plot, partly because of the location of the action. True lovers live in the woods, far from the seductions of the evil court.

Shakespeare's other romantic comedies, notably *Twelfth Night*, *The Merchant of Venice*, and *Much Ado About Nothing*, pretty much adhere to the same pattern. The false feeling of the effeminate courtier is trumped by the authentic feeling of the true lover. Viola disguises herself as a "eunuch" named Cesario to wait upon Orsino, himself in love with the Lady Olivia. Passionate about music, Orsino admires Cesario's voice, "like a maiden's organ, shrill and sound" (I.iv.32). And reminding us of "Ganymede" standing in for Rosalind in Orlando's wooing rehearsals, "Cesario" is commissioned by the duke to court Olivia in his place. This results in even more sexual confusion that in *As You Like It*, much commented upon by contemporary scholars, as Lady Olivia falls in love with the disguised Viola, who seems to interest Orsino as well, despite her male attire.

Viola's brother Sebastian is "adored" by Antonio, and commentators have spilled a lot of ink exploring the possible same-sex implications in that relationship. Antonio's love for Sebastian —

> His life I gave him and did thereto add
> My love without retention or restraint,
> All his in dedication (V.i.74–76)

— is not unlike Will's love for the "fair youth" of the sonnets. Like that relationship, it stops short of sexual consummation. But love plots aside, the real upstart courtier in this play is Malvolio, whose name means "bad will" (the reverse of the good-willed Benvolio in *Romeo and Juliet*). Sometimes a Puritan, sometimes a "time-pleaser, an affectioned ass" (II.iii.132), Malvolio is no thing constantly, except a counterfeit gentleman who would rise above his station. That makes him an ideal patsy, easily traduced into believing Olivia is urging him to "cast off" his "humble slough." Sir Toby, Feste, and Maria, playing upon him like an organ, encourage him to assume the outrageous fashions and manners of the upstart carpet knight—cross-gartered, smiling, kissing his hand—that are designed to offend Olivia. Not born to greatness, hardly likely to achieve it either, he waits for greatness to be thrust upon him. But Malvolio assumes stature only in folly and self-love. And had we any doubt about his upstart ambitions, we have only to examine his language—bloated and contorted like that of other Italianate courtiers in Shakespeare.[25]

Since the playwright is determined that virtually everyone in the play should find a proper mate, he resolves the relationships as perfunctorily as he did in *As You Like It*, again leaving one bachelor behind. The unwedded exception in that play was Jaques, who had no use for courtship or the court. In *Twelfth Night* the outsider is Malvolio, who longed to be a count but cannot even keep his job as steward. He leaves the stage half-mad, shrieking for revenge. In Illyria, as elsewhere in Shakespeare, the sinister intruder is the upstart Italianate courtier.

One more example of the curdled state of courtly love can be found in *Much Ado About Nothing*. The play begins with a report that Don Pedro has been much pleased by the soldierly comportment of young Claudio in the recent wars. Another soldier, his bachelor friend, Benedick, is teased by Beatrice, who promises, like the Lord Constable mocking the boastful Dauphin in *Henry V*, to eat all the soldiers he kills. Thus begins a "merry war" of wits between them (I.i.50). Unlike the Dauphin, Benedick is a truly brave soldier, conversant in the art of war. Where he needs instruction is in the art of love, for, unlike most of Shakespeare's romantic heroes, he starts out as a professed woman-hater. The wit play between him and Beatrice is a strong, and presumably healthy, antidote to the kind of insincere lovemaking common at the court. The object of these two, throughout the length of the play, is to find some way to express their feelings for each other without losing their reputations as wits.

Claudio, on the other hand, has no problem wooing Hero. When he went to war, he says, he looked on her with "a soldier's eye" that had "a rougher task in hand" than making love. Now that the war is over, he is subject once again to "soft and delicate desires" (I.i.244–45, 249), prepared, as Benedick describes him, to sacrifice the "drum and the fife" for "the tabour and the pipe." No longer simply "an honest man and a soldier" (II.iii.13–14, 17–18) he now wants to love. The obstacle to this desire is Don John, Don Pedro's brother, self-described not as "a flattering honest man," but as a "plain-dealing villain," an oxymoronic use of adjectives and nouns that also describe Iago.

As a result of Don John's Machiavellian conniving and dissembling, Claudio refuses that "rotten orange," as he dismissively calls Hero, and Shakespeare spends the remaining two acts of the play disabusing him of his error. Although Don John is the practiced dissimulator, it is Hero he accuses of "seeming," and Claudio, the most gullible character in the play, too readily believes him. Benedick is also in danger of losing his new inamorata, when Beatrice demands that he kill Claudio in order to retain her love. Like Hermione later in *The Winter's Tale*, Hero's only defense against slander is to feign her own death. And the strangest thing about this work is how Claudio continues to maintain his emotional reserve, with his love presumably lying dead and his friend Benedick challenging him to a duel.

Soon after, however, the play reverts to convention, with all the obstacles to love removed and Benedick clumsily trying to compose a poem to his lady. When in the last act Hero is resurrected as "another Hero" and Claudio realizes his mistake, Beatrice and Benedick are then allowed to couple, with Benedick sounding for all the world like John Tanner, backing reluctantly into domesticity. (Surely, the romance between Benedick and Beatrice in this play, along with that between Mirabel and Millamant in Congreve's *The Way of the World*, inspired John Tanner's and Ann Whitefield's relationship in Shaw's *Man and Superman*.)

Is Hamlet another member of this class of courtiers? Ophelia certainly seems to think so when, mourning the loss of his noble mind, she describes him as

> Th' expectancy and rose of the fair state,
> Th' glass of fashion and the mould of form,
> The observed of all observers. (III.i.151–53)

Claudius calls him "our chiefest courtier, cousin, and our son" (I.ii.117). But if Hamlet was once the king's "chiefest courtier," not to mention Ophelia's "glass of fashion" and "mould of form," that glass has broken, that mould has crumbled. Far from using courtly language, he is, as we have seen, a sworn enemy of the kind of flowery phrases practiced by the likes of Osric. He no longer dresses in the colorful fashions of the court but rather in "solemn black," wearing an "inky cloak" in mourning for his father. And even "the trappings and the suits of woe," as he calls his mourning clothes, are merely empty external accoutrements. Hamlet has "that within which passeth show." He is a man of true feeling, not appearances. As he says to Gertrude, "I know not 'seems'" (I.ii.76–86).

That explains his constitutional hatred of fawning. What gets him exiled from Denmark, apart from his murder of Polonius, his defiance of Claudius, and his menacing of Gertrude, is his refusal to defer to royalty. As he tells Horatio, explaining why he does not flatter him:

No, let the candied tongue lick absurd pomp,
And crook the pregnant hinges of the knee
Where thrift may follow feigning. (III.ii.53–55)

This is as good a statement as any about how Hamlet distinguishes himself from the typical Italianate courtier. Whatever one may say about his temperament, he neither sweetens his tongue nor bends the knee before "absurd pomp." A model of authenticity, he will be mordant, sarcastic, cutting, even insulting, rather than utter a flattering phrase.

Ophelia says that Hamlet has the courtier's eye, but it is not the eye of the courtly amorist. While she claims to have "suck'd the honey of his music vows" (III.i.155), those vows were all uttered in the past ("I did love you once" [116]). He sends her bad verses, gets sick at the numbers, and pays her a creepy visit, sloppily dressed. Hamlet tells us he loved Ophelia, a love worth "forty thousand brothers." His fustian "rant" at her graveside in act V suggests a powerful, if curiously wavering, grief. But Hamlet immediately shows that he has more pressing business on his mind than exchanging love vows. And however he later behaves at her graveside, he had earlier, in his act III scene, told her his feelings for her were dead, treated her like a whore, and proceeded to display the most intense disgust over the relations among men and women to be found anywhere in Shakespeare.

But in two important ways, Hamlet does fulfill the classic definition of the Italianate courtier—he avoids the battlefield, and he does not hesitate to dissemble. It is true that Hamlet's dissimulation is a survival tactic. One of the most overanalyzed puzzles in this play is why Hamlet takes so long to revenge himself on Claudius for his father's murder. Yes, the king controls the military, but surely this charismatic prince could have raised a people's army against his usurping uncle—Laertes does this easily enough, with considerably less popular support. But rather than seek an honest confrontation, Hamlet avoids direct argument, and goes willingly into exile. This noble Prince of Denmark, who has infinitely better reasons for taking action than Fortinbras, cannot exact his rightful revenge—until that moment when, his mother dead, Laertes dying, and himself expiring from a poisoned sword, he has no other choice. Hundreds of reasons have been offered to explain Hamlet's indecisiveness. Let me cautiously add another—like the courtiers he detests, he has lost his capacity for heroic action.

He also possesses more than a hint of Machiavellism. Hamlet charges Rosencrantz and Guildenstern with the very failing he possesses himself, namely hiding one's true feelings. If Rosencrantz and Guildenstern conceal their intentions under a pretense of friendship, Hamlet conceals his under a mask of madness and melancholy. Considering that it was Machiavelli who legitimized the political strategy of dissembling, or hiding one's true objectives in order to achieve one's secret goals, Hamlet behavior seems Italianate. He is continually criticizing false and artificial displays as "shows." Yet he is as much a disguised character, displaying an antic disposition he does not feel, as is Iago, pretending an honesty he does not possess. No matter how justified his dissembling, Hamlet certainly displays his share of playacting.

In assuming his "antic disposition," of course, Hamlet resembles many other figures in revenge tragedy (Hieronimo in Kyd's *The Spanish Tragedy,* for example, and Vindice in Tourneur's (or Middleton's) *The Revenger's Tragedy,* who must dissemble in order to survive. According to Marvin W. Hunt in *Looking for Hamlet,* he is also not unlike Shakespeare's "wise fools," whose riddles hide their meaning. But Hamlet's real or assumed madness, no matter how important to his safety or his resolve, stamps him as an actor playing a part rather than a man living authentically in his own skin. His histrionic talent is evident in his scene with the Players. But Hamlet is not only an actor, he is also a playwright (composing a speech of some dozen or sixteen lines for "The Murder of Gonzago"). He is also a critic of ham acting ("do not saw the air too much with your hand, thus . . . [or] tear a passion to tatters") and of excessive improvisation ("And let those that play your clowns speak no more than is set down for them" [III.ii.4-9, 34-35]). In his emphasis on truth and authenticity, Hamlet seems to favor what today is called Method acting. The question that has baffled so many commentators is how someone so sincere and honest can also be so hidden and unknowable.

This brings us back to the contradiction in Hamlet's nature, which is the basic puzzle in the Hamlet enigma. Why does this born prince feel such unease and discomfort inside a royal court? Surely, he is the least courtly courtier in Elizabethan drama. There is nothing effeminate about the man, he wears the simplest clothes, he will not flatter, he does not torture the language, he is not an amorist. But these noncourtly qualities are curiously combined with other forms of behavior springing from his aristocratic birth and breeding. He is unique among Shakespeare's heroes in being at once a hesitant character, an avenging nemesis and a mass murderer ("Nine lives are taken off for his father's one," as Joyce's Stephen Dedalus mordantly remarks about the body count in *Hamlet*). The stage is strewn with the people this fastidious man has killed out of his reluctance to act.

Most of Shakespeare's plays, despite occasional skepticism about the smooth course of true love, endorse the value of romantic passion. *Hamlet* is among the few that does not. *Troilus and Cressida* is another. Cressida is one of Shakespeare's raven ladies, with hair "somewhat darker than Helen's"—a hint that both of these enchantresses should be avoided. Just as Paris is besotted with Helen, Troilus professes to have fallen madly in love with Cressida. But his extravagantly amorous expressions (uttered to a pimp) only emphasize his unmanliness. So does his scorn for the battlefield. Despising its "ungracious clamors . . . rude sounds" (I.i.85), he reveals himself as another effeminate courtier who prefers making love to making war. When asked by Aeneas why he is not afield, he replies, "Because not there! This woman's answer sorts / For womanish it is to be from thence" (102–3). Remarks like this show an unusual self-awareness. Troilus admits that he has feminized himself for a woman's love.

But the next scene makes it abundantly clear that Cressida is not worthy of his sacrifice. She has eyes not only for Troilus but also for the entire Trojan court, ogling the warriors as they parade before her like models on a runway. She especially admires Hector, by contrast with whom she finds Troilus deficient. Indeed, in her scene with Pandarus, she disparages the man who will become her lover, though, in an aside, Cressida confesses her attraction to Troilus, feigning coyness because "Men price the thing ungained more than it is" (I.ii.267). It is Cressida's fault to be a thing too quickly gained.

The play is dripping with a kind of feverish eroticism, so it is not surprising that Ulysses' famous speech about degree should also refer to rampant sexuality. But this play revolves around more than the conduct of the appetitive will, or erotic lust. It is also about the conduct of a legendary war. Are the Trojans too courtly to prevail in such a war? When the Trojan herald Aeneas appears ponderously orating, Agamemnon concludes that either he is being mocked or the Trojans are "ceremonious courtiers." Proud that Trojans subscribe to courtly conduct, Aeneas proposes a medieval combat between Hector and a Greek who holds his mistress (or his wife) in equally high esteem.

"This shall be told our lovers," replies Agamemnon disdainfully, "We left them all at home" — an old soldier's way of saying that courtly chivalry is inappropriate on a battlefield (I.iii.281–83). Nevertheless, under counsel by Ulysses, he agrees to a traditional joust, complete with lances and shields, using Ajax as his stalking horse. The oafish Ajax would like to send Thersites to read the proclamation; Thersites would rather stay home and rail against the war.

It is Thersites who continually characterizes this war as the creation of whores and cuckolds. But despite Hector's sensible advice that Helen be returned to the Greeks, Troilus insists on preserving the "courtly," which is to say the amoristic, status quo. The thin line between true feeling and mere lust in this court surprises even Pandarus, who, after characterizing his countrymen as a "generation of love," wonders whether "love is a generation of vipers" (III.i.122–24). On their first meeting, Troilus and Cressida vow eternal constancy, and Troilus falls head over heels in love with her. But never in this wooing scene or after does anyone utter a single word about marriage.

Following the loss of what we are told, and do in part believe, is Cressida's maidenhead, Diomedes comes to fetch her to the Grecian camp as part of a prisoner exchange for Antenor. She resists strenuously and, of course, swears eternal fidelity to Troilus — she will be a "woeful Cressid 'mongst the merry Greeks" (IV.v.55). Even this promise has erotic overtones — *a merry greek* was Elizabethan slang for a woman of pleasure, a phrase already used to describe Helen. Troilus gives Cressida a sleeve, Cressida gives Troilus a glove, all in the time-honored tradition of chivalric exchange. But once in the Grecian camp, Cressida is embraced by each soldier in turn, even including Patroclus, and in a travesty of courtly love, she returns their kisses. Ulysses scorns her as a "daughter[] of the game" (IV.vi.64), who will "sing any man at first sight" (V.ii.9). For Thersites, the whole charade is "nothing but lechery" by "incontinent varlets" (V.i.88–89).

Troilus has the opportunity to witness firsthand Cressida's infidelity, and also how easily she gives away his sleeve, which Diomedes will wear upon his helm in battle. His response is not simply, Hamlet-like, to damn the entire female sex, but, Lear-like, to see the whole world in a state of disintegration: "The bonds of heaven are slipped, dissolved, and loosed" (V.ii.156). As for Thersites, he would rather see Diomedes fight with Troilus so "that same young Trojan ass that loves that whore there, might send the Greekish whoremasterly villain with the sleeve back to the dissembling luxurious drab of a sleeveless errand" (V.iv.4–7). Sex and war, traditionally opposed, have here become most hopelessly confused.

The skirmishes that follow are largely one-on-one encounters not unlike the perfunctory battle scenes in *1 Henry IV* (including a craven engagement between Thersites and Margarelon much like Falstaff's cowardly meeting with Douglas). These episodes seem like parodies of heroism, culminating in Achilles' murder of Hector not through single combat but rather with the aid of his army of Myrmidons. This shameful action, a grim violation of the chivalric code, underlines Cervantes' mordant perception in *Don Quixote,* written just three years after *Troilus and Cressida* in 1605, that the invention of gunpowder had at last made it possible for a base scoundrel to kill a noble gentleman. Potassium nitrate had initiated the Time of the Assassin.

In Shakespeare it is not a bullet but a battalion that overcomes this man of honor. But then much of *Troilus and Cressida* sounds the death knell of the chivalric world and its conventions of courtly love. Shakespeare's most cynical play ends, in totally unresolved fashion, with the diseased Pandarus, cursed by Troilus, pleading with his customers to weep for him.

Thersites' "Lechery, lechery. Still wars and lechery" (V.ii.193) seems to be the epigraph of a world, where—a rare thing in Shakespeare—the battlefield (action) and the bedroom (sexuality) are more related than opposed. Shakespeare never lets us forget that it was a sexual act, the seduction of Helen, that initiated the Trojan War, and that this event inevitably colored the war's conduct—brave men sacrificing their lives in a lubricious cause. The Trojans are defeated not just because they are more honorable and impractical than the Greeks but also because they behave more like courtiers than soldiers. Thus, however much Shakespeare may have admired the Trojans for their courtesy and despised the Greeks for their treachery, he is still looking at the lustful underside of chivalric love. *Troilus and Cressida* is Shakespeare's most penetrating probe into the bankruptcy of the courtly ideal, the main source of his effemiphobia. On the other hand, his distaste for the effeminate courtier is always balanced by considerable affection for the courtier's antitype, the plain-dealing soldier, who represents for Shakespeare the very embodiment of honesty and masculinity.

3

Machismo

THE HOTSPUR MODEL

This is some fellow,
Who, having been prais'd for bluntness, doth affect
A saucy roughness, and constrains the garb
Quite from his nature: he cannot flatter, he,
An honest mind and plain, he must speak truth:
An they will take it, so; if not, he's plain.
—King Lear, II.ii.87–92

This is Cornwall referring to Kent, after that "saucy" fellow has insulted every face in the room. Although intended as a snarl, it is the most accurate characterization of the plain-dealing soldier we have. It is the way Henry IV might have described Hotspur, or Beatrice Benedick, or Octavius Enobarbus, as a plain downright fellow who takes pride in his refusal to flatter. It describes the way Henry V woos Princess Catherine. It depicts Hamlet at his most dynamic before pretending to be a melancholy madman. It is the disguise assumed by Iago to mask his villainy. It is the most appealing side of Timon before he descends into snarling misanthropy. It is the positive expression of Thersites' currish negativism. It signifies the very antitype of the flattering courtier.

In refusing the idea of the courtier as personified by Castiglione, Shakespeare and his contemporaries rejected one of the most compelling models of the Renaissance. But this is not to say these writers dispensed with ideal lifestyles altogether. Together they created another highly admired figure who personified many of the nation's hopes and prejudices. Just as the courtier embodied effeminacy, this character personified masculinity. He was the courtier's opposite, generally identified—in satire, drama, and everyday parlance—as a "plain-dealer." Blunt in speech, rough in manner, simple in dress, honest to a fault, and above all manly in behavior, the plain-dealer was so scornful of frippery and flattery as to approach misanthropy. For the more cosmopolitan French, the plain-dealer was indeed indistinguishable from a misanthrope; Molière, in a famous play of that name, would treat his antisocial hero Alceste as an unmannerly extremist hardly fit for polite society. (In the next age, reaffirming the English admiration for honesty above manners, the Restoration dramatist William Wycherly would repatriate Molière's Alceste as a more heroic if more brutal Englishman, significantly named Manly, in a play appropriately retitled *The Plain Dealer*).

The plain-dealer originally enters drama in or around 1599, thanks to John Marston, as a theatrical surrogate for the discontented Juvenalian satirist, railing against the vices of the court. He also develops into one of Shakespeare's favorite later characters, the man (in rare cases, a woman) bold enough to speak truth to power, regardless of the consequences. The plain-dealer appears either in the guise of an aristocratic scholar like Hamlet, or a blunt soldier like Hotspur, Kent, or Enobarbus, or a fool like Feste and the Fool in *Lear*, or an honest countryman like Corin, or a truth teller like Cordelia, or a proud loner like Coriolanus, though (perhaps reflecting Shakespeare's darkening mood) he later devolves into a satiric railer like Thersites, and a festering misanthrope like Timon. He or she is almost invariably contrasted with a flattering figure from the court: Hotspur and the "certain Lord," Hamlet and Osric, Kent and Oswald, Cordelia and her faithless sisters.

No single philosopher or essayist, no Castiglione, championed the plain-dealer's way of life, though Montaigne displayed some affinity with the type in his essays ("I had rather be importunate and indiscreet," he wrote in "Of Presumption," "than a flatterer and a dissembler"). Unlike most of his more permissive countrymen, Montaigne admired the same kind of frankness and sincerity as the English idealized in their excoriation of courtly fakery. It might be stretching a point, however, to say that the plain-dealer, as a fictional character, has any literary existence at all outside of the drama, though historical models are plentiful.[1] The satirist does not write much about the plain-dealer in his pamphlets because the satirist considers *himself* the plain-dealer, displaying identical attitudes and postures—direct and unpretentious speech, fearless honesty, rough simple dress, and manly bearing. Further confirming his plain-dealing identity, the satirist pursues a noncourtly career, sometimes military, practices a restricted sexual life, and is motivated by strong patriotic sentiments. The plain-dealer follows the satirist in being defined as much by what he is against as by what he is for.

As the Italianate courtier's antitype, Shakespeare's plain-dealer is opposed in every particular to synthetic court life, which makes his link with the court tenuous. In the drama, he usually sits on the edges of power, where, through his special privilege as a pseudomadman (Hamlet), a jester (Lear's Fool), or a malcontent (Timon), he is allowed to speak his mind without fear of reprisals. (Hamlet's friend and schoolmate, Horatio, has the honesty of the plain-dealer but not his bluntness.) Very occasionally, the plain-dealer is a courtier, but if so he is an outsider, like Shakespeare's Hamlet or Chapman's Bussy D'Ambois or Tourneur's Vindice, soldiers and scholars who grab every opportunity to register disapproval of the court's affectations and vices. Taking his cue from the satirist, he hates flattery and compliment, dissimulation, fancy apparel, effeminacy, idleness, courtly love, and foreign—especially Italian—fashions. It is the English plain-dealer and not the Italianate courtier who fulfills Castiglione's demand that advice to the Prince be direct and free of selfish motives or ceremonious compliment. Sometimes the plain-dealer's advice, like that of the satirist, is so direct as to be brutal. If the Prince can suffer the plain-dealer's unbridled tongue, he profits from his virtue. More often, such honesty alienates him from the court. He is a rack, a scourge, a purge, a surgeon who lances the infected cankers of his time.

One of the earliest personifications of the plain-dealer in English literature is William Langland's fourteenth-century pastoral hero Piers Plowman. Following this rude rural example, a number of Elizabethan tractarians began to exalt the virtues of simple country cloth over luxurious court velvet. Robert Greene's *A Quip for an Upstart Courtier* (1592), for example, (itself plagiarized from Francis Thynne's *The Debate Between Pride and Lowliness* [1577]), while satirizing "Velvet Breeches" as guilty of every conceivable vice—"an upstart, come out of Italy, begot of pride, nursed up by self-love, and brought into this country by his companion Newfangleness"—praises "Cloth Breeches" as a plain-dealer devoted to the old English values. This honest countryman, a simple old-fashioned patriot, inveighs against the modern court as distinguished from a golden memory of the past when "charity flourished in the court, and young courtiers strove to exceed one another in virtue, not bravery." Although the courtier finds him simple and uncouth, the countryman effectively demolishes the courtier's polite amusements one by one, concluding that love in the court is destroyed by envy, malice, and jealousy, in contrast to love in the country, where "faith and troth are our bonds of love, plaine dealing, passages of honesty." The courtier, unable to get in another word, forfeits the victory by taking his leave.[2]

Shakespeare, as we have already noted, dramatized the traditional debate between the courtier and the countryman in *As You Like It* (1599) in the colloquy between Touchstone and Corin (III.ii). Touchstone believes the good old shepherd to be damned because he was never in court and "saw'st good manners." Corin argues that courtly manners in the country would be ridiculous and unclean, considering how greasy shepherds' hands get from handling sheep. Touchstone retorts that the hands of courtiers also sweat, and that "the grease of a mutton [is] as wholesome as the sweat of man" (48). Corin counters that he is an honest laborer, without hatred or envy of other men. Touchstone replies that Corin makes his living by the copulation of cattle, that he is a bawd to a bellwether and a pander to rams and lambs. In their comic debate over the appropriateness of Castiglione's precepts in a pastoral setting, Corin is finally forced to concede defeat to Touchstone: "You have too courtly a wit for me: I'll rest" (60)

This is a temperate version of an age-old conflict in which Corin gently replicates the savage arguments of the satirist. Like the good-natured Corin, the countryman is actually the mildest of the plain-dealers. When the satirist assumes that rustic role, his rebuke will be mixed with toxic virulence. The link to the countryside is preserved, however, largely because of the contemporary confusion between the words *satyr* (a figure from pastoral) and *satire* (a poem aimed at correcting vices and follies).[3]

For the typical Elizabethan satirist regards himself as one made malcontent by the vicious state of urban society. Driven by the savage indignation later associated with Jonathan Swift, he lays bare the abuses of the time in the tradition of his Roman forbears, notably Juvenal and the Stoic-Censors. Thus Greene, Rowlands, and Marston often identify themselves with Diogenes, that foul-mouthed celibate and beggar who, unlike Plato and Aristotle, paid no court to kings. (Marston frequently compares himself to Hercules as well, "an imbecility of corrupt nature," to be sure, for having enslaved himself to Omphale, but also a masculine paragon for purging the Augean stables of "muck" or "foul sin.")

Marston's effort to invent a language that would "purge the snottery of our slimy time" resulted in a remarkably ugly vocabulary that often exceeded the bounds of poetry altogether. It was no doubt intended as a corrective to the more feminine felicities of verse. In an amusing passage in *The Poetaster*, Ben Jonson makes Marston vomit up all his repulsive neologisms. But Jonson, who said his "language was never ground into such oyly colours, / To flatter vice and daube iniquitie," but rather was designed to "strip the ragged follies of the time, / Naked, as at their birth" (Induction to *Every Man Out of His Humour*), was not always the most musical of poets himself. The satirist's language was ugly because the truth was ugly, and his behavior was unmannerly because manners were corrupt (Diogenes was said to have defecated in the marketplace and urinated on a man who insulted him). In an age when the honest man was thought to have virtually disappeared ("one man picked out of ten thousand," according to Hamlet's exaggerated calculations), the satirist took it as his mission to be the plain-dealing conscience of the nation, however coarse his manners.

The plain-dealer also prided himself on his poverty because this was proof that he had not tried to enrich himself, like the courtier, through illegal activity. This explains why the figure of the poor scholar also comes to be included in the ranks of plain-dealers. As L. C. Knights has observed in *Drama and Society in the Age of Jonson*, there was a marked increase in the number of educated men toward the end of the sixteenth century, and a corresponding decrease in suitable jobs for them. In Marlowe's

Edward II (1592), for example, when the scholarly Baldock expresses his hope to thrive in his lady's service, the more realistic Spencer disabuses him of that silly notion:

> Then *Baldock,* you must cast the scholler off,
> And learne to court it like a Gentleman . . .
> You must be proud, bold, pleasant, resolute
> And now and then, stab as occasion serves. (II.i)

In short, Baldock must burn every one of his books except Machiavelli's *Il Principe.*

No wonder so many scholars developed into snarling satirists. Ben Jonson's poverty and Thomas Dekker's imprisonment for debt were signs that not much could be expected from writing for the stage, and the days of generous patronage were over. The consequence was a marked discontent among scholars, as reflected in Ben Jonson's character Macilente (in *Everyman Out of His Humour*), whose very name means "lean, meager, and bareboned." He has fallen into an "envious apoplexie," or malcontent humour, as a result of being displaced in the world. One sign of this "envious apoplexie" was a repudiation of erudition and philosophy, a metaphorical burning of the books.

In some minds, learning was equated with such external and inessential appendages as extravagant apparel, those civilized trappings that obscured rather than revealed the truth. Nashe's hero Pierce, in *Pierce Penilesse* (1592), tears up his papers in a "malecontent humor" and bites his pen, loudly repudiating his education because he has so little to show for it: "Ah worthless Wit, to traine me to this woe, / Deceitfull Artes, that nourish Discontent." Marston's Lampatho Doria, in *What You Will* (1601), experiences a similar disenchantment with the vanity of learning: "I was a scholler. . . . The More I learnt the more I learnt to doubt, / Knowledge and wit, faithes foes, turne fayth around" (II.ii). It is significant that Macilente in Jonson's

Everyman Out of His Humour, Bosola in Webster's *The Duchess of Malfi* and Flamineo in his *The White Devil,* Vindice in Tourneur's (or Middleton's) *The Revenger's Tragedy*—not to mention Hamlet himself—are all disenchanted scholars, each framing sentiments against the court identical with those in the prohibited satirical tracts.[4]

The final and most important group to which the plaindealer belonged was the military. It was the soldier who was more likely to spill his red blood on the battlefield than his dried blood (semen) in the bedroom. Considering how the satirist, following popular opinion, favored the active military man over the idle carpet knight, it was inevitable that he would invest the soldier with all his own prejudices about what constituted a virtuous life. Some satirists, notably George Gascoigne and Barnabe Rich, actually served as soldiers at some time in their careers. Rich bid "farewell to the militarie profession" in 1581 after having observed with extreme bitterness that "it is lesse painful to follow a Fiddle in the Gentlewomans chamber: then to march after a Drumme in the Field" (*Rich His Farewell to the Militarie Profession* [1606]). Rich added: "Princes have not so much scarcitie of any other thing as that of that, whereof they should be most plentifully stored, *Of such as should tell them the truth*" (emphasis in original).

Certainly, the change in regime from Elizabeth Tudor to James Stuart in 1603 created a radical change in court style in regard to honesty and plain-dealing. We have seen this change documented, among other places, in letters to and from the honest old Elizabethan courtier Sir John Harington, who could have been a model for Shakespeare's Kent or Enobarbus. They are worth mentioning again as evidence of how a plain-dealing old courtier from the court of Elizabeth might have expected to fare under the Stuart king—and how that change was reflected in Shakespeare's plays.[5]

As a matter of fact, in the tradition of English plain-dealers, Harington was not only a soldier but also a scholar, so the king, having completed a book on witchcraft called *Daemonologie,* at first welcomed him warmly because he was a learned man. Harington, however, soon tired of James's preoccupation with witches, and, hating the atmosphere of servile flattery, retired to the country. But when he thought of returning in 1611, his friend Lord Thomas Howard provided some sardonic advice about how to behave before the king, along with a vivid picture of how the court had degenerated further in the preceding eight years:

> I would wish you to be well trimmed, get a new jerkin well borderd, and not too short; the King saith he liketh a flowing garment. . . . We have lately had many gallants who failed in their suits, for want of due observance in these matters. Do not of yourself say, This is good or bad; but, If it were your Majesties good opinion, I myself should think so and so. . . . You have lived to see the trim of old times, and what passed in the Queens days: These things are no more the same; your Queen did talk of her subjects love and good affections, and in good truth she aimed well; our King talketh of his subjects fear and subjection. . . . You are not young, you are not handsome, you are not finely suited: and yet Will you come to Courte, and think to be favoured? Why, I say again, good Knight, that your learning may somewhat prove worthy hereunto . . . but these are not the thinges men live by now a days.

These two historical events, James's ascension to the throne in 1603, and the banning of verse satire in 1599, were both to have a significant effect on the direction of Shakespeare's theatre.

Certainly, the soldier who speaks plain truth to his prince is to become an even more recurrent character in the English drama of the Stuart period than of the Elizabethan.[6] For Shakespeare, the plain-dealer, whether as soldier, scholar, or malcontent, will become not only his chief exemplar of manliness but a central dramatic character. It is to Shakespeare's treatment of that figure that we now will turn our attention.

Although the plain-dealer makes his appearance from time to time in Shakespeare's earlier plays (Mercutio might be considered a member of the species, along with Benedick in *Much Ado About Nothing,* and perhaps the Bastard in *King John*), it is not until the last three parts of *The Henriad* (1597–98) that he emerges full-blown, first in the person of Hotspur and then in the maturing character of Prince Hal. Hotspur's plain-speaking is not just something revealed in his characterization of "the certain lord." It is virtually the sum total of his character. Shakespeare gives him a stammer, partly for historical reasons, but also no doubt to distinguish his unadorned speech from "the holiday and lady terms" of the carpet knight who talks "so like a waiting-gentlewoman" (I.iii.45).

In *As You Like It,* Jaques describes the soldier in his "Seven Ages of Man" speech as

> Jealous in honour, sudden and quick in quarrel,
> Seeking the bubble reputation
> Even in the cannon's mouth. (II.vii.150–52)

He seems to be characterizing Hotspur, even paraphrasing his celebrated boast: "By Heaven, methinks it were an easy leap, / To pluck bright honor from the pale-faced moon" (*1 Henry IV,* I.iii.199–200). Hotspur is hot-tempered, brash, unmannerly, and the soul of honor, which he prizes above all virtues. He brooks no contradiction, not even from his king ("My liege, I did deny no prisoners" [28]), and threatens to murmur the hated name of Mortimer even in the king's sleep as an exasperating way of speaking truth to power. He has no patience for the friends and allies who urge him to a more tactful, diplomatic course. He is a whip, a scourge, a whirlwind.

Hotspur is married, but he addresses his wife as bluntly as he does his fellow-soldiers.

> Love? I love thee not,
> I care not for thee, Kate. This is no world
> To play with maumets and to tilt with lips.
>   (II.iv.82–84)

Actually, he loves her dearly but does not have the time or temper for amorous dalliance; his place is on the battlefield, not the bedchamber. He is the ideal plain-dealer, representing the very light of chivalry, "indeed the glass / Wherein all the noble youth did dress themselves," as Lady Percy calls him after his death (II.iii.21–22), foreshadowing Ophelia's description of Hamlet as "the glass of fashion and the mould of form / The observed of all observers." This is the model whom the reprobate Prince Hal so envies in the first part of *Henry IV* and whom he will eventually kill in single combat, after bestowing upon him a fulsome eulogy: "This earth that bears thee dead / Bears not alive so stout a gentleman" (V.iv.91–92). Indeed, Hal will have no choice. He must displace Hotspur in order to expropriate for himself his rival's legendary function, plucking bright honor from the pale-faced moon.

It has been said that the two parts of *Henry IV* were conceived as a morality play, with Hal suspended among several renegade Vice figures, preeminently Sir John Falstaff ("that reverend Vice, that grey Iniquity" [II.v.413]), and several virtuous father figures, notably the Chief Justice. It could also be said that Hal is equally torn between two models of military men—the braggart soldier as represented by Falstaff, a figure of cowardice, lies, and deception, for whom honor is a breath, and the brave plain-dealing soldier as personified by Hotspur, a figure of absolute integrity, for whom honor is the ultimate value.

That may have been the plan, but it was not the way the play turned out. Falstaff, like Brecht's Mother Courage, escaped his author, transcending his traditional role as a Tempter Vice, to become a fully dimensioned epic figure, entertaining audiences and captivating critics from Maurice Morgann to Harold Bloom. In that sense Falstaff achieves that special Shakespearean status of being out of the moral limits of history, not of an age but for all time.

But in another sense, the fat knight is also very much in history and of his own age. Many scholars believe that Shakespeare's historical epic was originally designed to function as a moral crossroads where Hal finds the true path to virtue by abandoning the seductions of his youth and repudiating his old companions. Indeed, after his very first scene with Falstaff, in *1 Henry IV*, Hal is already informing the audience that the rejection of his bad companions is only a matter of time:

> I know you all, and will awhile uphold
> The unyoked humour of your idleness. . . .
> My reformation, glittering o'er my fault,
> Shall show more goodly and attract more eyes
> Than that which hath no foil to set it off.
>   (I.ii.173–93)

Using a glittering reformation to impress the public is hardly the most noble reason for reforming one's character. But Hal must reject his old companions in order to rule his country properly and overcome his enemies. Falstaff and his fellow braggart soldiers (notably Bardolph, Nym, and Ancient Pistol, whose often misquoted model is Marlowe's Tamburlaine) are lying rogues claiming victories on the battlefield they have not earned. In that sense, Falstaff contrasts with the honest soldier as much as does the effeminate courtier. He is both a literary type descended from the *Miles Gloriosus* of Latin drama, and an actual figure (originally based on Sir John Oldcastle) whom Shakespeare managed to elevate into one of the most glorious characters in literature. F. Scott Fitzgerald once remarked that a truly great mind is one that can manage two conflicting ideas at the same time. Shakespeare's concept of Falstaff embodies two great ideas in conflict—that cowardice is a vice and also a source of inexhaustible comedy.

Therefore, Falstaff's great speech on honor ("The better part of valour is discretion" [V.iv.117–18]) emerges as an inspired tribute to good sense—what George Orwell has called "the revolt of the belly against the soul"—an argument so reasonable that it has achieved a place in Bartlett's *Quotations*. But it is also a harsh condemnation of a coward's rationalizations on the field of battle. When Falstaff falls down and plays dead, he never fails to amuse an audience, but he is also disgracing an honored code of heroism. Thus he arouses divine laughter while destroying a chivalric ideal.

Hotspur, for all his defects, represents that chivalric ideal. And Hal will continue to regard him as a model after he ascends the throne, and later declares war on the French. There is, of course, not much chivalry in the king's decision to execute his French prisoners, after the French have killed all "the poys and the luggage" (*Henry V,* IV.vii.1). And there is not much honor or candor in the cunning way he entraps the conspirators, Scroop, Grey, and Cambridge, into condemning themselves out of their own mouths. But it is abundantly clear from Henry's wooing of the French princess Catherine that he regards himself as a legitimate military plain-dealer—and so perhaps does Shakespeare.

That wooing scene is perhaps the most revealing moment

in the play regarding Henry's perception of his role as warrior and king. Laurence Olivier's chiseled features and lazy eyes in the 1946 movie turned Henry into an irresistible matinee idol. But as a lover, this Plantagenet monarch is even less suited for courtship than is Benedick in *Much Ado About Nothing,* another soldier-wooer in a play written in the same year (1598). Henry has already soliloquized, in act IV, scene i, about the loneliness of a monarch, weighed down by the sins and troubles of his subjects. Now, in the great wooing scene of act V, scene ii, in the process of negotiating a highly political marriage with Princess Catherine, he describes himself more as a countryman than a ruler—"such a plain king that thou wouldst think I had sold my farm to buy my crown" (124–25). He asks Catherine, with her minimal command of English, to "vouchsafe to teach a soldier terms" that might help him woo her (99). He cannot "look greenly, nor gasp out" his eloquence (140–41). He would speak to her not as a lisping courtier but as "plain soldier" (146). Rather than flatter her beauty, he simply asks her to "clap hands and a bargain" (128). And that may be the best way to describe this hasty coupling, as an expedient bargain designed to bind the territories of France to the English crown. Unlike the prating poets who "rhyme themselves into ladies' favours" (and reason themselves out again), Henry will only, somewhat disingenuously, plead his good heart (V.ii.152).

In describing his encounter with Princess Catherine, Henry lists the qualities of the classic plain-dealer: "Our tongue is rough . . . and my condition is not smooth, so that, having neither the voice nor the heart of flattery about me, I cannot so conjure up the spirit of love in her, that he will appear in his true likeness" (266–69). He adds that he cannot see "many a fair French city for one fair maid that stands in my way" (293–94), though his vision is not clouded enough by love to obscure his claim to all of France. His marriage to Catherine will make that claim legal and binding—at least until England loses France again under the reign of his son, Henry VI.

Hamlet, written two years after *Henry V,* is in a sense its tragic counterpart. The eponymous heroes have much in common, including their passion for self-reflection, the major difference being that while Henry is a soldier who does not hesitate to claim his birthright, Hamlet is too steeped in melancholy and doubt to take strong action on his own behalf. More like King Henry is the forthright soldier Fortinbras, leading garrisons provisioned for a fight against Poland over "a little patch of ground that hath in it no profit but the name" (IV.iv.9.8–9). Like King Henry, Fortinbras does not hesitate to discharge his historical mission. He will risk two thousand men and twenty thousand ducats for acreage that is not even worth the farming,

> Exposing what is mortal and unsure
> To all that fortune, death, and danger dare,
> Even for an eggshell. (9.41–43)

If Fortinbras would risk his life and army "even for an eggshell," Hamlet's objectives are less ambitiously "bounded in a nut shell," within whose confines he could "count [him]self a king of infinite space" (II.ii.248–49). He claims to scorn all political ambitions; the reflective scholar in him constrains not just the climbing courtier but also the active military man. "Rightly to be great," Hamlet muses in this revealing scene,

> Is not to stir without great argument
> But greatly to find quarrel in a straw
> When honour's at the stake. (IV.iv.9.43–46)

Hamlet understands, in other words, that in order to achieve greatness one must risk lives like the daring Fortinbras, must challenge armies like the conquering Henry Plantagenet, must deliver vaunts like the heroic Hotspur, for whom "it were an easy leap / To pluck bright honour from the pale-faced moon."

But such ambitions are voided by too many inhibitions. Just as Hamlet's soldierly pluck is undermined by his meditative nature, so his plain-dealing instincts are occasionally contradicted by his need to play the misanthropic madman. But while his lunacy is a disguise, his misanthropy ("man delights not me") comes quite naturally. His scornful treatment of the tedious old logic-chopper Polonius, of the upstart courtier Osric, and of those opportunistic time-servers Rosencrantz and Guildenstern is familiar enough to us from the confrontations of other plain-dealers in Shakespeare's plays. But he wraps it in such a shroud of gauzy language that his meaning is often obscured. An unlicensed lunatic can exercise the same privilege as a licensed fool, which is the freedom to ridicule the objects of his contempt without directly insulting them. As a madman, Hamlet engages Polonius in a discourse on the shape of clouds; he satirizes Osric's overinflated language; and he channels the treachery of Rosencrantz and Guildenstern into a tirade on their inability to play the recorder. He postpones his revenge on his uncle Claudius, despite his father's command, with a pretext at the same time transparent and devious, putting on "an antic disposition," feigning a diseased wit. Always maintaining an edge of irony that preserves his authenticity and inner integrity, he nevertheless dissembles and dissimulates with everyone but Horatio.

Let us note once again what a paradox this is. Hamlet is the man who says, "I know not 'seems,'" who has "that within which passeth show," who scorns all "actions that a man might play," who disdains "the suits and trappings of woe." His open contempt for "showing," "playing," "seeming" (as opposed to the simple act of "being") mirrors one of the great oppositions of the Renaissance, the debate between Art and Nature (or

Appearance and Reality, or Form and Function). All the world may be a stage, as Jaques says in *As You Like It,* and every man and woman may be members of the same repertory company. But for Hamlet in his melancholy, the world of appearances is acceptable only on the stage, not in the real world. Hamlet the plain-dealer scorns dissembling (or acting any role but one's own character), for the same reason Plato rejected poetry, because it is riddled with artifice and lies.

Hamlet is, nonetheless, a consummate man of the theatre, and acting is a profession in which, under other circumstances, he might have excelled. In his first scene with the players, he recites a speech from Aeneas's tale to Dido so well that Polonius, another amateur actor (he once played Julius Caesar), offers him high praise: "'Fore God, my lord well spoken; with good accent and good discretion" (II.ii.446–47).[7] Hamlet's histrionic talent may be inconsistent with his sincere philosophy, but it is perfectly consistent with his character. For what is Hamlet anyway but a plain-dealer who, forced by circumstance to disguise his true feelings, turns into a playactor, potentially a more authentic one than the overly emotional Player King, who grows pale and breaks into tears describing the grief of Hecuba. The presence of an acting troupe in this tragedy (the only such professional theatre company in Shakespeare, if we discount the amateur rustics in *A Midsummer Night's Dream* and the masquers in *Love's Labour's Lost*) is not an accident. *Hamlet* is a play about performing and pretending, in which a plain-dealing soldier and scholar is forced against his will into the unwanted role of a dissembling courtier.

Only in the final scene, with Ophelia dead, with Laertes dying, with Gertrude poisoned by a toxic brew prepared for him by the king, can Hamlet finally face his villainous antagonist, as Hotspur and Fortinbras would have done instinctively, like a courageous son and soldier determined to avenge a murdered father and king. The epithets Hamlet showered on his uncle in private soliloquy ("treacherous, lecherous, kindless villain" [II.ii.558]) he can utter at last in public ("Here, thou incestuous murd'rous damned Dane, / Drink off this potion" [V.ii.267–68]), as he skewers Claudius with Laertes' poisoned blade and pours the remains of the poisoned chalice down his throat. Unable to take his revenge until the end of the play, Hamlet kills the king not once but twice. His final words are directed to another plain-dealing soldier, Fortinbras. He offers him, a man more fit for rule than the hesitant dreamer who proclaims him king, "my dying voice" (298). (The more forthright Fortinbras would probably have wrested the crown from him anyway, without his blessing.)[8]

By the time of *Othello* (1604), the blunt incorruptible soldier has become such a common, familiar figure of popular mythology that he has turned into stage convention. When Iago needs a disguise, which is to say a theatrical role, to achieve his insidious goals, he selects the character of the plain-dealer. (So, by the way, does his kissing cousin Richard III.) How cunning for an arch liar to choose the role of a man who cannot lie. This disguise requires no cross-dressing, no masks or buskins, only a capacity to perform. Iago will assume the qualities most frequently attributed to the type: frankness, openness, sincerity, simplicity, candor, and especially honesty. An arrant villain has transformed himself into "honest, honest Iago." The choice is highly ironic since there is in Shakespeare no character more untrustworthy. Iago is the archdissimulator. While Hamlet protests "I know not 'seems,'" Iago knows very little else. His true nature is hidden from everyone, even from his wife.

Everyone, that is, except the audience. We are given the roles of his confidants and confederates. When Christopher Walken played Iago in Central Park, his silken insinuating charm made the audience feel complicit in his evil. Soliloquizing to us, Iago confesses, "I am not what I am" (I.i.65), inverting the reply that God offered Moses ("I am what I am") when questioned about his identity. Shakespeare gives Viola the same inversion of the line in *Twelfth Night*. But if Viola feels compelled to disguise herself as a male page in order to protect her chastity, Iago must disguise himself as an honest soldier in order to advance his villainy. Despite Hamlet's abilities as an actor, he is often acting a role that has been forced on him. But while Hamlet seems to have been cast in somebody else's play, Iago is always in full command of his own. Iago functions not just as actor and playwright but as director, stage manager, and casting agent, choosing Othello as his tragic hero, and creating the Moor's tragedy by forcing him into the role of vengeful cuckold. He does this by playing one more theatrical role supremely—that of spitting critic. At the same time that he is Shakespeare's most hateful villain, he is also his most brilliant and analytical intellectual.

Shakespeare gives this skillful specialist in human nature some of the wittiest exchanges and most notable speeches in the play. Just as Hamlet criticizes the Danes for lack of sobriety, so Iago satirizes the English for outstripping all of Europe in this vice: "Why, he drinks you with facility your Dane dead drunk; he sweats not to overthrow your Almain; he gives your Hollander a vomit ere the next pottle can be filled" (II.iii.71–73). In libeling Desdemona to Roderigo, he expresses familiar Shakespearean prejudices regarding the lightness of women: "She must change for youth; when she is sated with his body, she will find the error of her choice" (I.iii.342–43). He delivers one of Shakespeare's most eloquent speeches about the power of reason over passion, and will over instinct, in a passage worth quoting in full:

> Virtue! A fig! 'tis in ourselves that we are thus, or
> thus. Our bodies are our gardens, to the which our

wills are gardeners. . . . If the beam of our lives had not one scale of reason to peise another of sensuality, the blood and baseness of our natures would conduct us to most preposterous conclusions; but we have reason to cool our raging motions, our carnal stings, our unbitted lusts, whereof I take this that you call love to be a sect or scion . . . merely a lust of the blood and a permission of the will. (316–29)

A lust of the blood and a permission of the will! In his capacity to control his every emotion toward a diabolical end, Iago is an early version of a figure who will continue to fascinate and terrify Shakespeare, the nihilist later resurrected by Dostoevsky in the characters of Raskolnikov and Stavrogin, for whom anything is possible in a world without God. Iago's paean to the power of Reason will later be rewritten by Rousseau and Robespierre, his tribute to the power of the Will later imagined by Nietzsche. Like Edmund's musings on a universe dominated by blind nature in *King Lear,* this speech sets the stage for the French Terror, and, ultimately, for Hitler's Third Reich.[9]

"I hate the Moor," Iago says. Why? Coleridge famously called him a "motiveless malignity," but he suffers not from a dearth of motives so much as an excess of them. Iago has so many reasons for entrapping the guileless Othello that it is impossible to identify a single cause. One is professional jealousy. Like Feste in *Twelfth Night,* who never forgets Malvolio's dismissive reference to him as a "barren knave," Iago has never forgiven Othello for passing him over for promotion in favor of Cassio. Another is revenge. He is maddened by rumors, whether true or not, that "the lusty Moor" has "leapt into my seat" and slept with his wife. A third is his hatred of goodness. Anticipating the bastard Edmund's resentment of his decent brother Edgar in *King Lear,*

Iago hates Othello because of his "constant, loving, noble nature" (II.i.276), the same "daily beauty in his life" (V.i.19) that sets him against Cassio. His chief motivation, however, seems to be an abstraction—a passion for civil chaos and destruction of the innocent. He may be the first pure terrorist in literature.

Regarding Iago's jealousy of Othello, we should note that it has nothing to do with the reality, only with the *appearance* of reality: "I hate the Moor," he soliloquizes,

> And it is thought abroad that 'twixt my sheets
> He has done my office: I know not if 't be true,
> But I, for mere suspicion in that kind,
> Will do as if for surety. (I.iii.368–72)

"It is thought," "I know not if 't be true," "for mere suspicion"— why does he take such extreme action without any proof? Because Iago, who does not believe in such intrinsic qualities as "virtue" or "honesty," is entirely committed to extrinsic appearances, to what people think. Othello thinks men honest "that but seem to be so." Iago is the opposite; he thinks men false who are actually true. Shakespeare gives this villain two brilliant but contradictory speeches on the subject of reputation. To Cassio, who fears that his good name has been dissolved in alcohol, Iago says, "Reputation is an idle and most false imposition; oft got without merit, and lost without deserving; you have lost no reputation at all, unless you repute yourself such a loser" (II.iii.351–53).

This is the plain-dealer's position, that one's interior merit cannot be measured by exterior opinion. And yet the idea of reputation, which he told Cassio was an "idle and false imposition," he defends to Othello as the very essence of humanity:

> Good name in man and woman, dear my lord,
> Is the immediate jewel of their souls:

> Who steals my purse steals trash, 'tis something,
> nothing;
> 'Twas mine, 'tis his, and has been slave to
> thousands;
> But he that filches from me my good name
> Robs me of that which not enriches him,
> And makes me poor indeed. (III.iii.160–66)

This speech (a favorite for rote memorization) seems to be the more accurate description of Iago's idea of reputation, and that of every Machiavellian dissembler, regardless of how piously it is expressed.[10] It is how you appear to the world, not what you are, that is your disguise when you need to hide your motives. It is the reason Iago assumes the postures and attitudes of the honest plain-dealer.[11]

Before he acts it out with Othello, he rehearses this role with Roderigo. In the same way that Sir Toby swindles Sir Andrew in *Twelfth Night* by enticing him with the prize of his niece Olivia, so Iago fleeces Roderigo with the promise of Desdemona. The face he offers to Roderigo—the sneering realist who thinks all women whores—is quite different from the one he shows Othello: the exceeding honest fellow who "knows all qualities, with a learned spirit, of human dealings" (III.iii.263–64). Because he is cold, passionless, cynical, and suspicious, because he truly believes that everything is driven by will, because he thinks the carnal appetites of humans and animals to be identical, but especially because he is able to disguise himself as a traditional plain-dealer, Iago can persuade Othello of Desdemona's infidelity and Cassio's treachery, simply by assigning them his own nasty motives. Thus he writes Othello's soaring tragedy; and thus he becomes the silent actor of his own.

King Lear has its own Iago figure called Edmund, a natural child (a bastard) who also identifies with Nature, with no belief whatever in transcendence. Being an atheist like Iago, he endorses the power of the individual will; being a naturalist like Iago, he considers pity and compassion to be signs of human weakness; and being a Machiavellian like Iago, he also assumes the disguise of an honest truth teller. *King Lear,* however, features a genuine plain-dealing soldier in the character of Kent, perhaps the purest example of the type in all of Shakespeare. As such, he is one of a handful of characters in the play, among them Edgar, Albany, and Cordelia, who retain the capacity to redeem the awfulness of the time. Barely.

In the opening scene, Cordelia, a female plain-dealer ("so young, my lord, and true" [I.i.107]), dooms herself by refusing to be a contestant in her father's love competition. Although her sisters, like true court ladies, are only too eager to tell their foolish father what he wants to hear, Cordelia lacks "that glib and oily art / To speak and purpose not" (225–26), otherwise known as dissembling.[12] She is, in other words, the female counterpart of Kent, who braves his master after Lear foolishly dispossesses his daughter for failing to flatter him sufficiently. "Come not between the dragon and his wrath" (122), Lear warns, but, like Cordelia, it is Kent's role to do precisely that. "To plainness honour's bound," he tells the furious king. "Be Kent unmannerly, when Lear is mad" (145, 148). He accuses Lear of "hideous rashness," he calls him blind, and tells him he does evil. He risks a charge of high treason, and is almost killed for his pains. Kent accepts his banishment with the same manly resignation he displays throughout the play.

Unlike the plain-dealing "all-licensed" Fool, who is allowed to speak truth to his master only by means of a wry, indirect, and anecdotal tone (and even this gets him in trouble when his reproaches become too clear), Kent has no strategies for softening his criticism. That is why he must spend most of the play in disguise. In this, he resembles Iago. But if Iago is a villain who acts the part of a blunt plain-dealer, Kent is a plain-dealer who, even in disguise, remains "a very honest-hearted fellow, and as poor as the king" (I.iv.17). Among the things he claims to have mastered is the intrinsic quality of his own nature: "I can keep honest counsel, ride, run, mar a curious tale in telling it, and deliver a plain message bluntly" (29–30). Only his speech is altered, only his accents disguised. It is a wonder that Lear does not recognize him, so little is he changed.

The scene in act II where Kent encounters Oswald is another of those familiar Shakespearean meetings between a manly soldier and an effeminate courtier. Kent even borrows some of Hotspur's phrasing and rhythms regarding the "certain lord" when recounting the meeting to Lear ("My Lord . . . came there a reeking post, / Stewed in his haste, half breathless, panting forth . . ." [II.iv.26–30]). Shakespeare, who rarely repeats himself, seems to relish such confrontations, and this one hardly deviates from the pattern. After advising Oswald to set his horses "I' the mire," Kent launches into his extended characterization of the whole breed of courtly narcissists that are currently poisoning the land: "a whoreson, glass-gazing, superserviceable, finical rogue; one trunk-inheriting slave; one that would'st be a bawd in way of good service, and art nothing but the composition of knave, beggar, coward, pandar, and the son and heir of a mongrel bitch . . . a tailor made thee" (II.ii.15–20, 48).

Aside from being an overdressed upstart created by a hem-stitcher, Oswald is also a vaunting coward (or effeminate braggart soldier) who refuses to draw when Kent challenges him to a duel. Kent's response encapsulates the whole courtly breed:

> Such smiling knaves as these
> Like rats, oft bite the holy cords a-twain
> Which are too intrinsic t'unloose; smooth every
>   passion

> That in the natures of their lords rebel;
> Bring oil to fire, snow to their colder moods,
> Renege, affirm, and turn their halycon beaks,
> With every gale and vary of their masters,
> Knowing nought, like dogs, but following.
> A plague upon your epileptic visage! (65–73)

Nor is he much taken with the looks of Oswald's master, the duke of Cornwall:

> Sir, 'tis my occupation to be plain:
> I have seen better faces in my time
> Than stands on any shoulder that I see
> Before me at this instant. (84–87)

In response, Cornwall attacks the character of the entire plain-dealing species in the speech that serves as the epigraph to this chapter. Though intended as a negative portrait, his contemptuous description is clearly endorsed by Shakespeare:

> He cannot flatter, he,
> An honest mind and plain, he must speak truth:
> An they will take it, so; if not, he's plain. (90–92)

Not to be outdone, Kent retaliates with a parody of courtly complement—

> Sir, in good sooth, in sincere verity
> Under the allowance of your great aspect,
> Whose influence, like the wreath of radiant fire
> On flickering Phoebus's front . . . (97–100)

—that reminds us of the way Hamlet ridiculed Osric's pretentious locutions. For his pains and for his plainness, Kent is placed in the stocks.

This is one of the events that will conspire to drive Lear mad, and, through his lucid madness, rocket him into the role of the fourth and most penetrating plain-dealer in the play. While Goneril and Regan play the parts of adulterous court ladies, competing for the affections of Edmund, Lear tries to preserve his retinue, his pride, and his sanity. Only when his five wits begin to fragment, and he is driven onto the heath to roar out his madness, is he finally able to think clearly, just as Gloucester could see clearly only once he was blinded.

Earlier, begging Goneril to "Reason not the need" (II.iv.259), Lear had argued that human beings require something more than the properties they were born with: "Allow not nature more than nature needs / Man's life's as cheap as beasts" (261–62). But the wisdom he acquires on the heath is that there may be nothing more than nature, that man and beast are one, and not just in the basic cheapness of their lives. The "dear goddess" Nature he once worshiped (I.iv.252) is proving now to be more like the blind indifferent force earlier celebrated by Edmund. But even nature at its most merciless is kinder than his two "unnatural" daughters.

Once before, in *As You Like It,* Shakespeare had associated the wintry blasts of nature with the thanklessness of humanity— in the song, "Blow, blow thou winter wind" ("Thou art not so unkind / As Man's ingratitude" [II.vii.174–76]). But Lear's ravings on the heath, while "contending with the fretful elements" (III.i.4), are not just descriptive but prescriptive. At times, he acquits the storm of malignant motives ("I tax not you, you elements, with unkindness"); at times, he considers the rain, wind, thunder, and fire the "servile ministers" of his thankless daughters (III.ii.15, 20). Still imagining himself a powerful monarch, he orders the storm to drench, drown, burn, singe, and strike flat "the thick rotundity of the world" (7). Worse, he commands it to spill "all germens . . . at once / That make ingrateful man" (8–9). Lear had earlier asked Nature to sterilize his daughter Goneril:

> Into her womb convey sterility,
> Dry up in her the organs of increase,
> And from her derogate body never spring
> A babe to honor her. (I.iv.255–58)

It is perhaps the most ghastly thing a father can wish upon his daughter, and in the Peter Brook production, when Paul Scofield's Lear delivered this pestilential blessing on Irene Worth's Goneril, it seemed to shrivel her up in a way from which she never recovered. Now Lear extends that curse to the entire world. The "germens" or seeds of life will be scattered to the winds, leaving a future without procreation or progeny. This is the first (not the last) example of a Shakespearean plain-dealer evolving into a total mankind-hater or misanthrope.

Attended only by Kent and the rapidly weakening Fool, Lear goes from reflections on filial ingratitude to a new understanding of universal injustice and inequality. This understanding awakens Lear's compassion for "poor naked wretches" with their "houseless heads and unfed sides" (III.iv.31). Lear believes poor Tom (Edgar in disguise) to be one of those wretches. But it is Lear himself, pelted by the rain, blown about by the wind, who most resembles unaccommodated man, for like the other naked wretches he also "owest the worm no silk, the beast no hide, the sheep no wool, the cat no perfume" (96–97). This physical and spiritual nakedness, in theory at least, happens to be the ideal state of the archetypal plain-dealer—Adam in the garden, Diogenes in the street. But there is no utopian past in this play, only ravening nature, and a predatory future that Albany describes in apocalyptic terms:

> If that the heavens do not their visible spirits
> Send quickly down to tame these vild offenses,
> It will come,

> Humanity must perforce prey on itself,
> Like monsters of the deep. (IV.ii.47–51)

It is honest Kent who tries to find some way to redeem the awfulness of the time, when, in act IV, noting the moral contrast between Cordelia and her sisters, he reaffirms the astrological view of life earlier scorned by Edmund:

> It is the stars,
> The stars above us, govern our conditions;
> Else one self mate and mate could not beget
> Such different issues. (IV.iii.31–34)

But despite a momentary glimmer of hope when honest Edgar triumphs over the knavish Edmund in an oddly anachronistic medieval tourney, despite the half-hearted restoration of order at the conclusion of the play, Cordelia's hanging and Lear's subsequent death suggest a world from which any benevolent God has long since fled, where you look up to heaven and only the moon shines down. As has often been noted, Lear's repeated negatives ("No, no, no life! . . . Thou'lt come no more,/Never, never, never, never, never" [V.iii.304–7]) reinforce the feeling that this is, indeed, "the promised end."

Kent is among a handful of survivors left on stage to restore this devastated kingdom, but like Horatio in *Hamlet* he would rather follow his master into oblivion. Hamlet prohibits Horatio's suicide, asking him to postpone "felicity" for a while to tell his story. Lear, having died with blistering negatives on his lips, is in no condition to ask the same of Kent. When Albany offers him and Edgar the kingdom, Kent tersely replies: "I have a journey, sir, shortly to go;/My master calls me, I must not say no" (V.iii.320–21). This leaves only Edgar and Albany to redeem the time from the "general woe" (318). The final stage direction—*Exeunt, with a dead march*—though probably not by

Shakespeare, is eloquence itself. The play ends with a funeral march in which the numberless dead join the handful of survivors in an exodus of ghosts, while the moon shines coldly down.

Shakespeare's Roman plays all have their plain-dealers, but instead of being paragons of honesty and truth, they are more often imperfect human beings in an imperfect world. In *Julius Caesar,* for example, Casca is a relatively minor figure whose malcontent personality accounts for both his cynical tone and his treasonous conduct. It is this laconic "blunt fellow" who sees through Caesar's simulated modesty when refusing the crown, and it is he who satirizes the pedantic pretensions of Cicero's oratory ("it was Greek to me" [I.ii.278]). Still, after his early plain-dealing remarks in act II, he lapses into the traditional role of conspirator.

In the sequel to this play, *Antony and Cleopatra,* however, Shakespeare uses the disintegrating quality of the plain-dealer as the basis for a splendid characterization. The honest soldier Enobarbus expresses all the familiar attitudes of his age toward logic-chopping and lovemaking. As Maurice Charney notes (in *Shakespeare on Love and Lust*), Enobarbus is a Roman soldier who, unlike Antony, is impervious to love. (Charney reminds us that Antony and Othello are among the few Shakespearean soldiers who seem to have a sexual life.) Upon his first entrance in act I, scene ii, Enobarbus is already grumbling about how sex has replaced warfare as the major Roman activity in Egypt. If Antony is forced to take his armies back to Rome because of his domestic business, "Why, then, we kill all our women" (121). His beady view of Cleopatra's wiles and temperament, however, is accompanied by his genuine admiration for this "wonderful piece of work." Enobarbus's description of Cleopatra's first appearance before Antony ("The barge she sat in, like a burnished throne,/Burned on the water" [II.ii.197–98]) is, of course, one of the most magnificent rhetorical flourishes in the English language. This speech, which also makes admiring reference to Cleopatra's gentlewomen ("like the Nereides, / So many mermaids" [212-13]), suggests that he is not totally impervious to female charms.

And there is no greater testimony in Shakespeare to a seductive woman's allure than Enobarbus's explanation of why Antony will never leave his Egyptian queen:

> Age cannot wither her, nor custom stale
> Her infinite variety; other women cloy
> The appetites they feed, but she makes hungry
> Where most she satisfies. (240-43)

Enobarbus is hardly blind to the way Cleopatra manipulates his master. And in his second act scene with Menas, he expresses the traditional satirical view of women's beauty: "There is never a fair woman has a true face" (II.vi.100). (Compare Hamlet: "That if you be honest and fair, your honesty should admit no discourse to your beauty" [III.i.109-10]). Perfectly willing to join in Antony's drunken wassails, even to lead the Romans in a Bacchic dance, Enobarbus still manages to speak the plain-dealing truth, often at the risk of incurring Antony's displeasure:

> Antony: Thou art a soldier only. Speak no more.
> Enobarbus: That truth should be silent I had almost forgot.
> Antony: You wrong this presence; therefore speak no more.
> Enobarbus: Go to, then; your considerate stone.
> (II.ii.112-15)

Enobarbus's stony silence in the face of rebuke is in marked contrast to Kent's defiance. And despite his shrugs, this "considerate stone" will start to turn when Antony reverses rudder in the midst of battle and deserts his fleet to follow the retreating Cleopatra. From that point on, Enobarbus's commitment to a master who "would make his will lord of his reason" (III.xiii.3–4) grows weaker and weaker. Torn between the steadfast loyalty of a Kent and the self-serving weakness of an Oswald or an Osric, he remains in a state of agonizing suspension for the rest of the play:

> Mine honesty and I begin to square.
> The loyalty well held to fools does make
> Our faith mere folly; yet he that can endure
> To follow with allegiance a fall'n lord
> Does conquer him that did his master conquer,
> And earns a place in the story. (40–45)

Should he follow self-interested gain or self-abnegating glory? Should he earn a place in somebody else's story, or write a part in his own?

Enobarbus soon concludes that Antony is "so leaky/That we must leave thee to thy sinking" (63–64), a nautical metaphor wonderfully appropriate to Antony's debacle at sea, which Enobarbus had vainly warned him to avoid. When his master again determines to fight at sea rather than land, with a broken army and a "sever'd navy," following "one other gaudy night" (185), Enobarbus finally makes his long-deferred determination to "seek some way to leave him" (203).

It is a Judas-like decision that will destroy this conscience-stricken soldier. He knows that, by this betrayal, he has ruined his peace forever:

> I am alone the villain of the earth,
> And feel I am so most . . . I will go seek
> Some ditch, wherein to die. (IV.vi.30–38)

And die he does, extolling Antony's nobility as compared with his own treachery, earning a place in the story only as "a master-leaver and a fugitive" (IV.x.21).

If Enobarbus is the most complicated of Shakespeare's plain-dealers, Coriolanus is the most compromised. Indeed, we do not always know whether his bluntness is a virtue or a vice. Neither do his fellow Romans. The qualities of his personality are endlessly anatomized (no other Shakespeare character is the subject of so much friendly chat and hostile discussion). In *King Lear,* Cornwall characterizes Kent as one who exults in his own directness. He is wrong about Kent, but regarding Caius Martius he could not make a better description. "Was ever man so proud as this Martius," asks the Tribune Sicinius, to which Junius Brutus answers, "He has no equal" (I.i.242-43). A few scenes later, we are introduced to the source of this pride—Volumnia, his overbearing mother, whose ambiguous sexual feelings toward her own child lead her into Oedipal revelations ("If my son were my husband, I should freelier rejoice in that absence wherein he won honour" I.iii.2-3). She often calls this mighty warrior "my boy"—a word that Martius will not accept from any other mouth. As many commentators have noticed, it may be his unresolved relationship with his mother that makes this boy-man so eager to prove his valor.

In battle he is a fury, and when his army is momentarily beaten back, he turns on them in rage:

> All the contagion of the south light on you,
> You shames of Rome! You herd of—Boils and
>   plagues
> Plaster you o'er. (I.v.1-3)

When he single-handedly carries the fight against the Volscians past the walls of their own city, his retreating soldiers are shamed into returning to Corioles and helping to turn the tide. Like all plain-dealing soldiers, Martius exults in his wounds ("The blood I drop is rather physical/Than dangerous to me" I.vi.18–19), for wounds symbolize his manly courage. He and Aufidius huff and puff at each other in battle like a couple of schoolyard bullies. When he is victorious, right before the end of the first act, he will be renamed after Corioles, the site of his victory: Caius Martius Coriolanus.

Pride, we are continually told, is Martius's greatest weakness. It is also the source of his strength. The man who tells us this is Menenius, Coriolanus's older friend, while berating the magistrates for their hypocrisy. Indeed, Menenius may be a more authentic plain-dealer than his model. "Master of the people/Your multiplying spawn how can he flatter?" (II.ii.73–74), Menenius asks, suggesting that the plain-dealer is not only too honest to lie to the king, he will not lie to his subjects either.

I shall examine Shakespeare's negative attitudes toward democracy in the next chapter, with *Coriolanus* as a chief example. It is sufficient to say about it here that Coriolanus is banished from Rome because his plain-dealing pride prevents him from displaying sufficient deference to the mob. Reluctantly, he will wear a garb of humility, but he will not show his wounds, nor will he placate "the tongues of th' common mouth" (III.i.23) in order to become their consul. Goaded by the treacherous tribunes, filled with contempt for the unruly rabble, Coriolanus grows so insulting that soon the whole state is calling for his head.

Menenius tries to save the day by telling the crowd:

> His nature is too noble for the world:
> He would not flatter Neptune for his trident
> Or Jove for's power to thunder. (255–57)

He offers to mediate between the lion and his wrath, calling Coriolanus "a limb that has but a disease," easy enough to cure (297). As for Coriolanus, he only wants his mother to sufficiently admire his defiance of the plebeians. She doesn't, and answers with a maternal rebuke: "You might have been enough the man you are/With striving less to be so" (III.ii.18-19).[13] Volumnia's reservations about her son's manliness explain a lot about his pride, especially toward the mob. Between them, Volumnia and Menenius manage to persuade this self-absorbed plain-dealer to make one more stab at placating the people and the tribunes: "Mother, I am going to the market-place;/Chide me no more. I'll mountebank their loves" (131-32). The honest soldier will turn playactor solely to placate his mother.

But the tribunes know full well how to use his weaknesses to undermine his ambitions. A few lines into the scene, they have aroused his wrath by calling him traitor, and have banished him from Rome. This triggers the best-known speech in the play. Coriolanus, in yet another Shakespearean tirade against ingratitude, calls his enemies a "common cry of curs" and shouts defiantly, "I banish you!" (III.iii.124, 127) Pouring bile on their infamous heads, the defender of the city, so recently honored for his military victories, renounces his people, his heritage, and his home:

> Despising
> For you, the city, thus I turn my back:
> There is a world elsewhere. (137-39)

It is not that Coriolanus has chosen to die as a plain-dealer rather than live as an equivocator. Rather, he has been goaded into blurting out his extreme feelings because of his wounded pride. The rest of the play dramatizes the consequences. In Antium, he joins Aufidius, who, comparing Coriolanus to Mars, suggests that seeing him

> more dances my rapt heart
> Than when I first my wedded mistress saw
> Bestride my threshold (IV.v.115–17),

curiously suggesting that Coriolanus excites him more than his own wife. When the two warriors lead a great power against Rome, one by one his friends and family come to plead with Coriolanus to spare the city—first Menenius, whom he sends away bearing a "crack'd heart" (V.iii.9), and then his equally hapless wife, Virgilia, accompanied by their child, young Martius. Only his mother, Volumnia, manages to change his mind, at the end of the longest speech in the play, by once again chiding him like a child:

> There is no man in the world
> More bound to's mother; yet here he lets me prate
> Like one i' the stocks. (159–61)

Volumnia's success in subduing Coriolanus's wrath ultimately causes his death. Aufidius will not stand still and be denied his conquest by a tearful family scene. He calls him traitor, cancels out his "borrowed" name of Coriolanus, and, most insulting of all, calls him a "boy of tears" (V.vi.103). Like all of his other antagonists, Aufidius drives this plain-dealer mad by insulting his manhood. Coriolanus responds in typical fashion:

> Boy! False hound!
> If you have writ your annals true, 'tis there,
> That, like an eagle in a dove-cote, I
> Fluttered your Volscians in Corioles:
> Alone I did it. Boy! (113–17)

Aufidius gives the signal, and the conspirators fall upon him with their swords. After treading on the dead body, Aufidius is persuaded to honor the corpse. Coriolanus is more exalted in his death than in his life, this most proud and easily provoked of all the plain-dealers remembered as a "noble memory" (154).

Shakespeare's two later Greek plays, *Troilus and Cressida* (1601) and *Timon of Athens* (c. 1607), also have imperfect plain-dealers at their center, suggesting that something dark and bilious was turning this character, and possibly the author, into a misanthrope. In *Troilus and Cressida*, the character of Thersites ("a deformed and scurrilous Grecian," according to one rendering of the dramatis personae) is clearly a hangover from the *Satiromachia*, the War of the Satirists. Indeed, he seems less a theatrical figure than a satirical railer. His view of sex is remarkably similar to that of Iago. What passes for romantic love is nothing but a lust of the blood and a permission of the will. And in this play, that mean interpretation appears to be correct. *Troilus and Cressida* is mainly populated with whores, customers, and panders.

In *Troilus and Cressida*, Thersites acts the part of the licensed jester, closer to the bitter Fool in *Lear* than to such sunnier clowns as Feste or Touchstone. But Thersites also plays the role of a traditional satirist. As O. J. Campbell has remarked in *Comicall Satyre and Shakespeare's Troilus and Cressida*, Shakespeare in this play (as before in *Hamlet*) is recognizing the presence of those poetic and prose satirists who, stymied by the bishop's ban of 1599, were pouring their bile into dramatic works. Thersites joins Jonson's Macilente and Marston's Malevole as a theatrical stalking horse of knaves and villains. Indeed, he may even be a hidden portrait of one of Shakespeare's rival satirical playwrights.

Is he a typical plain-dealer? Only in the sense that Elizabethan satirists were all self-proclaimed plain-dealers. In the minds of more moderate beings, and perhaps sometimes even in Shakespeare's, they were often little more than scurrilous whiners. The dull-witted Ajax calls Thersites a "bitch-wolf's son," and Thersites has equally ripe expletives for Ajax ("thou mongrel beef-witted lord" II.i.10–12). He has the fearlessness of the plain-dealer, but hardly his gravitas. "I would thou didst itch from head to foot and I had the scratching of thee," he tells Ajax, using the prevalent disease imagery of the play. "I would make thee the loathsomest scab in Greece" (27–29). They go at each other this way until Ajax finally summons up the energy to beat him out of doors.

Thersites claims to be a volunteer, but he has really been impressed into service. Whatever the truth, he has no use for this war and takes every opportunity to insult the people who fight it. Like a licensed fool, he is humored a little in this, as when Patroclus invites him to "come in and rail" (II.iii.19–20). (Patroclus himself is said to spend his days "like a strutting player," mocking the Greek generals [51].) Patroclus's lover Achilles acknowledges that Thersites is "a privileged man," and allows him to abuse them both. A critic himself, Thersites has nothing but contempt for facile judgments: "A plague of opinion! A man may wear it on both sides, like a leather jerkin" (III.iii.254–56). (Not a bad way to describe the opinionating of not a few drama critics.) Nevertheless, he is an absolute anthology of insults, with a particular genius for scabrous inventions. He is contemptuous of the Greeks, however, for lacking brains (a fact they demonstrate in every scene), and also for being lechers, "incontinent varlets" a truth that is demonstrated throughout the play (V.i.88–89).

Thersites' sex nausea is enough to identify him as a plain-dealer, if not a Shakespearean mouthpiece. But he is a coward, too, and when Hector finds him on the battlefield, he saves his own life by claiming to be "a rascal; a scurvy railing knave, a very filthy rogue" (V.iv.254–55). Confronted by another Trojan warrior—Margarelon, a bastard son of Priam—he claims to be a bastard, too, and accepts the name of coward rather than lose his life. Thersites is one of the strangest characters Shakespeare ever conceived, a compound of many conventions, attractive and repellent at the same time. He is a scurvy railing knave, but he also carries the play's central theme, as well as Shakespeare's recurrent obsession that all human actions, including the Trojan War, have their origin in lechery.

That strange late play *Timon of Athens* is to a large extent a revision of *King Lear,* but it also carries resonant echoes of *Troilus and Cressida* and *Coriolanus* (which was written at about the same time). Each of the previous plays seems to have contributed another plain-dealing character to *Timon:* the "churlish philosopher" Apemantus looks and sounds a lot like Thersites; the Athenian Captain Alcibiades, when banished, behaves like another Coriolanus; and Timon, following his bankruptcy, evolves into a second Lear. Equally interesting, the play combines three of Shakespeare's continuing obsessions—his hatred of flattery, his suspicion of women, and his distaste for ingratitude.

The earliest reference to Apemantus (by a character named the Poet) identifies him as the very opposite of "the glass-faced flatterer" (I.i.59). Indeed, on his very first appearance, Apemantus is railing against the simpering lords who feed off generous hosts ("O you gods! What a number of men eats Timon, and he sees 'em not" I.ii.38–39). The expletives *flattery* and *flatterer* are central to his vocabulary. One lord calls him "opposite to humanity" (I.i.272). And indeed, he has the lowest opinion of humankind in all of Shakespeare, except for Lear. "Who lives," he asks, "that's not depraved or depraves?" (I.ii.132) Sometimes his philosophy sounds like a reverse species of Darwinism. Instead of having descended from primates, humans may be ascending toward them: "The strain of man's bred out / Into baboon and monkey" (I.i.251–52). Only Apemantus refuses Timon's bounty: "I scorn thy meat," he snarls; "'twould choke me, for I should ne'er flatter thee" (I.ii.37–38). Later he adds:

"No, I'll nothing; for if I should be bribed too, there would be none left to rail upon thee" (236–37). In other words, he is honest not so much out of conviction as out of affectation. He does not want to lose his reputation for railing and snarling.

Alcibiades functions in a plot parallel to Timon's. The soldier's victories on the battlefield carry as little weight as the nobleman's generosity in a moment of need. Seeking amnesty for a friend who has killed another in a drunken quarrel, Alcibiades appeals to the senators on the basis of the man's service record and his own. "Call me to your remembrances," he pleads, and when they refuse, cries "My wounds ache at you" (III.vi.94). For his pains, he is permanently banished, but, just like Coriolanus, he turns this banishment back on them:

> Banish me!
> Banish your dotage, banish usury,
> That makes the senate ugly. (96–98)

Like Timon, Alcibiades is a late learner regarding human ingratitude: "Is this the balsam that the usurping senate / Pours into captain's wounds? Banishment!" (108–9).

Again like Coriolanus, Alcibiades raises an army and marches on his own country. His wrath is terrible, but—and this is rare among the characters in this play—he has the capacity for forgiveness. And when the senators agree to let him reenter the city, he offers them the glove of peace. Alone among the plaindealers in *Timon of Athens*, Alcibiades has the virtues of charity and humanity.

So of course does Timon when the play begins. Indeed, his unconditional largesse is his undoing. When he goes bankrupt and calls upon his guests for help, he discovers they are but "mouth-friends" (III.vii.81). But just as Timon's material descent is from generous benefactor to penniless wretch, so his spiritual journey is from warmhearted patron to bitter enemy of all humanity: "I am Misanthropos," he snarls, "and hate mankind" (IV.iii.53). If Hamlet is the plain-dealer as melancholic, and Enobarbus is the plain-dealer as renegade, and Coriolanus is the plain-dealer as egotist, then Timon is the ultimate development of the type, the plain-dealer as spitting misanthrope.

Timon demonstrates how close under the skin of the honest truth teller lies the bile of the caustic mankind-hater. Repairing to his cave in the woods to rail against flatterers, as Lear retreated to the blasted heath to curse his daughters, he reminds us of all those figures who exchanged the corruption, promiscuity, and flattery of the court for the artlessness and simplicity of nature. He feeds on roots, like Diogenes. And like Diogenes, he despairs of finding a honest man (though he ultimately discovers one in his steward Flavius).

Timon's scene with Apemantus in the fourth act shows how much deeper lies the misanthropy of the disappointed humanitarian than that of the posturing pessimist. Apemantus has come to Timon because he has heard report "Thou dost affect my manners." But what he finds is far from affectation. And when Timon refuses even to accept Apemantus's admiration ("I love thee better than e'er I did," he tells him, to which Timon replies, "I hate thee worse" [IV.iii.233–34]), he correctly concludes: "The middle of humanity thou never knewest, but the extremity of both ends" (300–301).

In his lack of moderation, as well as in his revulsion against courtly hypocrites, in fact, Timon far exceeds Apemantus. When he first emerges from the cave, in act IV, scene iii, he is already obsessing on the subject of universal flattery:

> The learnèd pate
> Ducks to the golden fool: all's obliquy;
> There's nothing level in our cursèd natures
> But direct villainy. (17–20)

Indeed, in their competitive ranting toward the end of the scene, Timon makes Apemantus look like an amateur. To the thieves who come to steal his newly discovered gold, he demonstrates that every person is a thief, as well as every celestial object, including planet, sea, earth, and moon ("her pale fire she snatches from the sun" [431]). His argument persuades the thieves to give up their trade. He wishes on mankind a literal pox, the disease that would flatten the bridge of their noses and make the hairy bald, crack lawyers' voices, suppress the source of all erection, and turn the whole world impotent: "Let it no more bring out ingrateful man" (188).

These echoes of Lear on the subject of ingratitude reverberate again in Timon's attacks on women. He not only abuses Alcibiades' whores ("Paint till a horse may mire upon your face" [147]) but suggests that all women are prostitutes. "Strike me the counterfeit matron," he raves. "It is her habit only that is honest,/Herself's a bawd" (112–14). Elsewhere, Timon adds: "Maid, to thy master's bed;/Thy mistress is o' the brothel" (IV.i.112–13).

Let us listen once more to Lear's remarks about the lechery in the heart of the purest-seeming woman:

> Behold yond simpering dame,
> Whose face between her forks presages snow;
> That minces virtue, and does shake the head
> To hear of pleasure's name;
> The fitchew nor the soilèd horse goes to't
> With a more riotous appetite. (IV.vi.115–20)

"But to the girdle do the gods inherit," Lear concludes, "Beneath is all the fiends'" (123–24). This disgusted misogyny, if it be Shakespeare's, has now exploded into an apocalyptic call for the end of the world and the extermination of the human race. In *Lear*, doomsday is expressed through the spilling of germens or seeds, in *Timon* through a future of sterility and suicide. When the senators come to beg Timon for gold to resist the rebels, he offers them instead a way "to prevent wild Alcibiades' wrath" (V.ii.88), namely a tree on which to hang themselves.

With *Timon of Athens*, Shakespeare has reached the end of the road for plain-dealers and plain-dealing. A snarling anger that blasts all hope for man or faith in woman has taken the place of honest, blunt directness; and the powerful diatribe against ingratitude has thinned into a hysterical shriek. There have been many hints of Shakespeare's misanthropy in earlier plays, particularly in Hamlet's morbid reflections on the "quintessence of dust" we call humankind (II.ii.298). As many commentators have noted, the plays that follow *Timon*, Shakespeare's final works, will be elegies of reconciliation, often between fathers and daughters. But being fantasies and romances, they glance only occasionally toward the Shakespearean obsessions.

If you accept the thesis that Shakespeare's plays tend to reflect his states of mind, I do not think it fanciful to say that for whatever reason—the death of his son Hamnet, strained relations with his wife Anne, the trial of his daughter Judith on charges of adultery, the marital problems of his daughter Susanna—during the ten-year period of his greatest plays (1601-11) Shakespeare was looking into an abyss. He had suffered some kind of severe spiritual crisis, and managed to avoid breakdown, I would guess, only by objectifying his obsessions in his art. It also seems likely that by the time of his late romances (1608-13), just before his retirement to Stratford, this bitter plain-dealer had managed to conquer his misogyny and misanthropy, emerging from the dark night of anger and recrimination into the bright warm air of forgiveness.

4

Elitism and Mobocracy

FROM JACK CADE TO CALIBAN

*The rabblement hooted, and clapped their chapped hands, and
threw up their sweaty nightcaps, and uttered such a deal of stinking
breath . . . I durst not laugh for fear of opening my lips and
receiving the bad air.*
—*Julius Caesar, I.ii.243–48*

It is a generally accepted principle of Renaissance scholarship
that a prime function of Elizabethan drama, particularly historical and chronicle plays, was to build up confidence in what
historians have called the Tudor Myth. Since Queen Elizabeth's family line had a dubious claim to the crown stemming from the deposition of a legitimate ruler (Richard III),
and since her claim to the throne was under dispute by other
pretenders, Elizabeth expected poets and dramatists to justify
her royal authority through political propaganda exalting her
family line. She also expected them to proclaim her wisdom and
flatter her beauty—indeed, to treat her as something akin to a
goddess. This affirmation of immortality was not just a form of
sycophancy, it was also a kind of magical thinking, in light of
the fact that, since the execution of Mary Stuart in 1587, there
had been a number of attempts on the queen's life. The pope
himself had promised absolution for anyone involved in her assassination.

Far from being a dissenter from this royal imperative, Shakespeare was probably one of Elizabeth's most dedicated myth-
makers, a willing cog in the propaganda apparatus of the time.

As a dramatist he helped perpetuate the image of a beauteous Virgin Queen who remained forever young, forever desirable, forever unattainable. Playwrights and poets were generally forbidden to put a living monarch on the stage or into print in her own persona, but Elizabeth was a continual spiritual presence being exalted in one art form or another—for example, as Spenser's "divine Gloriana" and "faerie queene," possibly also as Shakespeare's queen of the fairies, Titania, and certainly as "the imperial vot'ress" (II.i.163) cited by Oberon to Puck. She even makes an appearance, in her own infant person, as "the maiden phoenix" (V.iv.40) born to Anne Boleyn in the Fletcher-Shakespeare *Henry VIII*.

Shakespeare did more than help immortalize the queen. He also joined the effort to legitimize her reign. This was done through a pair of epic tetralogies, namely the three parts of *Henry VI*, along with *Richard III*, sometimes called *The War of the Roses*, and the two parts of *Henry IV*, sandwiched between *Richard II* and *Henry V*, sometimes called the *Henriad*.[1] The primary political purpose of these eight chronicles was to establish, through a process of revisionist English history, the legal prerogatives of the Tudor line. Playing a vital part in this mythmaking, Shakespeare seems to have used Richmond in *Richard III* (he will later ascend the throne as the Tudor Henry VII), and particularly Henry Plantagenet (Henry V) in the *Henriad*, as his political mouthpieces, at least on the subject of usurpation and its political consequences.

The two tetralogies are written in reverse chronological order. Put in proper historical perspective, the story begins, in *Henry IV*, with the illegal deposition of a legitimate king, Richard II. This causes not only civil tumult (the War of the Roses between the houses of Lancaster and York) but also a severe disruption in the Great Chain of Being. Now through sincere repentance on the part of Bolingbroke, and through the heroic actions of his son Henry V in conquering France, the rights of the Plantagenets to the English throne are in process of being validated. In the earlier plays, Shakespeare had tried to justify Elizabeth's weak hold on the throne through the overthrow of the putatively diabolical Richard III, last of the Plantagenets, at the Battle of Bosworth by the earl of Richmond, later Henry VII, who thereupon united the two warring dynasties by marrying the heiress of the House of York. (It was a happy coincidence that Richmond's queen was also named Elizabeth.)

However well established Elizabeth was in the hearts of her subjects, however, the last years of her reign, from about 1599 until her death in 1603, were filled with considerable anxiety and apprehension, as well as a mood approaching despondency. These feelings were, no doubt, exacerbated by the queen's despair over the rebellion in 1601 of her young former favorite, the earl of Essex. It is common knowledge that Elizabeth identified herself at the time of the Essex uprising with the deposed Plantagenet, Richard II ("I am Richard II," she said. "Know ye not that?"). It is also a fact that Essex had commissioned Shakespeare's play on the day of the rebellion in order to encourage the citizenry to rise up against her. (Since nobody stirred, Essex had overestimated either his own personal appeal or the political power of the stage.)

Perhaps as a result of that betrayal, one finds in the queen's poetry at this time a brooding sense of displacement and disillusionment regarding the loyalty of her people, as suggested in these lines from one of her sonnets:

> The dread of future foes
> Exyles my present joye,
> And wit me warns to shunne such snares,
> As thretten myne annoye. . . .
> For falsehood now dothe flowe

And subjects faith doth ebbe;
Which should not be if reason rul'd,
Or wisdom wove the webbe.

The ebbing of her subjects' faith was taking place almost in tandem with the waning of her life.

The ascension of James Stuart of Scotland to the English throne in 1603 confirmed the misgivings of many regarding the direction in which the country was heading. James had previously published his *Demonologie,* in which, contrary to the best educated opinion, he ascribed evil supernatural powers to witches. This is a belief that Shakespeare would also embrace in *Macbeth,* at the same time validating the Stuart claim to the English throne through the character of James's ancestor, Banquo. Where scholars and artists were once happy to praise Elizabeth's poetry, they were now forced to flatter James's scholarly pretensions.[2] Where courtiers were once obliged to exaggerate Elizabeth's aging beauty as part of the myth of Gloriana, they were now required to praise James's roan jennet horse as a way of gaining preferment at the Jacobean court.

It is not too much to say that in kind if not intensity, James's court was characterized by the same opportunistic conditions as the fictional Italianate courts of the Jacobean dramatists, where flatterers abound and honest men go hungry. Young, handsome, and well-dressed upstarts, jostling for position, unconscionable in their desire to gain favor, were to become the preferred figures at Whitehall. Of course, Elizabeth's courtiers were hardly immune from such criticism, In a scandalous 1584 pamphlet called *Leicester's Commonwealth,* the queen's then-favorite was accused (by an anonymous Jesuit priest) of flattery, atheism, and the use of aphrodisiacs, poison, and murder (of his own wife) in order to advance himself in the affections of his sovereign.

But such tabloid accusations were less common in the queen's time. Even allowing for understandable nostalgia about the previous age, the rumors about James's court were much more numerous and scurrilous. Whereas Elizabeth's anonymous critics were largely Catholics, the most severe critics of the formerly Romanist James were almost exclusively Puritans. In fact, a number of Puritan histories have come down to us, describing courtly conditions at Whitehall that are almost identical with those found in Italianate court plays by Shakespeare and his contemporaries. These Puritan accounts were, admittedly, written some decades after James was dead, motivated partly by an effort to justify Cromwell's execution of James's son, Charles I. But although these writings are largely undependable, they no doubt reflect what many people believed was going on behind the scenes, and thus provide us with a vivid sense of the haunted cultural atmosphere of the time.

Francis Osborne, for example, in his *Historical Memoires on the Reigns of Queen Elizabeth and King James* (1658), concedes that Elizabeth attracted flatterers who "bred in her a higher esteeme [of her beauty] than an impartiall eare or eye can think due from others report or her owne pictures." But even though she was a woman, Osborne found her more manly than her successor, James, whom he criticized for "the intombing of the spirit of a brave soldier in the corps of a lesse sightly courtier."

To his Puritan critics, James was an effeminate monarch who preferred peacocks at his elbow. Osborne takes the king to task for the "Pride and Lust" of his spectacles and masques, and the "universall vanity in Cloathes" displayed by his courtiers. But not surprisingly the strongest Puritan charge against James is the imputation of homosexuality. Osborne writes that James's bosom was

> a place reserved for younger men and of more in-deering Countenances: And these went under the

appelation of his *Favorites* or *Minions*. . . . Now as no other Reason appeared in favour of their choice but handsomnesse, so the love the King shewed was as amorously conveyed as if he had mistaken their Sex, and thought them Ladies. Which I have seen Sommerset and Buckingham labour to resemble, in the effeminatenesse of their dressings . . . for the Kings kissing them after so lascivious a mode in publick . . . prompted many to imagine some things done in the Tyring-house, that exceed my expressions no lesse then they do my experience.

This malicious (and delicious) tabloid gossip cannot be confirmed as fact, though the author claims to be an eyewitness. And Osborne's writing style is so gross that Samuel Johnson once urged little boys to throw some stones at him. But the litany of Puritan charges against the excesses of James's court—its effeminacy, riotousness, gluttony, sexual depravity, and cheapening of the nobility (as already noted, James sold off knighthoods for a hundred pounds apiece)—perfectly mirrors the conditions of the Italianate court in Stuart drama.

Those charges are seconded in a number of Puritan histories. Sir Anthony Weldon, in *The Court and Characters of King James* (1650), even suggests that the king's love of the courtier was stimulated by his hatred of the military ("He naturally loved not the sight of a Souldier, nor of any Valiant man"). And Arthur Wilson, in *The History of Great Britain* (1653), claims that the long period of peace under James was a sign less of good fortune than of pestilence: "Peace is a great blessing," he wrote, "if it bring not a Curse with it; but War is more happy in its effects than it, especially if it takes away the distemper that grows by long surfeits, without destroying the body." Do we not hear echoes of Shakespeare's Hamlet here complaining about "the imposthume of much wealth and peace" (IV.iv.9.17)?

Along with scurrilous imputations about the king and his courtiers inevitably came insinuations regarding James's queen, Anne of Denmark, and her court ladies. Sir Edward Peyton, for example, in *The Divine Catastrophe of the Kingly Family of the House of Stuarts* (1652), describes how Anne satisfied her "unruly appetite" with any number of James's courtiers. (Anne was also charged with initiating her adolescent son Charles "in the Court of Cupid" by locking him up at night with a beautiful court lady, "indeed more like a Bawd than a discreet mother.")

"Now King *James*," Peyton continues, "more addicted to love males than females, though for complement he visited Queen Anne, yet never lodged with her a night for many years." The insinuation is that he lodged with Robert Carr, and after Carr with the duke of Buckingham, and after him with Henry Howard. And to this court vice of pederasty, Peyton adds the mortal sin of drunkenness: "And generally the Courtiers were then so debauched in that beastly sin, as at that time, in the wayters chamber at supper, a Courtier was found dead on the Table, the wine foaming out of his mouth: a horrid sight to behold."

All of this could be a description of court conditions in Venice, Urbino, or Florence, in plays by Marston or Middleton, Tourneur, Webster or Ford. For that matter, it could be a description of Claudius's Elsinore in *Hamlet* ("They clepe us drunkards, and with swinish phrase / Soil our addition" I.iv.18.3–4), even though that play was written toward the end of Elizabeth's reign. To be sure, since cultural channels usually flowed in both directions, between literature and life, the Puritan histories may have been influenced to some extent by the theatrical representations of the preceding age. But surely those plays had been influenced earlier by the kind of rumors circulating first around Elizabeth and then around the Jacobean court, not to be published until after the Cromwellian revolution. And it is such imputed vices, I believe, that help to explain the growing darkness of tone in late Elizabethan and Jacobean drama.

Shakespeare, as has been noted, was never reluctant to flatter both Elizabeth and James whenever possible. But although a confirmed monarchist devoted to the crown, he seemed like most of his literary contemporaries to have developed increasing doubts about the court in the years immediately preceding Elizabeth's death and following James's ascension to the throne. In this, he may have merely been following tradition. Anticourt satire, a literary staple since Juvenal, had entered English literature centuries before, beginning with reforming poets like Langland, Lollards like Wycliffe, and stern monks like Bishop Broyard and Robert Rypon, who had agitated for years against flattery, insincerity, and the excessive splendor of the papal court.

Sixteenth-century court satire immediately preceding Shakespeare shows the influence of medieval writings as well as classical influences. John Skelton's *The Bowge of Courte* (1499) and, especially, his *Magnyfycence* (1530), involve such courtly personifications as Counterfeit Countenance, Cloaked Collusion, and Courtly Abusion, all representing the double-dealing, backbiting, and affectedness universally associated with the court. Some years before the Italian infiltration, Skelton is already finding the court guilty of what will later be considered exclusively Italianate crimes and follies: murder, lust, envy, affectation, pride, flattery, and idleness. After this, Sir Thomas Wyatt, Edmund Spenser, Thomas Nashe, Robert Greene, Gabriel Harvey, John Marston, and dozens of other satirists would continue these themes in the form of verse satire until being suppressed by the Bishop's Edict of 1599.

I do not think it too farfetched to say that these writings

laid some of the groundwork for later Puritan grumbles against the crown. Eventually the Long Parliament in 1640–42 toppled the Stuart regime for the next eighteen years during the Cromwellian Interregnum. In no way was Shakespeare involved in the conspiracies leading up to this revolution, but he may have secretly shared a number of its assumptions—implicit, for example, in his misogyny and his effemiphobia. A committed royalist, he would never have supported the Puritan political leveling that led to the execution of Charles I and the Protectorate. But just as some people can concur with a negative Marxist critique (corporate greed and economic determinism) without embracing a positive Marxist ideology (dictatorship of the proletariat and withering away of the state), so I suspect that Shakespeare could secretly deplore the excesses of the court without having any faith in the populist alternative.

If Shakespeare is guarded about his attitudes toward royalty, his characters have little hesitation about expressing their disgust with popular rule, later to be called democracy. Democracy was not only a danger to the state, it was a threat to the very structure of religious and family life, which God intended to be hierarchical, like the celestial realm. To consider government without an ordained ruler was tantamount to accepting a family without an authoritative patriarch or a faith without a Heavenly Father. That is why the Puritans posed such a threat not only to existing religion but also to existing government. They were ready to depose a sitting monarch and establish a crude form of parliamentary rule in his place.[3]

To sum up, however Shakespeare may have endorsed some Puritan criticisms of the court, he clearly had no use for Puritan political theory. Shaw once defined democracy as a system that "substitutes rule by the incompetent many for rule by the corrupt few." That could have been Shakespeare's mantra as well. It is impossible not to hear his voice in some of the more virulent antidemocratic rants of his characters.⁴ Most of these can be found in his Roman plays. But an early example of Shakespeare's contempt for popular rule — as it was evolving in England, interestingly enough — can be found in *2 Henry VI,* particularly in the playwright's treatment of the Jack Cade rebellion.

Cade (whose real name may have been Mortimer) had led a mob of discontented peasants, workers, and soldiers against King Henry in 1450, looting London and beheading the lord treasurer. The rebellion failed, and Cade was executed, but the implications of this popular uprising obviously worried a lot of people, including Shakespeare. It was one of the earliest expressions of what two centuries later would come to be called Jacobinism, and, a hundred years after that, Marxism. As A. D. Nuttall has noted, in *Shakespeare the Thinker,* Cade was one of the earliest communists in his belief in the abolition of private property.

What seems to have most disturbed Shakespeare, apart from the bloodiness of the revolt, was the arrant stupidity of its leaders. Does he sympathize at all with the democratic aims of the rebellion? In her introduction to the play in the Norton Shakespeare, Jean E. Howard makes the argument that although Cade is "vilified and discredited" in the body of the play, he is correct about the "unspeakable selfishness of the English nobles."

That is true, just as the mob in *Coriolanus* is correct about the selfishness of the Roman patricians. But a mob is still a mob. Cade remains one of the most stupid, vicious, and self-important characters Shakespeare ever created. In an early mention of him in *2 Henry VI,* a rebel tells us that "Jack Cade the clothier" intends to give a whole new look to the "threadbare" Commonwealth, and that tanners, butchers, and weavers will become the new justices (IV.ii.4, 6). In Edward Hall's 2005 production for the Chicago Shakespeare Theater, Cade and his proletarian army came on stage chanting Reformation hip-hop ("Down with the government, down with the gentry"), while banging drums and smashing bats on a metallic floor in rhythm with their raucous shouts. Cade considers himself the law of the land. In his opening speech, he announces new statutes for England—seven halfpenny loaves of bread will be sold for a pence, and "I will make it felony to drink small beer" (IV.ii.64). Perhaps under the influence of too many flagons of large beer, he is also preparing to abolish money and make every parcel of land the property of all—a basic Marxist principle, except for the fact that he also expects to be worshiped as a lord (a basic Stalinist principle).

Cade inspires one of his followers, a butcher, to declare: "The first thing we do let's kill all the lawyers" (70), a sentiment that has evoked some sympathy in certain quarters. A Clerk who can read and write Cade declares to be a "villain" and a "conjuror," and sentences him to be hanged "with his pen and inkhorn around his neck" (81, 83, 98–99). A Lord who can speak French is declared a traitor. A soldier who calls him by his common name, Jack Cade, and not by his assumed title, Lord Mortimer, is executed. Henceforth, all the records of the realm will be burned—and Cade's "mouth shall be the Parliament of England" (IV.vii.12–13).

Like Harpo Marx tearing a book to pieces in *Animal Crackers*, Cade gets angry because he can't read. But the most debased example of Cade's democratic leveling is when he confronts the aged Lord Saye, accusing him of a variety of thought crimes: "Thou has most traitorously corrupted the youth of the realm in erecting a grammar school . . . thou has caused printing to be used . . . thou hast men about thee that usually talk of a noun and a verb and such abominable words as no Christian ear can endure to hear" (IV.vii.27–34). Part clown, part bumpkin, part savage, part political theorist, Cade is the very embodiment of the benighted subject of the realm, raging against learning, seething with grievances, desperate for power. He is almost a caricature of the ignorant *polis*, predicating a future of bigotry, stupidity, and tyranny.

Of course, Shakespeare always had considerable sympathy for the common man. He was hardly of noble birth himself. But he expressed this sympathy mainly for individuals, never for the mob. The contentious soldier Michael Williams, in *Henry V*, makes the disguised king angry by questioning the monarch's motives and his cause. But Williams's critique of the war ("I am afeard there are few die well that die in a battle, for how can they charitably dispose of anything, when blood is their argument?" [IV.i.134–36]) has profound Christian humanist roots. And his companion John Bates absolves the king of responsibility for each soldier's spiritual state, determining "to fight lustily for him" (175–76).

These are just two examples in Shakespeare of the wisdom of the common folk. However goofy are such comics as Dogberry, Pistol, Don Armado, and other Shakespeare clowns, his peasants and citizens, taken one by one, are often highly appealing salty individuals. It is only in mob scenes that they take on qualities of thuggish brutality.

Shakespeare extends his criticism of this type of rude commoner into his Roman plays, where the playwright's contempt for the "rabblement," indeed for democratic politics as a whole, is never far from the surface. The central political issue of *Julius Caesar*, for example, is whether Rome is to remain a republic, ruled by an enlightened Senate, or an empire, under the sway of a dictator installed by the people. There are at least four different views of the situation, embodied in the four central characters. Julius Caesar, an incipient dictator, believes in the rule of the strong, namely himself. Marcus Brutus, a parliamentary liberal, believes in the rule of an enlightened citizenry acting through its more sophisticated representatives. Caius Cassius, a backroom schemer, believes in political wheeling and dealing, and eventual political assassination, to maintain his own power in the Senate. And Marcus Antonius (Mark Antony) believes, like his mentor Julius Caesar, in swaying the people through demagogical oratory. In each case, it is the Roman populace that holds the key to power, and the irony of the play is how easily a democratic system can be subverted by the very people who benefit from it most.

In the very first lines of *Julius Caesar,* the commoners are being reviled. The tribune Flavius calls them "idle creatures" (I.i.1), or lowly workmen, who walk abroad with no tools of their trade about them. They have come to celebrate the triumphs of Caesar, newly returned from his victory over Pompey at Pharsalus. This leads Murellus to abuse them further—"You blocks, you stones, you worse than senseless things!" (34)— because they once celebrated their fallen idol Pompey in exactly the same way. Instead of following the man who put down the Spartacus revolt, they are embracing Caesar, his conqueror, and, some will later say, his murderer. Having shamed them, Flavius sends these commoners on their way to "weep your tears / Into the channel" (57–58). The ease with which men of "basest mettle" (60) can be moved and persuaded, back and forth, by oratory is one of the more demoralizing themes in this play.

Flavius believes that if he can drive the "vulgar" from the streets, Caesar will be unable to rise. But in the very next scene, Caesar enters followed by a large crowd of working-class admirers. He is superstitious enough to believe a runner's touch can cure Calpurnia's barrenness, but not sufficiently mystical to credit the Soothsayer's warning to beware the ides of March ("He is a dreamer. Let us leave him. Pass!" [I.ii.26]). The off-stage cries of the people make Brutus fear they would "choose

Caesar for their King" (82). Brutus recoils before the "general shout" (133), distrusting commoners as much as Caesar distrusts intellectuals ("He thinks too much," Caesar famously says of Cassius. "Such men are dangerous" [195]).

The fact that Cassius loves no plays (nor music neither, as Antony does) makes him an object of suspicion to Caesar and, one would guess, to Shakespeare as well. He cannot behold anyone "greater than [himself]" (210), whether a dictator or a king. While Brutus hates tyranny, Cassius hates the tyrant. His resistance is personal rather than political. But the threat is nonetheless real. While the conspirators stew, the "rabblement," as Casca calls the crowd at the races, are offering Caesar a crown or a coronet (Casca is not absolutely certain of the object), clapping their "chopped hands" and throwing up their "sweaty nightcaps," and uttering "such a deal of stinking breath . . . that it had almost choked Caesar" (243–46). To these antipopulist insults, Casca offers the ultimate put-down—that the "tag-rag people" applauded and hissed Caesar, depending on their disposition, "as they use to do the players in the theatre" (257–58). Brutus will later compare himself and the other conspirators to Roman actors ("with untired spirits and formal constancy" [II.i.246]). But for Brutus it is the actor, not the spectator, who carries the nobler deportment. Casca agrees, because he considers the groundlings, at least those who applaud for Caesar, to be mindless sheep, stimulating his contempt for the democratic *polis*.

We learn one more crucial fact from the plain-dealing Casca in this scene—that the two tribunes from scene i, Flavius and Murellus, have been put to death for pulling the people's scarves off Caesar's busts. This does not augur well for the future of civil liberties in Caesar's Rome. Using any device at hand, Cassius works on Brutus in the same way that Iago will later work on Othello and Edmund on Gloucester, through wiles and insinuations. And just as Iago manipulates Othello's jealous nature, and Edmund plays on Gloucester's gullibility, so Cassius exploits Brutus's sense of pride and self-importance.

The irony of this play, from a political perspective, is that the royalist Shakespeare, like the democrat Brutus, seems to be criticizing the populace for wanting a king. But as Cicero remarks, this is a "strange-disposèd time," when "men may construe things after their fashion, / Clean from the purpose of the things themselves" (I.iii.33–35). Come to think of it, that would not be a bad epigraph for the entire play. Casca, for example, construes the tempest in act I as signifying "civil strife in heaven" (11); Cassius attributes it to Caesar's growing imperial tyranny. Both are mystical subjective misconstructions. But it is Brutus who will most construe (or misconstrue) things after his fashion—albeit manipulated by Cassius's strategic flattery— "clean from the purpose of the things themselves."

Brutus is the traditional liberal humanist. In conceiving him, Shakespeare may have been thinking of Sir Thomas More, though Brutus is more active than was More in confronting perceived wrongs. He has nothing against Caesar personally "but for the general" (II.i.12), which is to say the populace. Caesar has not yet shown himself to be an abuser of power, but if, as Brutus believes, power is always abused by men who seek it, then Caesar, like the serpent egg, must be killed "in the shell" (34). This kind of preventive vengeance is very rare in Shakespeare. In fact, it may be unique to this play. To overthrow a man *before* he assumes power for abuses you think he *might* commit is to foment the very tyranny that Brutus deplores. (Of course, Shakespeare has telescoped history in this play, since Caesar had already been dictator, if not king, for nine years before his assassination.)

Brutus's liberal instincts are responsible both for his greatness of heart and for his softness of mind. He certainly makes a ghastly series of errors. First, he imagines the assassination of Caesar as a form of artistry ("Let's carve him as a dish fit for the gods" [II.i.173]) instead of what it clearly is, an act of butchery. Second, he spares Mark Antony's life to avoid the appearance of excessive cruelty, and because he totally mistakes his character (this misreading is the fatal error that ultimately destroys Brutus). And third, he allows this popular idol to speak at Caesar's funeral, despite Cassius's passionate entreaties and accurate apprehensions.

Antony recognizes the malleable nature of the populace infinitely better than Brutus does. Brutus believes in simple truths rather than flowery rhetoric; Antony understands the use of ornate language as a means of manipulating a crowd. Thus while Brutus is a plain-dealer, Antony is a press agent, with instinctual knowledge of the power of advertising. Shakespeare signals the superiority of Antony's oratory by putting his speech into blank verse and Brutus's into prose. He also shares Antony's deeper insights into the weaknesses of the human heart. Brutus offers the citizens freedom through the medium of Caesar's death. Antony offers them cash through the medium of Caesar's will. And while they are momentarily roused by Brutus's talk about how to enjoy their liberty, they are more effectively rabble-roused by Antony's rhetoric about how to stuff their coffers. By the conclusion of his speech, the "free" Roman citizens have turned into a lynch mob, screaming for blood, and slaughtering innocent bystanders like Cinna the poet.

Brutus has failed to properly understand the darker side of human motive, including his own. He has such a lofty estimate of his own character ("I am armed so strong in honesty" [IV.ii.122]) that he disdains even to seek financial backing for his own war ("For I can raise no money by vile means" [126]). Imagine an American presidential candidate who honestly expected to be elected on the basis of his character rather than his contributed funds or his campaign promises; the party would quickly write him off the ticket.[5] At the same time that Brutus is waxing sentimental over "the hard hands of peasants," he is calling their money "vile trash" (129). And just as he miscalculates in peace, so he miscalculates in war, yet again ignoring the advice of the older soldier, Cassius, and prematurely marching on Philippi.

As a result, when he loses the battle, he chooses death rather than capture because, as Brutus says in praise of himself (inevitably using the third person), "He bears too great a mind" (V.i.113). Titinius might have declared of Brutus—even more than of Cassius who dies in error—"Alas, Thou hast misconstrued everything" (V.iii.83). Even in the act of committing suicide, Brutus misconstrues everything, believing, quite wrongly, "that yet, in all my life,/I found no man but he was true to me" (V.v.34–35). And this from the naïf whom Cassius and the other conspirators have been gulling as completely as Iago duped Roderigo, as Sir Toby hoodwinked Sir Andrew. Brutus has killed his best friend for nothing, becoming responsible for an even more repressive political regime than Caesar's, and one that will last for centuries.

Thus Shakespeare makes his subtle commentary on this complicated, self-deluded man. Even Antony's tribute to Brutus— "This was the noblest Roman of them all" (V.v.67)—is high praise only out of context. He is not calling Brutus the noblest of the Romans. That superlative he had already lavished on Caesar ("the noblest man/That ever livèd in the tide of times" [III.i.259–60]). He is saying Brutus was the noblest and best-intentioned of the *conspirators*, which is a considerably more limited kind of compliment.

If the democratic *polis* in *Julius Caesar* is a mob of easily manipulated yokels, in *Coriolanus* it is a crowd of fickle and ungrateful commoners. Like *Julius Caesar, Coriolanus* begins with a gathering of Roman citizens. (A stage direction calls them "a rabble of Plebeians" [III.i].) They are starving because they are unable to control the price of corn, and the patricians, with their goodly share, are showing no inclination to yield the "super-fluity" (I.i.14—what Lear had called the "superflux" [III.iv.36]) to lesser mortals. It is this economic inequality between rich and poor (a pervasive theme of recent American political campaigns) that will later persuade Bertolt Brecht to adapt the play for the Berliner Ensemble into a treatise about the economic consequences of a famine. But Shakespeare's citizens are a far cry from the Stalinist peasantry, posing on their tractors with their muscles rippling. Indeed, they sometimes sound a bit like the mad dogs of Jack Cade.

From the very first, they want to kill Caius Martius (later Coriolanus) for being "a very dog to the commonality"—an "enemy to the people"(I.i.5–6, 24)—despite his heroic services to his country.[6] The First Citizen, introducing an important theme of the play, says that the courage of Caius Martius on the battlefield was actually "to please his mother" (33). The patrician Menenius, who enjoys some of Antony's capacity to sweet-talk the citizenry, tries to dissuade them from rebellion with an extended metaphor about how the body once rebelled against the belly for receiving the most food, and how the belly replied that it needed all it could get in order to feed the rest of the system.

But the natives are too restive to accept this rather wonky wisdom, and Caius Martius, sensing this when he enters, calls them "dissentious rogues" (153). This Roman hero almost considers it a point of pride to insult the populace (elsewhere called "the many-headed multitude" [II.iii.13]). But while he clearly is excessively proud and captious, he is not wrong about the fickleness of the commoners: "With every minute you do change a mind, / And call him noble that was now your hate"

(I.i.171–72)—the same charges leveled against the commoners who deserted Pompey in *Julius Caesar.*

There are enough of these instances in the plays to persuade us that Shakespeare was "no democrat," as Allan Bloom recognized. But Bloom believed that Shakespeare despised the poor because they did not possess the virtues of patricians when of course they didn't. Patrician virtues were luxuries they could not afford. But despite some sympathy for the populace, Shakespeare, living under monarchist rule, certainly had strong royalist sympathies, and usually admired strong leaders. As Robert Nisbet observes in *Prejudices: A Philosophical Dictionary,* even Ulysses' speech on degree "makes clear that . . . authority is the absolute condition of any culture." Indeed, Shakespeare's appreciation for great kings like Henry V was paralleled by his respect for great if sometimes testy military heroes like Hotspur, Macduff, Richmond, and Coriolanus. There are, of course, a host of malevolent royals in his plays as well (Queen Tamora, Goneril and Regan, Cornwall, and Cloten, among others), as well as an army of imperfect rulers (Richard II, Richard III, Claudius, Caesar, Octavius Caesar, Macbeth, Leontes, Cymbeline). But Shakespeare never ceased to believe in the divinity that doth hedge a king.

This does not mean that he could not conceive of deposing royals when the occasion warranted. In a recent article in the *New York Review of Books,* Stephen Greenblatt even makes the point that Shakespeare may have approved of usurpation (or "regime change") as a proper way of getting rid of a bad ruler. Greenblatt also suggests that Shakespeare, for all his flattery of Elizabeth and James, was deeply suspicious of authority: "In Shakespeare," writes Greenblatt, "*no* character with a clear moral vision has a will to power and, conversely, no character with a strong desire to rule over others has an ethically adequate object." This is an interesting argument, one with the strength to make us modify our assumptions that Shakespeare loved the powerful. I believe it to be fully supported by all of the Shakespeare characters who, according to Greenblatt, are involved in or affected by "regime change"—not only ambitious schemers like Macbeth, Richard III, Cornwall, and Claudius but also those who "pull back from power" like Richard II, the mature Antony (in *Antony and Cleopatra*), Coriolanus, Prospero, and Lear after his divestiture. In short, Shakespeare under special circumstances could contemplate changing monarchs—for example, a weak king like Richard II, or an evil one like Richard III or Macbeth.

For Greenblatt, the truly great rulers in Shakespeare are those who come reluctantly into power. "Rule in Shakespeare is the fate of those who have been born to it. It is the fate of those as well who have been driven to exercise it out of desperation, forced, like Richmond in *Richard III*, Edgar in *Lear*, or Malcolm in *Macbeth*, to confront an evil so appalling that they have no choice but to act." This is why in Shakespeare the heads that bear the crown are often so uneasy. "Governance, as Shakespeare imagines it," says Greenblatt, "is an immense weight whose great emblem is the insomnia that afflicts the competent, tough-minded usurper Bolingbroke after he has become Henry IV. . . . Sleeplessness, tormenting, constant sleeplessness, is one of the only principles that he consistently depicts."

This plague of insomnia not only troubles Bolingbroke in *Henry IV*, it is a source of concern as well for the monarch whom Bolingbroke deposes, namely Richard II. It also afflicts Bolingbroke's son, Henry Plantagenet in *Henry V*, as he wanders among his troops the night before the battle of Agincourt, reflecting on the burdens of kingship. And, of course, it destroys the sleep of Macbeth after he has assassinated Duncan, king of Scotland. Macbeth, who seems to act mainly in darkness, tells us he has murdered sleep and will sleep no more, though he apparently drops off regularly enough to experience "these terrible dreams/That shake us nightly" (III.ii.20–21).

Considering the red-eyed nature of kingship in Shakespeare, it is a wonder that anyone would want the crown at all. And the ending of *Lear*, as Greenblatt observes, is noteworthy for the way, after the old man's death, so many characters repudiate the prospect of the throne—first Albany, who offers the crown to Edgar and Kent, and then Kent, who says he prefers an honorable Roman suicide. Edgar himself remains silent, though, as Greenblatt notes, in the Folio the final lines are assigned to him (to Albany in the Quarto), and concluding lines are usually the possession of those left to assume the reins of government.

For Shakespeare, then, people in political authority assume greatness only when they lose their power, or when they recognize the burdens of their power, or when they set their power aside. Richard II is a strong example of the first condition, Henry V of the second, and of the third, the duke (in *Measure for Measure*), Lear, and Prospero. Let us look at each of them in turn.

Richard II is the deposed king whom Henry V identifies as the fault his father made "in compassing the crown" (IV.i.276). His illegitimate removal causes Bolingbroke to lose a lot of sleep after he becomes Henry IV. It is ironic, considering that Bolingbroke will eventually unseat the king, that when we first meet him, he is claiming to defend his cousin Richard against a treasonous plot contrived by Norfolk to overthrow him.

The theatrical Richard, having failed to make them friends, allows Bolingbroke and Norfolk to meet in combat, only to interrupt the event before it has even begun—his first piece of stagecraft! No doubt smarting over the refusal of both combatants to accept his amnesty ("We were not born to sue, but to command" [I.i.196]), the king banishes Bolingbroke for six years and Norfolk for life. It is the beginning of his downfall. The dying Gaunt, visited by Richard, sees "a thousand flatterers sit within thy crown" (II.i.100), the certain sign of a deteriorating regime. Another sign is Richard's unjust expropriation of Gaunt's lands following his death. But Bushy, Bagot, and Green, those "caterpillars of the commonwealth" (II.iii.165), are part of a much wider general decline than that suggested by courtly flatteries or illegal seizures. There is even a hint that Richard (following Marlowe's Edward II) may have been having homosexual relations with these courtiers. After their capture, Bolingbroke charges them with misleading the prince in a very specific way:

> You have, in manner, with your sinful hours
> Made a divorce betwixt his queen and him,
> Broke the possession of a royal bed. (III.i.11–13)

This is innuendo rather than statement, hardly as flagrant as the open relationship between Edward and Gaveston in Marlowe's work. But the play is obviously written in imitation of *Edward II*, where a sovereign's love for another man is unequivocally erotic. As a result, at least one recent production of *Richard II* (Robert Woodruff's at the American Repertory Theatre) portrayed the king, played by Thomas Derrah, as a modern drag queen, first seen in a dressing room strewn with wigs and cosmetics.

Almost from the moment Richard believes his cause is lost, he begins to evolve into a much more delicate and poetic character than the coarse tyrant who insulted Gaunt and stole his lands. Representing himself as a poet of the ephemeral, he sometimes sounds like a philosopher of the eternal: "Not all the water in the rough rude sea," he proclaims in a time-worn line, "Can wash the balm from an anointed king" (III.ii.50–51).

On the other hand, Richard seems to find more interest in the histrionic potential of his various roles—as victim, as prisoner, and finally as deposed monarch—than in the reality of his condition. He must continually remind himself of who and where he is. And in his famous speech about the death of kings, he shows an awareness well beyond his age or experience of the transience of life and the impermanence of station.

At Flint Castle, Richard tells Bolingbroke he does "profane, steal, or usurp" (III.iii.80), and accuses him of treason. But almost immediately he agrees to submit, to be deposed, and lose the name of king. In a touching monologue, resembling Henry V's hankering for the simple life before the Battle of Agincourt ("What infinite heartsease / Must kings neglect that private men enjoy?" [IV.i.219–20]), Richard envies the idealized state of the poor anchorite ("I'll give my jewels for a set of beads, / My gorgeous palace for a hermitage" [III.iii.146–47]). And then, having repudiated the base court and all its trappings, he begins the process of translating his surrender into classical myth: "Down, down I come like glist'ring Phaethon, / Wanting the manage of unruly jades" (177–78). (A relative of Icarus, Phaeton was the son of Helios, the sun god, who drowned trying to manage his father's chariot.)

Having discharged his histrionic function, Richard nevertheless hesitates to resign his throne to Bolingbroke until he is allowed to transform his crown and scepter into theatrical props, handing them over to the new king with ostentatious ritualism. The climactic looking-glass scene, where Richard, peering into a mirror, becomes a self-conscious actor, recalling his own former powers—

> Was this face the face
> That every day under his household roof
> Did keep ten thousand men! (IV.i.271–73)

—contains echoes of Marlowe's Faustus eulogizing Helen of Troy ("Was this the face that launched a thousand ships?" [V.i]). But Richard is talking about his own face here, not that of some beauteous vision conjured up for the occasion. It is this self-absorbed quality that makes York compare the deposed monarch to "a well-graced actor" (V.ii.24) leaving the stage, rejected by his audience, patiently composed even when they throw rubbish on his head.

Before he is murdered, the imprisoned Richard will metamorphose not just into a performer reflecting on his roles ("Thus play I in one person many people" [V.v.31]) but also into a poet and a penitent, reflecting on his sins. In all of these guises, Richard seems to be expressing Shakespeare's views about power and powerlessness—how only when human beings withdraw from politics can they achieve kinship with God. Richard, nonetheless, is allowed one last moment of participation in life. He strikes down two of his assassins before being murdered himself. Bolingbroke, now King Henry IV, reminding us of how Henry II recoiled from the murder he ordered of Thomas Becket, refuses to reward the men he paid to kill Richard. It is a symptom of the chaos that will follow this unlawful deposition. The play ends with Henry promising to travel to the Holy Land, where he will wash the blood from his guilty hands.

He never makes that journey. He is too preoccupied, in the two parts of *Henry IV,* with trying to stem the unrest resulting from his seizure of the throne. The wild behavior of his son, Hal, he interprets as God's revenge on him for his sins. And when this intemperate youth, at his father's sickbed, prematurely puts on his crown, Bolingbroke doubtless remembers how he stole the crown from Richard. The prince's misconduct hardly bodes well for good government. Still, when Hal, rejecting his tavern friends and youthful follies, transforms into King Henry V at the conclusion of *2 Henry IV*, he seems to undergo a radical change of character as well, only partially prepared for by this premonitory pledge to break with his old companions:

> I know you all, and will a while uphold
> The unyoked humour of your idleness. . . .
> My reformation, glit'ring o'er my fault,
> Shall show more goodly and attract more eyes
> Than that which hath no foil to set it off.
> (*1 Henry IV*, I.ii.173–93)

No longer Falstaff's partner in downing sack and cutting purses, Hal turns, after his father's death, into a stiff-necked, straitlaced moralist whose first royal action is to banish his best friend from his sight on pain of death.

Falstaff's response ("Master Shallow, I owe you a thousand pound" [*2 Henry IV*, V.v.70]) is a shrug to hide a heartbreak, one of the saddest lines in literature, and a lot more deeply felt than Henry's Puritan posturing. Hal is equally indifferent to the fate of his other cohorts at the Boar's Head Tavern, not only allowing the rejected Falstaff to die ("the King has killed his heart" [*Henry V*, II.i.79]) without a hint of sympathy, but letting Bardolph be hanged without a thought of intercession. Furthermore, his order to kill all the French prisoners after the raid on the "poys and the luggage" (IV.vii.1) seems particularly heartless in the context of the scene, hardly the noble action of the "star of England" he is called in the Epilogue.

But Henry is involved now with greater challenges than friendship or forgiveness, the forging of an iconic legend of sin and redemption: "I'll so offend to make offence a skill, / Redeeming time when men think least I will" (*1 Henry IV*, I.iii.194–95). This is a highly convoluted way to dramatize his conversion to virtue. Heroic as he is, Henry has more than a few drops of his ancestor Richard III's Machiavellian blood in his veins. He is not quite as ruthless as his brother Lancaster, but he is perfectly capable of concealing his true intentions. And he is not above contracting a marriage with a princess he has barely met in order to consolidate his hold on her country. Henry has been played either as a perfect ruler both in peace and war (Laurence Olivier), or as man who grows increasingly brutalized by the horrors of the battlefield (Kenneth Branagh). He is probably a bit of both, though Shakespeare would often have us believe he represents the ideal ruler.

He is never more kingly than when reflecting on the burdens of kingship, as in his great fourth-act speech on the eve of the battle of Agincourt. Following a harsh exchange with the common soldier Williams, Henry delivers his famous soliloquy on royal responsibility, and on a king's possession of nothing that commoners do not enjoy except for "ceremony" (a synonym for "poisoned flattery" [*Henry IV*, IV.i.233]). All of his advantages, "the balm, the sceptre, and the ball" (242), are mere vanity. He cannot heal the sickness of his subjects or himself, or even enjoy the restful slumber of the typical laboring man who "all night / Sleeps in Elysium" (255–56).

Much as Henry disdains kingship, he never thinks of abdicating. Let us look at three Shakespeare royals who do.

The first is Duke Vincentio in *Measure for Measure*. For reasons that will later become more clear, the duke (whose opening words refer to "government") has decided to temporarily abandon his seat and install his deputy Angelo in his place with "absolute power" (I.iii.13). Such a decision is fraught with danger, as Shakespeare will demonstrate a year later when he writes *King Lear*. But for the moment, Angelo—"a man of stricture and firm abstinence" (12)—looks like a likely candidate for office. The old lord Escalus has testified to his upright character, and the duke has no reason to doubt his virtue. Angelo himself insists that he be tested further before he assumes such powers, but the duke will not consider it. "In our remove," he tells him, "be thou at full ourself" (43).

Why does the duke make such a fateful decision? He is leaving in great haste, ostensibly for Poland, as Lucio thinks, to conclude a pact with the king of Hungary (this may be a later interpolation by Thomas Middleton). He has installed a Puritan in his place. In the first act of his new regime, Angelo orders all the whorehouses in the Viennese suburbs to be razed to the ground. And in his second move against the lusts of the flesh, he has Claudio imprisoned for getting Juliet pregnant before marriage. (Since Shakespeare's prenuptial relations with Anne Hathaway led to the same result, it is not hard to guess his opinion of Angelo's excessive justice.)

Clearly, this cleaning out of the Augean stables is precisely what the duke has desired. He has been a liberal and permissive ruler, unwilling, for fourteen years, to enforce the strict laws of his duchy. As a result, his statutes have been mocked and his laws ignored, and "Liberty plucks Justice by the nose" (I.iii.29). Having governed as a blue-state ruler, in other words, he now wants to enforce some red-state laws. Angelo would seem to be the perfect surrogate for the task.

He is also curious, as a student of human nature, about how Angelo's new power might change his character, and of course it will. In one sense, then, *Measure for Measure* is a play about hypocrisy, revealing that at the base of every severe morality is a sensual itch that mocks it. *Measure for Measure* is Shakespeare's *Tartuffe*. Like Molière's later comedy, it is a fierce critique of Puritanism as embodied in an easily aroused hypocrite. True, Shakespeare's character, unlike Molière's, does not begin as a lecher. Lord Angelo, according to the duke,

scarce confesses
That his blood flows, or that his appetite
Is more to bread than stone. (I.iii.51–53)

Is this constraint a form of dissimulation or the essence of the man? That is the question to be resolved by the duke's temporary abdication of power.

It is also not surprising that in this absolutely corrupt Vienna—populated with bawds and whores and sensualists, not to mention the likes of Lucio, Mistress Overdone, and Pompey—Isabella, the heroine, should be a lustrous light of virtue. She is not at all shocked that her brother has gotten Juliet with child, and suggests an obvious solution ("O, let him marry her!" I.iv.48). What shocks her to the very roots is Angelo's proposal that the only way to save her brother from the gallows is to yield to him her chastity.

Angelo, a man "whose blood / Is very snow-broth," who "never feels / The wanton stings and motions of the sense" (56–58), is represented as a man of unimpeachable virtue. He concedes the power of temptation, but "'Tis one thing to be tempted . . . Another thing to fall" (II.i.17–18). In language that sounds like a rehearsal for Lear on the heath, he also recognizes that members of a jury passing judgment on a thief may be guiltier than the accused. But he is as strictly wedded to the law as Inspector Javert, his lineal descendant in Hugo's *Les Misérables*.

Isabella, seeking her brother's pardon, wants Angelo to treat sexual indiscretions as the duke did in the past, and forgive them. But Angelo refuses to "Condemn the fault, and not the actor of it" (II.ii.37). Isabella, borrowing from Portia in *The Merchant of Venice*, speaks of "mercy" as the greatest form of ceremony, and begs for pity. "I show it most of all when I show justice", Angelo responds (102). It is an early confrontation between right-wing rectitude and left-wing compassion, between strict constructionism and progressive permissiveness, a conflict that will stir the courts for centuries to come. Finally, Isabella wins her suit—not through her arguments but through her beauty. The Puritan in Angelo is overcome by the satyr.

His prayers, like those of Claudius, fly up while his thoughts remain below—"heaven hath my empty words" (II.iv.2). When he reveals to Isabella "his pernicious purpose," she shows herself to be as morally extreme as he is: "More than our brother is our chastity" (150, 185). With extremists operating on both sides of this political spectrum, who occupies the moderate position? Well, Claudio for one. In a weak moment, he begs his sister to commit a sin in order to save a brother's life, only to invoke Isabella's wrath in an outburst of unusual savagery ("Die, perish! . . ./I'll pray a thousand prayers for thy death" [III.i.145–47]). And then there is the duke himself, though speaking in disguise as Claudio's ghostly confessor, who draws a picture of existence ("What's in this/That bears the name of life?" [38–39]) that makes dying appear to be the more appealing alternative.

But this is no tragedy, and the duke, functioning as a ghostly stage manager, is present to ensure a happy ending through one of Shakespeare's favorite theatrical devices, a sexual substitute. A former fiancée of Angelo's, whom he abandoned when she lost her dowry, Mariana of the moated grange will take Isabella's place in darkness. For all intents and purposes, the play is over at the beginning of act III, when the duke discovers the hypocrisy of his deputy and the vices in his state. His debate with Lucio regarding "lenity to lechery," and whether premarital sex can ever be legislated out of existence (Duke: "It is too general a vice, and severity must cure it"; Lucio: "It is impossible to extirp it quite, friar, till eating and drinking be put down" III.i.344, 348–49), advances Shakespeare's central thematic conflict in its most specific form.

Commentators have faulted the duke for failing to correct

his errors sooner, but if he had, like Hamlet seeking earlier revenge, there would have been no play. From the duke's point
of view, everything that happens contributes to his education
in the subjects of justice and the law, and makes him a better
ruler. Having confounded Angelo with a bed trick (Mariana
losing her maidenhead instead of Isabella), he now confounds
him further with a head trick (Ragozine being decapitated instead of Claudio). When the duke finally reappears in his own
character, he dissimulates as well as any Machiavellian in praising Angelo's stewardship in his absence, and in defending him
against Isabella's charges. In the brilliant denouement, Mariana
appears to accuse Angelo of the selfsame premarital crime that
would have sent Claudio to the gallows. The duke makes him
marry her, then forces Lucio to marry the whore he once impregnated, thus fulfilling his pledge to provide "measure still
for measure" (V.i.403). He pardons Angelo and Barnardine,
and offers his hand to Isabella, who is understandably silent at
this unexpected turn of events. What new thing has he learned
from this elaborate journey into subterfuge? To temper justice
with mercy? That he knew before. No, he has learned the opposite—to temper his merciful nature with a just application of
the law.

In *King Lear,* the play Shakespeare wrote a year later, he
creates another ruler who becomes wiser only after he loosens
his hold on his crown. But the wisdom Lear gains is hardly as
rational or judicial. Actually, the politics of this pre-Christian
play are quite unusual for Shakespeare, and the lessons are altogether different. The duke in *Measure for Measure* steps aside;
the king in *King Lear* steps down. The Viennese duke can re-
gain his power; the king of Britain has abdicated his. Or is this
true? Some scholars have been debating recently whether Lear
has actually abdicated his throne at all. He divides his physical
kingdom, to be sure, in order to divest himself of "interest of

territory, cares of state," and thus "unburthened crawl toward death" (I.i.48, 39). But he also insists on retaining the name and all the ceremony of a king (symbolized by his hundred knights).

This is a highly contradictory demand, and fairly characteristic of a man who has grown old before he has grown wise. Yet Harry V. Jaffa, for example (in his essay "The Limits of Politics" in *Shakespeare's Politics*), makes the argument that Lear is Shakespeare's "greatest" king, and not just in the magnitude of his soul but rather in the quality of his kingship. After all, he chooses to divide his kingdom at a time of peace and stability unknown in Shakespeare's history plays, when England's traditional enemies (France and Burgundy) are suing for his daughter's hand rather than defending their territories against invasion. (Jaffa also observes that only a very wise, sagacious ruler would have kept such blunt plain-speaking counselors by his side as Kent and Cordelia.)

But this is to argue outside the box of the play. The fact is that the life of Lear, like that of all of Shakespeare characters, begins with his first appearance. He has no dramatic existence apart from what he shows us in the present action and no historical reality apart from what he tells us about his past (just as Lady Macbeth, as L. C. Knights once reminded us in a famous essay, has no living children if they are not mentioned in the play).[7]

No, Lear is not a great king at the beginning of the play. Indeed, the political trajectory of the action follows Lear's growth in wisdom from a self-protected absolutist into a sympathetic and compassionate human being. But he develops these qualities only after he has surrendered the power to make amends. He is a rash and self-regarding monarch, a prey to the sycophancy he insists on, and totally unable to distinguish loyal friends from flatterers. Like Oedipus, Gloucester is able to *see* only after he goes blind ("I stumbled when I saw" [IV.i.20]). In the same way, Lear, like the duke in *Measure for Measure,* can make discriminating judgments about his subjects only after he has become one of them himself.

And only when his wits have turned. Lear's lucid madness provides this play with its most extraordinary insights. Until this point, he continues to quantify and evaluate love as a statistic, just as he does the number of his knights. Although he has blistered Goneril with the most harrowing curse in literature, the curse of sterility, he is still willing to live with her because she will accept more of his followers than Regan ("Thy fifty yet doth double five and twenty, / And thou art twice her love" [II.iv.253–54]). He has learned nothing yet from his encounter with Cordelia. And when Regan asks him, "What need one?" his justifying answer is that nothing in nature is truly essential: "O, reason not the need! Our basest beggars / Are in the poorest things superfluous" (258–60).

But Lear, after being battered on the heath, will go on to recognize that even the basest beggars have less than their basic needs, that the true human condition is that of a poor, bare, forked animal. Instead of turning inward and dissolving in self-pity, he begins to empathize with the suffering of others—beginning with the Fool ("How dost my boy? Art cold? / I am cold myself" [III.ii.66–67]), and continuing with Poor Tom. And he begins to recognize that everything we consider ours by divine right—our clothes, our speech, even our five wits—is ours only by sufferance, merely another form of borrowing.

As for his growing apprehension that injustice is universal, this is probably the most radical idea one finds in all of Shakespeare. In the "mad" Edgar, Lear has discovered a true Theban philosopher, thus underlining Shakespeare's unsettling insight in this play that the mad are more visionary than the sane. The injustice being practiced by Cornwall and Regan is vivid enough in the way Gloucester is condemned without judge or jury, and sentenced on the spot to have his eyes plucked from his head.

Lear's justice is infinitely more merciful now, reminding us of the duke in *Measure for Measure* before he commissioned Angelo to put some spine in the law.

> I pardon that man's life. What was thy cause?
> Adultery?
> Thou shalt not die. Die for adultery? (IV.vi.107–9)

Lear would have pardoned Claudio for impregnating Juliet, because he now recognizes that fornication is a basic function of nature:

> No.
> The wren goes to't, and the small gilded fly
> Does lecher in my sight. (109–11)

Lear not only expresses a very dark view of female virtue — "Down from the waist they are Centaurs, / Though women all above" (121–22). He also extends this morbid opinion to every animal, every insect, every living creature.

Lear will soon see corruption everywhere, not just in the heart of humans but also in the very palace of justice. A beadle beating a whore longs for her himself, the usurer hangs the moneylender. Meanwhile, ceremonial costumes ("Robes and furred gowns" [159]) are layers of deception, concealing the fact that the entire human race is equally lascivious and universally corrupt:

> Plate sin with gold,
> And the strong lance of justice hurtless breaks;
> Arm it in rags, a pygmy's straw does pierce it.
>   (159–61)

His pity directed toward the "poor naked wretches" with whom he has shared the fury of the elements, Lear begins to regret his former indifference to the suffering of his subjects:

> O, I have ta'en
> Too little care of this. Take physic, pomp,
> Expose thyself to feel what wretches feel,
> That thou mayst shake the superflux to them
> And show the heavens more just. (III.iv.29, 33–37)

The only antidote to universal injustice, then, is a more equitable distribution of wealth—a solution, ironically, not so different from Jack Cade's primitive communism—showing generosity to the needy, shaking the "superflux" to the "poor, bare, forked animal" (99–100). Thus, although Lear hardly begins as the wisest king in Shakespeare, he most certainly ends that way. The greatness of this play is that only after its hero looks into the vast abyss of madness does he become truly, luminously sane.

My final example of Shakespeare's ambiguous attitude toward regime change is Prospero in *The Tempest.* The play is perhaps Shakespeare's culminating exploration of the vanity of power, and the futility, impotence, and ultimate exhaustion of the powerful. (It also contains another splendid example of Shakespeare's capacity for creating storm scenes—and a typical illustration of the way the sea can separate families.)[8] Prospero, like so many Shakespearean royals, has been the victim of a usurpation. In a striking parallel with the way Claudius treats his brother King Hamlet, Prospero's brother Antonio has stolen his dukedom through treachery and deceit. A major difference (*The Tempest,* after all, is a comedy) is that Prospero is not poisoned, but rather put to sea in a bark. Another is that he has not been cuckolded by his brother. Still another is that this Ghost survives to tell the story. In a speech that almost puts

Miranda to sleep, Prospero informs his daughter of her perfidious "false uncle," who, having won the friendship of the king of Naples, and after purchasing the loyalty of Prospero's courtiers while the true duke was engaged in his studies, has managed to become "absolute Milan" (I.ii.77, 109).

Note that even in the telling of a story where there are no imputations of adultery regarding Prospero's wife, traces of Shakespeare's misogyny still echo. "Sir, are not you my father?" Miranda asks upon learning that Prospero is duke of Milan, to which he replies: "Thy mother was a piece of virtue and/She said thou wast my daughter" (55–57). The remark is a jest, but not entirely free of skepticism. Soon after, Miranda hints that her uncle's behavior may reflect upon his mother's virtue:

> I should sin
> To think but nobly of my grandmother:
> Good wombs have borne bad sons. (117–19)

But Antonio's usurpation is much less criminal in nature than that of Claudius, and Prospero's exile is more like the banishment of Duke Senior in *As You Like It* than like the murder of King Hamlet. The political events have resulted not in the death of a ruler but in his education regarding the true purpose of life, rather like Lear. Duke Senior discovers the blessings of nature, finding sermons in stones and good in everything. (He also learns, like Jaques, that every man is an actor on the seven stages of life.) Prospero, already a scholar in magical arts, goes well beyond Jaques' conviction that "all the world's a stage" (II.vii.138) to conclude that all of life is a dream (IV.i), anticipating Segismundo's titular epiphany in Calderón's *La vida es sueño*. Prospero also anticipates Segismundo's discovery that the only way to validate this dream is through a virtuous life.

In disposition, however, Prospero is quite different from

Duke Senior. For one thing, unlike that mild-mannered philosopher, he is something of a crank. Given Caliban's erotic designs on Miranda, one can understand why Prospero would become so furious with such a "bestial thing," though the way this Italian colonialist stole his island from the its natives is not that different from the way Antonio swiped his brother's kingdom. But how do we explain his often testy attitude ("Thou liest, malignant thing" [I.ii.258]) toward Ariel, whom he loves, or his punitive "crabbed" treatment of Ferdinand, who is courting his daughter? Admittedly, Prospero's bad temper is partly feigned. But either he is meant to be something of a tyrant, or he may be reflecting some of Shakespeare's cranky paternalism in his own advancing age. "My father's of a better nature, sir, / Than he appears by speech" (500–501), says Miranda, and it is probable that Prospero's severity is meant to enhance, as in a fairy tale, his warm embrace of the couple at the end. But his often "ungentle" behavior clearly marks a new kind of hero in the Shakespearean gallery of characters. Even at the end, in the act of blessing the union of Ferdinand and Miranda, he is warning Ferdinand not to "break her virgin-knot" (IV.i.15) before the ceremonies are completed—a stricture Shakespeare hardly bothered to observe himself.

As for the politics of the play, while there is much ado about the inhumanity of man to man, and the evils of usurpation, the issue of succession, about whom will eventually govern Prospero's usurped dukedom, seems to lose its urgency as the play proceeds. Indeed, the musings on governance by Gonzalo, a kindly if longwinded old courtier who sometimes seems to have spent some time in the company of Polonius, remind us of Lear's late conclusions on the need for more equality of wealth. Together, these speeches hint at a growing skepticism on the part of Shakespeare toward authority and rule:

I' the commonwealth I would by contraries
Execute all things; for no kind of traffic
Would I admit; no name of magistrate;
Letters should not be known; riches, poverty,
And use of service, none; contract, succession,
Bourn, bound of land, tilth, vineyard, none;
No use of metal, corn, or wine, or oil;
No occupation; all men idle, all;
And women too, but innocent and pure;
No sovereignty. . . .
All things in common nature should produce
Without sweat or endeavour: treason, felony,
Sword, pike, knife, gun, or need of any engine,
Would I not have; but nature should bring forth,
Of its own kind, all foison, all abundance,
To feed my innocent people. (II.i.147–64)

No judges, no sovereignty, no police, no labor, no law—the scheme reminds one of the nineteenth-century anarchist Alexander Bukunin's revolutionary utopianism.[9] This is, of course, a model for ideal government, an image of the Golden Age, a gloss on Plato's Republic, hardly to be taken as a serious political proposition. One even wonders whether Shakespeare was serious about it. For one thing, it would spell the end of drama, humans having achieved that ethical perfection toward which Plato always aspired, and Aristotle always rejected as being untrue to life or art. But given the fact that, almost immediately after Gonzalo's peroration, Sebastian and Antonio begin plotting the deaths of Alonso and Gonzalo, there is no convincing sign that perfect people will soon be ruling the commonwealth.

The monster Caliban is likewise involved in a conspiracy to overthrow a master—namely, Prospero—this time in collusion with Trinculo and Stephano. The "celestial liquor" of these two clowns has totally won his worship and obedience: "I'll kiss thy foot; I'll swear myself thy subject" (II.ii.109, 144). "Has a new master: get a new man," chants the drunken "Cacaliban" (175–76). Ferdinand, meanwhile, has sworn allegiance to the "peerless" Miranda in a convention of courtly love that accepts the woman's dominance and sway:

> The very instant that I saw you, did
> My heart fly to your service; there resides
> To make me slave to it; and for your sake
> Am I this patient log-man. (III.i.64–67)

In this play, even romantic love is structured on the model of hierarchical politics.

But when Prospero is reawakened from the reveries created by his masque to confront the various conspiracies that threaten him, he grows angry and disappointed. Politics for him, as for Lear, is just another form of human vanity. The spirits of the masque are faded into thin air, dissolving as the globe will soon dissolve, and "like this insubstantial pageant faded / Leave not a rack behind" (IV.i.155–56). These, among the most quoted lines in the play, represent a vision of life that makes ambition and aspiration, indeed all human striving, seem to be destined for disillusionment and disappointment—

> We are such stuff
> As dreams are made on, and our little life
> Is rounded with a sleep. (156–58)

Richard II compared the world to a prison—and so did Hamlet thinking on suicide—the Viennese duke likens it to an after-dinner sleep. They are Prospero's seconds in his dreamlike view of the afterlife.

Under the influence of Ariel, Prospero allows his harsh feelings to soften a bit. And after an eclogue in the elegiac style of Oberon ("Ye elves of hills, brooks, standing lakes and groves" [V.i.33]), he promises to abjure his rough art and potent magic, burying his staff and drowning his book. He liberates Ariel, pardons Caliban, and forgives the brother who usurped his crown. He will "retire" to Milan, but will he rule there? His very tired epitaph, in which "every third thought shall be my grave" (314), suggests not. Prospero, perhaps reflecting Shakespeare's fatigue, has lost interest in politics, grown tired of conspiracies, and with stoic fortitude is preparing himself for death. He is the last of Shakespeare's elite leaders, defective like all those mortal rulers, yet still capable of transforming acts.

5

Racialism

THE MOOR AND THE JEW

But thy vile race,
Though thou didst learn, had that in't which good natures
Could not abide to be with.
— The Tempest, I.ii.361–63

Shakespeare's prejudice toward minorities, as one might expect, was less inflamed than that of other writers of the day. But it existed, even though Shakespeare managed to overcome his preconceptions at times through his special qualities of humanity and compassion. An annotated bibliography by Parvin Kujoory and Bruce T. Sajdak lists essentially five minority groups that appear with some regularity in Shakespeare plays: women, blacks, Jews, homosexuals, and slaves. I have already touched on two of these categories (women and homosexuals). In this chapter I concentrate on Shakespeare's treatment of Moors, Jews, and other subjugated people.

Blacks in the drama of this time are usually called "Black Moors" (or blackamoors), a group that originated in North Africa before colonizing much of Spain, and then was brought into England in the fifteenth century by the Vikings. Although most frequently called Moors, they could have been of Negro, Berber, Spanish, or Arab descent, or a mixture of the four. Blacks in England usually worked as servants and laborers, and despite William Harrison's proud boast ("As for slaves and bondmen, we have none"), they might have been indentured property as well. Although Elizabeth was reported to have called slave trading "detestable" and prophesied that it would bring down "the Vengeance of Heaven upon the Undertakers," the queen was probably secretly involved in that lucrative business. We know that she employed a black maidservant and used black musicians. Indeed, it was not unusual for freed or indentured blacks to play instruments at court—John Blanke, for one, a famous black trumpeter for Henry VII and Henry VIII.

The queen tried to expel her black population both in 1599 and 1601, complaining "of late divers blackamores brought into this realme, of which kind of people there are already here too manie." (Here she sounds a bit like Lou Dobbs, inveighing against illegal aliens.) In a proclamation issued in 1601, right before she died, Elizabeth tried to scapegoat black people for the poverty and vagrancy of her realm, saying that "most of them are infidels having no understanding of Christ or his Gospels." (Pope Paul IV had earlier made a similar assault on minorities, "that breed of Moors and Jews, those dregs of earth.") The attempt at expatriation was not successful—England's Moors could be neither dislodged nor deported. But since, like Jews, they were circumcised foreigners, they were usually considered a source of darkness and villainy.

The first appearance of a black character in Shakespeare's plays—and he is the darkest of villains—is Aaron the Moor in *Titus Andronicus.* Marlowe had already created a similar character—Ithamore in *The Jew of Malta* (1590)—and Shakespeare in this early stage of his career is not much inclined to deviate from models he admires. Despite the resonance in his name, and the fact that he is sometimes identified as a blackamoor ("This Moor is comeliest, is he not," one of Marlowe's characters says [II.iii]), Ithamore is, in a later version, also identified as "A Turkish slave" (when Barabas offers to buy him, Ithamore claims that he was born in "Trace" and "brought up in Arabia"). But aside from the assonance in his name, Ithamore (Ithimer in some versions), there are signs that he is a man of Moorish descent who accepts his subjugated status.[1] Elizabethans did not make very subtle distinctions among people of color.

Or sometimes even among foreigners. In the wonderfully written scene in which Barabas and Ithamore compete in infamy, Barabas embraces him as a fellow spirit: "we are villaines both:/Both circumcized, we hate Christians both" (II.iii). Ithamore is the essence of hyperbolic evil. He sets Christian villages on fire, cripples pilgrims, cuts the throats of travelers, and performs similar diabolical improvisations that delight Barabas. Like most black men, Ithamore is also assumed to have singularly voracious sexual appetites, and any number of women in the play are eager to go to bed with him. Furthermore, he possesses a gift of gab, echoing lines from Marlowe's "The Passionate Shepherd to his Love" ("Thou in those Groves, by Dis above,/Shall live with me and be my love" [IV.iv]). Embracing the Courtesan, he sounds a little like Faustus kissing Helen: "That kisse againe; she runs division of my lips" (IV.ii).[2] Ithamore helps Barabas poison all the nuns, including his own daughter, Abigail. Inevitably, he will get too big for his breeches, and Barabas will poison him, too.

In Shakespeare's *Titus Andronicus,* Aaron the Moor bears a number of Ithamore's qualities. He swears the same allegiance to his mistress, Queen Tamora, as does Ithamore to Barabas, and is as wanton with her as Marlowe's Moor is with his Courtesan. Aaron has the vocabulary of a seasoned Machiavellian, speaking of "policy" and "stratagems," and the like. He conceives the plan that will allow Tamora's sons, Demetrius and Chiron, to satisfy their lust with Titus's daughter, Lavinia. He is totally dedicated to "blood and revenge" and argues that even his appearance, his "deadly-standing eye" and "fleece of woolly hair" (II.iii.32–34), is symbolic of his evil intentions.

Not only does Aaron plan the rape and mutilation of Lavinia, he conceives the ghastly notion that Titus should cut off his hand in return for the safety of his (already murdered) sons. Aaron grows fat from villainy. It is his nourishment and his destiny: "Let fools do good, and fair men call for grace: / Aaron will have his soul black like his face" (III.i.203–4). Tamora conceives a son by him—"a joyless, dismal, black, and sorrowful issue" (IV.ii.66), as the Nurse describes the child. And in the only moment of decency Shakespeare allows him, Aaron protects his baby against all efforts to kill it, using huffe-snuffe Marlovian apostrophes to announce his defiance:

> Not Enceladus
> With all his threat'ning band of Typhon's brood,
> Nor great Alcides, nor the god of war
> Shall seize this prey out of his father's hands.
> (92–95)

Aaron's capacity for filial love ("Look how the black slave smiles upon the father" [119]) gives him a fleeting moment of humanity, though he is soon back in character, stabbing the Nurse to ensure her silence.

In order to save the child, Aaron confesses all of Tamora's villainy, and his own, to Lucius. Asked whether he is sorry he has done these heinous things, he answers, "Ay, that I had not done a thousand more" (V.i.124). Heroic only in treachery, he curses each day he failed to do an evil deed. And in an obvious effort to compete with Marlowe's Ithamore in inventive villainy, he boasts, "Oft have I digged up dead men from their graves / And set them upright at their dear friends' door" (135–36). He longs to be a devil, willing even to burn in everlasting fire if he could torment his enemies "with my bitter tongue" (150). After Titus serves Tamora the bloody banquet—her two sons baked in a pie—and the play approaches its conclusion through an orgy of murder, Aaron is sentenced to be buried "breast-deep" in the earth and starved to death. He remains exultant, unashamed in his dedication to evil: "If one good deed in all my life I did / I do repent it from my very soul" (V.iii.188–89). Actually, the one good deed he will not repent is conceiving his baby boy, who somehow manages to survive the general slaughter at the end.

Shakespeare was never again to create such a diabolical black man. *Titus* was written around the same year that Marlowe died (1593), but three years later, when Shakespeare was composing *The Merchant of Venice,* he had already kicked his Marlovian dependency. Like *The Jew of Malta, The Merchant of Venice* features a Jew and a black man. Both Barabas and Shylock are stage Jews in conflict with Christians. Even the two titles share some resonance. But what a world of difference there is between Shakespeare's Shylock and Marlowe's Barabas. As for Shakespeare's black man, the Prince of Morocco, he is of an infinitely nobler class, both by birth and by temperament, than either Ithamore or Aaron.

Shakespeare's black Prince is probably intended to be a Moor as well, a race that some believe originated in the Numidian kingdom of Maure in what is now Morocco, though Elizabethans doubtfully understood such distinctions. He is, of course, one of Portia's many suitors, none of whom she much cares for. Still, she reveals a sneaking admiration for this Moroccan. The Prince begins by asking her not to judge him by the color of his skin ("Mislike me not for my complexion, / The shadowed livery of the burnished sun" II.i.1–2). His blood, he says, is redder than that of her paler suitors, and hotter, too, as he hints in describing how many Moroccan virgins have been attracted to him.

Portia concedes that he is just as "fair" as any of his rivals, while cautioning that the choice of husband will not be hers. The Prince, of course, selects the wrong casket and dooms himself to a life of bachelorhood, if not of celibacy. Portia thereupon bids him "a gentle riddance," with a parting racist shot—"Let all of his complexion choose me so" (II.vii.79)—a remark that inspires little confidence in Portia's racial tolerance. Or Shakespeare's.

A minor character in this play, the Prince of Morocco is an early sketch for a major character Shakespeare would create eight years later in 1604—namely, Othello, the Moor of Venice. Othello is not a prince, but he is clearly of noble birth, and his exploits on the battlefield have given him high status in the Venetian state. This makes him the object of considerable envy and prejudice, particularly from Iago. Iago hates the Moor because he is what Roderigo calls a "thick-lips" (I.i.66). But his mind is inflamed not only by racism, and by the fact that a black should be his superior, but by a sense of sexual inferiority as well. Having suffered from a licentious canard regarding his wife, he knows the power of salacious rumors planted in people's heads. To Brabanzio, he shouts, "Even now, now, very now, an old black ram / Is tupping your white ewe" (88–89), adding to the barnyard metaphor the image of "a Barbary horse" mounting Desdemona, and finally materializing a creature out of erotic mythology, "Your daughter and the Moor are now making the beast with two backs" (117–18).

The animal references are relentless and chilling. Iago believes that black people are the children of Lucifer, which is why he urges Brabanzio to act quickly lest "the Devil . . . make a grandsire of you" (91). But Brabanzio is equally prejudiced. Although he has much admired Othello's exploits on the battlefield, he does not want him in his bedrooms. He cannot believe his daughter would willingly give up the "wealthy curlèd darlings of our nation" for one with such a "sooty bosom" (I.ii.69, 71), "to fall in love with what she feared to look on!" (I.iii.98) Rather than believe that, he suspects that she had been drugged. Othello believes Desdemona's love for him to be a result of the way she reacted to his exploits with cannibal anthropophagi "and men whose heads / Do grow beneath their shoulders" (143–44). These adventures seem farfetched to skeptical ears, leading Iago (and later Bernard Shaw) to conclude that Othello is an epic liar. Nevertheless, Shakespeare obviously intended these adventures as authentic evidence of Othello's heroism and intrepidity. Desdemona, after expressing much more respect for her father than did any of his daughters for Lear, declares the Moor her lord. And having received Brabanzio's unwilling consent, Othello is commissioned as the Venetian general in the coming battle with the Turks.

Unlike Shakespeare's other black characters, and despite Iago's insinuations about his animal nature, Othello is not a fully functioning sexual being. He is attracted more to Desdemona's mind and soul than to her body ("She loved me for the dangers I had passed, / And I loved her that she did pity them" [166–67]). He has reached an age — "the young affects in me defunct" (262–63) — when he no longer needs much in the way of physical satisfaction. There is even some question whether he ever finds the time on his wedding night to consummate the marriage, so busy and compressed are the events of the play. As a result, Iago is convinced, at least in his conversations with Roderigo, that Desdemona will soon be lusting after younger men, and that Othello himself will look for change in his appetites.

He is, of course, wrong about both. Desdemona is totally devoted to her husband, and Othello cannot remember a time when he did not adore Desdemona, or imagine a time when he will not — "and when I love thee not, / Chaos is come again" (III.iii.92–93). Chaos does come again, however, after Iago manages to turn Othello's better qualities against him. He attributes to Desdemona the defective character he possesses himself, particularly his aptitude for "seeming." He claims that Venetian women do "pranks" that "they dare not show their husbands" (207). He expresses wonder that she has turned down matches "of her own clime, complexion, and degree" (235).

In his growing jealousy, Othello quickly picks up first on the race issue, and then on the class issue, and then on the age issue:

> Haply for I am black
> And have not those soft parts of conversation
> That chamberers have; or for I am declined
> Into the vale of years . . . (267–70)

He imagines "the forkèd plague" (280) to be the lot of man the moment he is born. He believes that Desdemona's name, though once

> as fresh
> As Dian's visage . . . is now begrimed and black
> As mine own face. (391–93)

Iago thereupon plants in Othello's brain the picture of Cassio and Desdemona as animals in heat—"Were they as prime as goats, as hot as monkeys, / As salt as wolves in pride" (408–9)—describing their imagined attraction to each other in his most indelible images. These are images that will haunt Othello throughout the play, becoming for him the very embodiments of stampeding lust.

Convinced of Desdemona's infidelity, Othello is ready to "tear her all to pieces." Shakespeare will now demonstrate what happens when the veneer of civilization is stripped away to expose the erupting seething morass below. It is significant that Othello calls vengeance black ("Arise, black vengeance, from they hollow hell!" [451]), though the devil he refers to (Desdemona) is now considered "fair." His language becomes bloated with words like *blood, revenge, violence,* and *tyrannous hate.* It is no accident that at this point Othello begins to speak of his origins, revealing that his mother was a "charmer," with the capacity to weave "magic" into the "web" of a handkerchief. He is being pulled back into the world from which he came, a world of sorcery and voodoo.

Othello's epileptic fit in act IV—his second in two days according to Iago—is no doubt caused by his suspicions about Desdemona. But Shakespeare may also be suggesting that the malady derives from his African heritage—if the epilepsy is not allowed to run its course, he will foam at the mouth and break out into "savage madness" (IV.i.52). When Iago brings on Cassio and Bianca to help prove Desdemona's faithlessness, audiences are usually expectant that they will prove the opposite. Does not Cassio's intimacy with Bianca confirm that she, not Desdemona, is his mistress? Will not this relationship persuade Othello of Desdemona's innocence? But Iago plays on the Moor's suspicions so artfully, aided by the handkerchief prop, that Bianca and Desdemona become confused in Othello's mind as if they constituted a single wanton mistress. He is ready now to cut off Cassio's nose and throw it to the dogs.

Regarding Desdemona, his heart has turned to stone. And then it melts again. He would "chop her into messes" (IV.i.190), until he remembers the softness of her voice, the gentleness of her condition. "But yet the pity of it, Iago! O Iago, the pity of it" (186-87). But Iago is pitiless, and the murder, and the means of the murder (not poison but strangulation), are left for Iago to choose. Othello's *hysterico passio*, so similar to Lear's, continues to climb. In front of the Venetian visitors, he calls her devil and strikes her. Nobody recognizes this "much changed" man(265) who once was thought a noble Moor.

Indeed, he is much changed. Othello is now convinced that Emilia is a bawd and Desdemona a whore, a "cistern for foul toads / To knot and gender in!" (IV.ii.63-64) Enlisting in

Shakespeare's army of misogynists, he cannot imagine a woman who is not corrupted and befouled. Preparing to kill Desdemona, he entreats her to pray, to confess, to solicit heaven for forgiveness, all Christian safeguards against the murder of her soul. He speaks of her death as a sacrifice, as if it were a familiar Christian ritual, like the Mass. Yet, Othello is continuing his descent into the dark primeval world whence he came. In his fierce exchange with Emilia over Desdemona's death, Emilia calls his wife an angel and "you the blacker devil" (V.ii.140).

When the smoke clears, and Othello finally begins to realize what he has done, he begins to talk of journeys—more accurately, of the end of journeys: "Here is my butt, / And very sea-mark of my utmost sail" (274–75). The voyages to exotic far-off lands, the visits to cannibal anthropophagi, to men whose heads do grow beneath their shoulders, have reached their final port. Now his only butt and sea-mark is in hell, where he is doomed to reside eternally in torment: "Whip me ye devils, / From the possession of this heavenly sight" (284–85). He awaits the conventional Christian inferno of sulfur and liquid fire, and he imagines Iago to be among the cloven-footed devils: "I look down towards his feet, but that's a fable" (292).

In his last speech, Othello replants his alien roots. He identifies himself with the Indian who threw a pearl away "richer than all his tribe" (357). He compares his falling tears to Arabian trees dropping medicinal gum. And he ends his life remembering a day in the Syrian city of Aleppo, "where a malignant and a turbaned Turk / Beat a Venetian and traduced the state," adding, "I took by th' throat the circumcisèd dog / And smote him, thus" (362–65). Although Othello is presumably a Muslim, therefore circumcised himself, he speaks here as a Christian general defending a European state. On the other hand, his final memories are of Africa, and his last action an atavistic evocation of African territories and primal customs.

Othello is a great heart, and a considerable advance beyond the good-natured Prince of Morocco, not to mention the evil-spirited Aaron the Moor. But he inhabits a society permeated with considerable racism, in which the color black is still associated with devils and hell, even in the mind of his admiring creator.

Shakespeare usually employed the same associations in the sonnets. Describing his dark-colored mistress, he harps incessantly on the color black as the opposite of virtue and beauty: "In the old age black was not counted fair" (sonnet 127). When he suspects her of deceiving him, even the blackness of her hair and eyes inspire thoughts of devils and hell: "For I have sworn thee fair, and thought thee bright, / Who are as black as hell, as dark as night" (sonnet 147). In sonnet 144, he compares his dark mistress with the fair youth he loves, imagining her as a devilish temptress:

> The better angel is a man right fair
> The worser spirit a woman color'd ill. . . .
> To win me soon to hell, my female evil
> Tempteth my better angel from my side,
> And would corrupt my saint to be a devil.[3]

In this sonnet, the black entity is the sexual corrupter rather than the sexual victim. Since Shakespeare is speaking here in his character as "Will," it is not implausible to guess that this prejudice against the color black is something he shares with his dramatic characters.

In the figure of Shylock in *The Merchant of Venice*, Shakespeare gives us an example of another despised Elizabethan minority that was probably inspired by a Marlovian creation, namely Barabas in *The Jew of Malta*. But unlike Shakespeare's Moorish Aaron, who closely imitated Ithamore's unadulterated evil, Shakespeare's Jewish Shylock is considerably more fully dimensioned than Barabas, indeed, a genuine attempt to give a little complexity to a much detested ethnic figure.

An effort to add dimension to a Jew is rare in this period, and virtually unique in Shakespeare. Most of his other allusions to Jews are defamatory references to an inferior, blaspheming race. In *Two Gentlemen of Verona*, for example, Lance tells Speed that if he doesn't accompany him to the alehouse, he is "an Hebrew, a Jew, and not worth the name of a Christian" (II.v.45). Falstaff in *1 Henry IV* swears that his prisoners "were bound, every man of them, or I am a Jew else, an Hebrew Jew" (II.v.164–65). Benedick, in *Much Ado About Nothing*, affirms that "If I do not love her [Beatrice], I am a Jew" (II.iii.231–32). The Third Witch in *Macbeth* includes among the contents of her cauldron "Liver of blaspheming Jew" (IV.i.26). There are many other examples in Shakespeare of the inferior nature of Jews.

A number of helpful studies have been published regarding the place of the Jew in Elizabethan England, including the pioneer research of M. J. Landa's *The Jew in Drama*, Hermann Sinsheimer's *Shylock: The History of a Character*, James Shapiro's compendious *Shakespeare and the Jews*, and, most recently, Stephen Greenblatt's *Will in the World*. These studies note that after having been expelled from England in 1290, Jews became, in Greenblatt's words, "symbolic tokens of all that was heartless, vicious, rapacious, and unnatural." Shapiro enumerates the various crimes associated with Jews, citing the astonishment of Samuel Coleridge upon reading a sermon in which John Donne spoke of the Jewish custom of anointing the dead with the blood of a Christian. It was common wisdom that Jews stank, that Jewish males menstruated, that Jews abducted Christian children and castrated Christian men. These suspicions were enough to create considerable hatred, fear, and abhorrence toward Jews among the people of England, most of whom had never seen a Jew. But as a result of the execution of the queen's physician, a converted Jew named Roderigo Lopez, on trumped-up charges of trying to poison Elizabeth, English anti-Semitism erupted with unprecedented savagery.

Greenblatt speculates that Shakespeare's treatment of the trial scene in *The Merchant of Venice* was inspired by the prospect of spectators watching the execution of Lopez in 1594, and laughing when he announced that "he loved the Queen as well as he loved Jesus Christ." The fact that the play was written so soon after this public execution clearly suggests a link between the two events, though I am not yet fully convinced that Shakespeare had the crowd's amused doubts about Lopez's Christian piety in mind when he wrote the trial scene. He certainly had Barabas in mind, and it is hard not to conclude that, writing *The Merchant of Venice* one year after the death of Marlowe, Shakespeare was trying to demonstrate his superior capacity not only for creating dubious characters but for partially redeeming them.

Certainly, Barabas is the very embodiment of the Machiavellian villain, as Marlowe himself makes clear in *The Jew of Malta*.[4] "I count religion but a childish toy," the character named Machiavel says in the Prologue, "And hold there is no sin but ignorance." The fact that Marlowe himself held religion but a childish toy suggests that he used Barabas partly as a foil for satirizing Christianity. And in the opening scenes of the play, Marlowe's Jew is a character more sinned against than sinning. When we first meet Barabas, he is in his counting house, irritably fingering the coin he has obtained through ocean commerce (he prefers gold): "What a trouble 'tis to count this trash" (I.i). When the Turks come demanding tribute, the Maltese officials extort money from the Jews, particularly the wealthy Barabas.

Marlowe's ironic take on Christian hypocrisy is strong. "What? Bring you Scripture to confirm your wrongs?" says Barabas, "Preach me not out of our possessions" (I.ii). Shakespeare's Antonio will echo this sardonic comment in *The Merchant of Venice* against Shylock ("The devil can cite Scripture for his purpose" [I.iii.94]). But at this point in Marlowe's play, the Christians are more treacherous than the Jews. It is not long before Barabas's desire for revenge assumes monstrous proportions and starts driving the action. And the Jew who begins as a victim very quickly evolves into a self-delighted victimizer:

> As for myself, I walk abroad at nights
> And kill sick people groaning under walls:
> Sometimes I go about and poison wells. (II.iii)

He has studied how to poison through his medical studies, how to blow up people through his engineering practices, how to extort, cheat, lie, and drive young bankrupts to suicide through his banking procedures. He even arranges for his own daughter to be murdered when, out of love for a Christian, she deviates from the true path of Judaism.

In all of these character traits—the Jew's desire for vengeance, the way he alternates between paternal love and homicidal rage, his maritime connections—Shakespeare's Shylock closely follows Marlowe's Barabas.[5] But Shakespeare breaks decisively with his model and his master by refusing to demonize Shylock totally. Unlike Marlowe, he provides his Jew with a few recognizably human qualities beyond his murderous thirst for revenge, in the same way that he tried to humanize the traditionally despised minority figure of a black Moor in *Othello*. On the other hand, Shakespeare's Christian characters, so warm and comradely toward each other, are quite brutal to Shylock, treating him in much the same way that the Maltese treated Barabas. This cruelty is especially true of the otherwise humanitarian Antonio.

When we first meet Shylock negotiating with Bassanio over Antonio's loan, he is discussing interest and terms. Shylock is willing to do business with Christians but not to dine (or "smell pork") with them. He clearly detests Antonio, partly for his charity (he lends money without interest), but mostly for his anti-Semitism ("he hates our sacred nation" [I.iii.43]). Following the advice of Polonius, Antonio has never been a lender or a borrower, but his love for Bassanio plunges him into this fateful exception. Shylock, on the other hand, has a secret motive for lending money to Antonio—revenge. He hates Antonio for some of the same reasons Iago hates Othello, because of his different race and nationality and because of his superior character. But he also hates him because he has been deeply insulted. Antonio has reviled him, called him "cut-throat dog," and "spit upon my Jewish gaberdine" (108). The last insult is the vilest, and it will be avenged. He will extend his "friendship" and seal the bond, with the "merry" provision that Antonio provide a pound of flesh if he forfeits.

Shylock's servant Launcelot Gobbo shares the general Venetian fear, distrust, and hatred of Jews. In his first speech, he declares that the "fiend" is urging him to desert Shylock. On the other hand, Shylock himself "is the very devil incarnal" (II.ii.21-22), so either way he moves, he is damned. Lancelot decides that the fiend is the more friendly counselor and he will run—"for I am a Jew, if I serve the Jew any longer" (99-100). Shylock solves his problem by giving him away to Bassanio.

Shylock's daughter Jessica, like Barabas's daughter Angela, is Christian in temperament, though Jewish in blood—"a Gentile and no Jew," Lorenzo calls her. She has, therefore, resolved to wed out of her faith. Salario later describes Shylock and his daughter as if they were from two separate races—"There is more difference between thy flesh and hers than between jet and ivory; more between your bloods than there is between red wine and Rhenish" (III.i.33-35). Jessica seems to confirm these differences. She is one of the few daughters in Shakespeare, outside of Goneril and Regan, who has no feeling whatsoever for her father. Indeed, she is planning to rob Shylock and give all his ducats to Lorenzo. Shakespeare justifies the betrayal, in the elopement scene, by showing Shylock at his most stereotypical: dreaming of moneybags, stopping the ears of his house against music and masques, pinching his pennies and hoarding his kitchen stores.

Antonio's catastrophe is the loss of his ship, Shylock's is the loss of his daughter. Shylock's rage against Antonio—"a bankrupt, a prodigal . . . let him look to his bond" (III.i.37–40)—is no doubt fueled by Jessica's betrayal. But his revenge is instigated entirely by Antonio's hatred of Jews: "He hath disgraced me, and hindered me half a million; laughed at my losses, mocked at my gains, scorned my nation, thwarted my bargains, cooled my friends, heated mine enemies; and what's his reason?—I am a Jew" (46–49).

This is a prologue to the most famous speech in the play, where Shylock defends the Jew's place in the lists of humanity, and where Shakespeare for the first time modifies his otherwise consistently jaundiced attitude toward Jews. "Hath not a Jew eyes? Hath not a Jew hands, organs, dimensions, senses, affections, passions? Fed with the same food, hurt with the same weapons, subject to the same diseases, healed by the same means, warmed and cooled by the same winter and summer as a Christian is? If you prick us, do we not bleed? If you tickle us, do we not laugh? If you poison us, do we do not die" (50–55)?[6]

This famous speech is a spirited and eloquent defense of a persecuted minority group (although one could argue that the same reasoning might be used in defense of a chimpanzee). Shylock's demand that Christians extend the same charity to all persecuted groups has become a central tenet of modern Liberalism. Indeed, it is a sentiment that will next be expressed by Lear. Since all human creatures are made in the image of God, the despised and the oppressed deserve to be treated with the same compassion as the privileged.

Approaches to acting Shylock have often depended on how this speech was delivered. Although such nineteenth-century actors as Macready, Booth, and Irving followed a tradition of portraying Shylock as a comic villain with a red wig and a big nose, Edmund Kean, following the lead of the great eighteenth-century Irish actor Charles Macklin, reportedly made an effort to play him as a tragic figure. In the twentieth century, however, and especially after the concentration camps of the Nazis and their extermination policies, actors became all too eager to turn Shylock into a suffering victim of adversity. One thinks of Morris Carnovsky's Holocaust martyr at Stratford in 1957, and Charles Marowitz's 1977 version of the play, set in Palestine in 1946, with Antonio cast as a villainous Ernest Bevin and Shylock as a wily Zionist. Dustin Hoffman's performance, under the direction of Peter Cook, turned Shylock into a suffering intellectual, more sinned against then sinning. Even Sir Laurence Olivier's Shylock, played as an elegant Victorian businessman under the direction of Jonathan Miller, had its highly sympathetic side, while the actor playing Shylock in Peter Sellars's 1994 production of the play at the Goodman Theatre in Chicago was a black man, whose trial was televised on Court TV, observed by members of a lynch mob.[7] By the time Andrei Serban directed the play at the American Repertory Theatre in 1998, Shylock had recovered his original comic identity, played (by Will Lebow) as a Borscht Belt tummler.

These interpretations undoubtedly drew their inspiration from Shylock's celebrated appeal for tolerance in a racially charged society. But the rest of his speech is hardly an argument for sympathy, despite its demand for equality: "And if you wrong us, shall we not revenge? If we are like you in the rest, we will resemble you in that. If a Jew wrong a Christian, what is his humility? Revenge. If a Christian wrong a Jew, what should his sufferance be by Christian example? Why, revenge. The villainy you teach me, I will execute, and it shall go hard but I will better the instruction" (III.i.56–61). Note that Shylock speaks of revenge, not of justice. That is something he will demand later. What he is following here is the Mosaic code, an eye for an eye, not Christian forgiveness, with its injunction to turn the other cheek.

A servant announces the arrival of Tubal before Salerio can frame an adequate answer to Shylock's argument. But he uses Tubal's entrance to repeat his libels about the satanic nature of the Jew ("Here comes another of the tribe; a third cannot be matched, unless the devil himself turn Jew" [65–66]). Tubal has come with the news of Jessica's elopement, and her squandering of Shylock's stolen ducats. What drives Shylock into fury is not the loss of his daughter but the loss of his precious diamond ("cost me two thousand ducats in Frankfurt" [71–72]). This is the primal curse on Jewry, he thinks, to lose a fortune, so he wishes the same kind of death on Jessica that Barabas actually visited on Abigail. The only thing that consoles him is the ill luck of Antonio in the wreck of his argosy on its way from Tripoli. Tubal's alternating accounts of Jessica's profligacy and Antonio's misfortune evoke contrasting emotions in Shylock of rage and joy that are clearly intended as comedy. But never again in the play, except perhaps for a single moment at the end, are we to glimpse his "human" side.

The one exception is that curious moment in Tubal's narrative when he mentions a ring that Jessica exchanged for a monkey, and Shylock moans: "Out upon her! Thou torturest me, Tubal. It was my turquoise. I had it of Leah when I was a bachelor. I would not have given it for a wilderness of monkeys" (100–102). It is by far the most touching thing Shylock is permitted to say in the play, and the most personal—much more affecting than his long speech on equal opportunity suffering. This is the only moment when his sentiment outweighs his greed, rapacity, and hatred, the single time that we are allowed to glimpse a younger Shylock capable of conjugal love.

But now all of Shylock's murderous instincts have been unleashed. He wants his enemy's bleeding heart, not his gold. In Jessica's words,

> He would rather have Antonio's flesh
> Than twenty times the value of the sum
> That he did owe him. (III.ii.285–87)

The most repeated word in Shylock's vocabulary is *justice*. "Justice" and his "bond." Salario calls him "the most impenetrable cur / That ever kept with men" (III.iii.18–19), and Antonio, now grown absolute for death, speculates that Shylock hates him because he helped others with their forfeitures.

Antonio, or Shakespeare, seems to be indicting Shylock for contradictory reasons—his greed and his vindictiveness. He hates Antonio for paying off others people's bonds, yet he will not let anyone pay for Antonio's. The Venetian duke in *The Merchant of Venice*, like the Viennese duke in *Measure for Measure*, is charged with upholding the justice of the state in the face of two relentless plaintiffs. In both plays, the statutes are clear. But in both plays, Shakespeare invents a stratagem to rescue the defendants from certain death.

Before this happens in the trial scene, a curious encounter occurs between Lancelot and Jessica (III.v). Lancelot has been suggesting to Jessica that the only way she might be saved is on the basis of a mistaken birthright, if her mother played her father false with a Christian. When Jessica responds that her husband Lorenzo has made her a Christian, Lancelot begins to whine about the subsequent rise in the price of pork caused by the increase in the Christian population. When Jessica informs

Lorenzo of Lancelot's charges, he replies that Lancelot has impregnated a Moorish woman. Even a simple love scene between a husband and a wife seems to carry racialist overtones in this play.

Virtually the whole of act IV is devoted to the trial of Antonio and the ultimate humiliation of Shylock. The duke is already badly disposed toward Shylock—

> A stony adversary, an inhuman wretch
> Uncapable of pity, void and empty
> From any dram of mercy (IV.i.3–5)

—but is helpless to release Antonio. When Shylock enters, the duke invokes Christian images of forgiveness, gentleness, pity, and love to say he expects a compassionate response from the Jew. But they fall on deaf and pitiless Jewish ears, on a "stony" and "inhuman" Jewish heart.

Shylock replies that the reason he prefers a pound of flesh to the payment of the bond is simply his "humour." As some men hate a rat, a pig, a cat, a bagpipe, and would pay to have it removed, so he hates Antonio. "Do all men kill the things they do not love?" asks Bassanio, to which Shylock replies, "Hates any man the thing he would not kill" (65–66)?[8] Antonio sees no sense in trying to soften Shylock's "Jewish heart," and, Stoic that he is, accepts the judgment. Shylock, still justifying his decision, compares his right to Antonio's flesh with any Venetian's right to a "purchased slave" (89). The slaves do not enjoy the comfort of soft beds, or marriage to their masters' children, because they were bought. Antonio's pound of flesh was similarly bought, and now belongs to Shylock.

While Portia prepares her case, Shylock whets his knife, leading Gratiano to find Pythagoras correct in assuming that animals possessed the souls of men. Shylock is unmoved by Christian insults. He demands only justice and the "law." After

Portia has vainly tried to persuade the Jew to drop his suit with her anthology speech about mercy ("It is an attribute to God himself" [190]), Antonio's death seems to be ordained. The law must be upheld. Any precedent would encourage further violations. As for Shylock, his passion for revenge has completely eclipsed his miserly instincts. He will not accept three times the value of the bond (he has already rejected twenty times that sum). Shylock prepares his scales to weigh the pound of flesh, and will not even agree to a surgeon to save the life of his victim ("Is it so nominated in the bond?" [254]). At this point, Portia brings up her famous legal technicality (one wonders why she didn't mention it earlier), that Shylock can have his pound of flesh but not one drop of blood, and no more or less than a single pound. Shylock now is willing to forfeit his revenge, but not his greed, and asks for the offer of three times the value of the bond. Refused that, he asks for the principal only, and is further denied.

Portia then invokes a law against those "aliens" who would threaten the lives of legitimate citizens, and Shylock is ordered to give one-half of his fortune to Antonio, the other half to the state. (More than one modern production has emphasized the similarity between this judgment and the way the Nazis expropriated the property of Jews after sending them to death camps.) Antonio, more merciful than the Jew, appeals to the court to let Shylock keep one-half of his goods so long as he bestows them on Jessica and Lorenzo at his death. Shylock, forced to agree, obliged to give away his patrimony and convert to Christianity, leaves the court, not surprisingly with the words, "I am not well" (392).

It is the last we see of Shylock. The fifth act is entirely devoted to romantic relationships. Lorenzo and Jessica, among the three sets of lovers who couple at the end, utter some lines that recall Mercutio's reflections on Cressida, Thisbe, and Dido, with a blighted new addition, Medea. And much of the act is devoted to Portia's mock-serious indictment of Bassanio for giving away her ring, bringing the play back to the romantic comedy it was originally intended to be. The alien and vengeful Jew has been expunged from the state and the stage, left to cough out his last breaths in a sadly depleted household, while the Christian characters reconstitute themselves into a blissful connubial community. As a Jewish character, Shylock indeed represents a considerable advance over the Barabas of Marlowe. But except for a few moments when Shakespeare's own humanity distracts him from his racialism, the character is far from the suffering victim that modern actors would like to play and modern liberals would like to pity.

The third category of minorities in Shakespeare is represented by his indentured characters, some of them slaves, some servants, some fools. Still, in Shakespeare, servants and fools are more often freedmen than bondsmen, reflecting the fact that despite its economic interest in slave-trading, Europe usually paid for its help. Perhaps as a result, even characters in Shakespeare's Roman plays who might normally be considered slaves (such as Eros in *Antony and Cleopatra*) are referred to in the *dramatis personae* as "friends" or "servants."⁹ A somewhat different example is provided by the twin Dromios in *A Comedy of Errors*. They are identified as "bondsmen" of their twin masters, therefore slaves, and they certainly endure enough beatings on their pates and shoulders to qualify as members of the slave community. But so do various members of Shakespeare's large servant class—characters like Tranio, Biondello, and Grumio in *Taming of the Shrew;* Peter, Sampson, and Gregory in *Romeo and Juliet;* and the various Fools—Touchstone, Feste, Lavatch, and the Fool in *Lear*—in the comedies and tragedies. The Dromios help build the paths of these servants, and sometimes act out their comic function. But, however knocked about they are by their masters, they are of a different species than the subjugated characters in Shakespeare's plays.

Shakespeare's slaves are more often unworldly characters, such as Puck, Caliban, and Ariel. In this final section I intend to focus on these three subjugated figures, though the first, Puck in *A Midsummer Night's Dream*, could very well have doubled as a Shakespearean fool or jester.

Puck is the servant of a very cranky master, Oberon, king of the fairies, which makes his merry mischief-making all the more daring. When he first appears, he is accosting one of Titania's fairies, busy dropping orbs and rubies, dewdrops and pearls in the nocturnal environment. He tells of a quarrel between Oberon and Titania, and the Fairy instantly recognizes him as "that shrewd and knavish sprite,/Called Robin Goodfellow" (II.i.33–34). Puck is happy to embrace the identification, celebrating his status as neighborhood nuisance ("he/That frights the maidens of the villagery" [34–35]) and Oberon's Fool ("I jest to Oberon and make him smile" [44]).

Oberon gives Puck one major task in the play, which either out of incompetence or more likely out of mischief he manages to bungle—to fetch the fairy juice intended for Titania and lay some of it on the eyes of Demetrius. This is exactly the kind of monkey business Puck delights in (and I can still hear the trilling laughter that issued out of the mouth of Mickey Rooney, playing the part in the 1935 Max Reinhardt movie version). Indeed, Puck's relationship with Oberon is extremely delicate. He is always at risk of being beaten by the testy Oberon, especially after he lays the love juice on eyes of the wrong lover (Lysander rather than Demetrius). "This is thy negligence; still thou mistak'st,/Or else committ'st thy knaveries willfully" (III.ii.346–47), says Oberon. He is half right. Nothing amuses Puck more than the confusion of others. By the end of act III, however, he has made restitution for his error, assuring us that

Jack shall have Jill;

Naught shall go ill,

The man shall have his mare again, and all shall be

well. (III.iii.45-47)

And by the end of the play, he has turned into a benign tutelary spirit, sweeping the dust behind the door, and, in an epilogue, asking pardon from the audience if "we shadows have
offended".

In this early play, Puck never gives the slightest sense of
being less than happy in his subservient role. By the time of
Shakespeare's late play *The Tempest*, not just the malignant slave
Caliban but also the gentle sprite Ariel is chafing in slavish sub-
jugation, yearning to be free. *The Tempest* was written sixteen
years after *A Midsummer Night's Dream*, soon before Shakespeare's retirement from the stage. It is the work of a sadder
and more resigned man, and those qualities are nowhere more
evident than in the writing of Ariel's role. Ariel is Puck's kissing cousin, as functionally close to him, say, as the bitter clown
Feste in *Twelfth Night* is to the Fool in *Lear*. But whereas Puck's
mischief-making is a token of his freedom, Ariel's miracle-
working is always subject to Prospero's powerful will.

After the opening storm scene, Miranda pleads with her
father, Prospero, to subdue the tempest he has created. Miranda
is one of those young girls—Perdita, Marina, and Imogen are
others—who appear in Shakespeare's later plays from time to
time to redeem the female sex from the libels men (including
Shakespeare) have poured on it. Her heart is full of pity for the
poor victims until Prospero informs her that not a soul has per-
ished through this the exercise of this, "mine art" (I.ii.293).

The agent of his art is Ariel, and upon her first appearance
(she is clearly female and later appears as a water nymph), Ariel
expresses full submission to Prospero: "All hail, great master,

grave sir, hail! I come / To answer thy best pleasure . . ." (190–91). But soon after delivering her account of the tempest she has stage-managed, Ariel is begging Prospero to fulfill his promise and set her free. Prospero had agreed to reduce her sentence by one year if she served him truly, without "grudge or grumblings" (250). And she has been slavish in her duty and devotion, to the point of waking at midnight "to fetch dew / From the still-vexed Bermudas" (229–30). (Just the sort of geographical task that Oberon assigned to Puck.) Her relationship to Prospero, in fact, seems pretty much the same as Puck's to Oberon—though she fetches dew rather than aphrodisiacs for her master, and serves with more compliance than enthusiasm. Still Ariel's premature request for liberty puts Prospero into a towering rage, which provides the impetus for some exposition about Ariel's history and that of Caliban.

While Caliban is made for hard labor, Ariel is designed for softer tasks. What she does best, apart from supervising storms, is making music. She has two of the loveliest lyrics in Shakespeare—"Come unto these yellow sands" (378–83) and "Full fathom five thy father lies" (400–406)—sung within two minutes of each other as a means of drawing Ferdinand into the presence of Prospero and his daughter. Ariel has played her part so well in providing an enchanting male partner for Miranda that Prospero promises this "fine spirit" her freedom "within two days" (424).

Caliban, of course, is Ariel's antitype. Where Ariel is air, Caliban is earth. Prospero repeatedly refers to him as "my slave" when he is not dismissing him as "hag-seed" (272, 368). He is ugly, murderous, treacherous, lecherous, mindless, kindless. His mother, "the foul witch" Sycorax, was born in Argier (or Algiers), which suggests that Caliban might have had some Moorish blood—odd, considering that Caliban's mother was a "blue-eyed hag" (259, 368).[10] Odder still is the god beloved of Sycorax, namely Setebos, a deity or devil believed in Shakespeare's time to be worshiped by American Indians. Shakespeare is deliberately vague about the location of the island where Sycorax gave birth to Caliban, because in addition to references to Argier, there is that curious allusion to "the still-vexed Bermudas" (230), suggesting that this particular piece of real estate might be situated somewhere off the coast of North Carolina. Geography was never Shakespeare's strong point. He erroneously put a seacoast in Bohemia (in *The Winter's Tale*), and a wood near ancient Athens (in *A Midsummer Night's Dream*), populated with London artisans and journeymen. Shakespeare may have had a chance to see a Native American paraded through London (as Trinculo suggests when he says that his countrymen "will lay out ten to see a dead Indian" II.ii.30–31); if so, that captive may have served as a model for Caliban.

To return to the history of the island, having won the power contest over control of the place, Prospero thereupon freed Ariel from her imprisonment in a cloven pine and enslaved Caliban, who now, he tells Miranda,

> does make our fire,
> Fetch in our wood and serve[] in offices
> That profit us. (I.ii.314–16)

Never having been totally subdued, however, Caliban continues to regard Prospero's presence on the island as a form of foreign imperialism. (In Lee Breuer's production of the play at the New York Shakespeare Festival in 1981, as a matter of fact, all of the Italians were treated as colonialists.) "This island's mine," Caliban roars, "by Sycorax my mother,/Which thou tak'st from me" (334–35). And indeed, there was a time when Prospero and Caliban lived in peace, when Prospero instructed him about the sun and the moon, and treated him with kindness, which is why Caliban introduced his new master to all the secrets of the island.

When this lecherous monster tried to force himself upon Miranda, however, Caliban was inured in a hard rock, restricting his free motion. Nor does he express any remorse over that attempted rape:

> O ho, O ho! Would't had been done!
> Thou didst prevent me; I had peopled else
> This isle with Calibans. (352–54)

It is interesting that Caliban is less regretful about his thwarted pleasure than about failing to populate the island with offspring.[11] This atavistic instinct to increase and multiply is precisely what Prospero finds so brutish and uncivil in the species, along with Caliban's lack of inner grace:

> But thy vile race,
> Though thou didst learn, had that in't which good
>   natures
> Could not abide to be with. (I.ii.361–63)

The remark comes perilously close to racialism, the kind of prejudice we feel lurking behind the creation of Aaron the Moor, the kind of exclusiveness that made Shylock such an outlander in *The Merchant of Venice*. Later in the play, Prospero will identify Caliban with "a devil, a born devil, on whose nature / Nurture can never stick" (IV.i.188–89), which is the way the age usually characterized foreign and darker races. Prospero's remark also reveals the typical impatience of the frustrated colonialist, who tried to bring civilization to the benighted savage and failed: "I endowed thy purposes / With words that made them known" (I.ii.360–61), he says, and received only ingratitude in return. "You taught me language," Caliban replies, "and my profit on't / Is I know how to curse" (366–67). In fact, Caliban's vocabulary is now almost entirely composed of curses, partly because Prospero, like many occupying forces, is not above torturing his prisoners:

> I'll rack thee with old cramps,
> Fill all thy bones with aches, make thee roar
> That beasts shall tremble at thy din. (373–74)

He has also had Caliban pinched and thrown into the mud, bitten by apes, pricked by hedgehogs, and hissed by snakes. If this island sometimes reminds one of Guantánamo, Caliban's treatment is Prospero's equivalent of extreme rendition. No wonder Caliban awaits the day when he can turn his ineffectual hatred into violent insurgency.

Bearing his burden of wood and dreaming of revenge, Caliban comes upon a deity he thinks can save him—namely, the butler Stephano. The vaudeville in which Trinculo and Caliban share the same gabardine convinces the drunken butler that he has discovered a four-legged monster he can haul back to Naples for profit. (The original film of *King Kong* may have drawn some inspiration from this scene.) Caliban embraces the new magician who has awakened his appetite for strong spirits, singing "'Ban, 'Ban, Cacaliban / Has a new master.—Get a new man!" (II.ii.175–76). Later, he offers to kiss his foot and worship him as a god. Obviously, Caliban has been so thoroughly enslaved that, unable to imagine life beyond servitude, he is capable only of exchanging one prison for another, and embracing yet another keeper. Got a new master; but still a caged man.

Caliban is not Prospero's only slave. He has, of course, subjugated Ariel as well, and continually dangles the hope of freedom before her to keep her loyalty. He condemns the king's son Ferdinand to a regimen of hard labor, lugging logs for no apparent purpose. He barks a lot at Miranda. And more often than not, he behaves like a testy, splenetic man, continually threatening even the people he loves most in his disappointment over their inability to live up to his expectations.

In an increasingly drunken scene, Caliban tells Trinculo and Stephano how Prospero cheated him out of the island, while Ariel, invisible, screeches "Thou liest" (III.ii.23). Her function here is similar to Puck's in the Athenian wood, speaking out of the mouths of mortal characters, and getting them to quarrel with each other as a result. (Just as Puck ventriloquizes insults between Lysander and Demetrius, so Ariel improvises a quarrel between Caliban and Trinculo.) When things settle down, Caliban suggests the ways to conquer Prospero—battering his skull, disemboweling him with a stake, slitting his throat. Stephano begins to fantasize about becoming both king of the island and its queen, with Trinculo and Caliban as his viceroys. Ariel's music suddenly terrifies them, stimulating one of Caliban's rare lyric stanzas: "Be not afeard, the isle is full of noises, / Sounds, and sweet airs, that give delight and hurt not" (130-31). And in one of those lovely passages that sometimes make *The Tempest* sound like a riper version of *A Midsummer Night's Dream*, Caliban strikes the theme of waking and dreaming that is the subtext of both plays:

> Sometimes a thousand twangling instruments
> Will hum about mine ears, and sometime voices
> That if I then had waked after long sleep,
> Will make me sleep again: and then in dreaming
> The clouds methought would open and show
>   riches
> Ready to drop upon me, that when I waked,
> I cried to dream again. (132–38)

While Stephano obsesses on the profitable possibilities of free streaming audio, Caliban, forgetting for a moment his fantasy of destroying Prospero, muses on the freedom of the dream.

While the three men plot a usurpation, Ariel demonstrates another function of her servitude, which is to create theatrical representations. She has earlier stage-managed a storm. Now she functions as playwright and actor (in the role of a harpy) in a scene designed to chasten Alonso, Sebastian, and Antonio for their treatment of Prospero. The latter, functioning as a drama critic, praises her performance ("Bravely the figure of this harpy has thou / Performed, my Ariel; a grace it had devouring . . ." III.iii.83–84). And the relationship between the two of them deepens to the point where Ariel, at the end of a song, asks wistfully: "Do you love me, master? no?" (IV.i.48)

Prospero replies that he does indeed love her, "dearly," and Ariel, with the aid of Prospero's "art," immediately concocts another diversion—this time a masque, involving Iris, Ceres, Juno, and a few stray nymphs and reapers. The entertainment, doubtless designed to please the taste for spectacle of King James and Queen Anne, is broken off when Prospero remembers the conspiracy of his rebellious slave and his confederates. The three conspirators enter, smelling all of horse piss. Trinculo and Stephano quarrel over theft; Caliban is preoccupied with murder. Ariel hounds them with spirits, and Prospero promises even more painful tortures to come-"dry convulsions" and "agèd cramps" (256). Ariel sings her last song—"Where the bee sucks, there suck I"—as Prospero, ravished by "my dainty Ariel" (V.i.97), guarantees her freedom.

But not before she accomplishes one last task—to unite the mariners with the nobles and repair their ship. Ariel promises to "return / O ere your pulse twice beat" (104–5; compare Puck's "I go, I go, look how I go! / Swifter than arrow from the Tartar's bow" [III.ii.100–101]). And the delighted Prospero pledges that when she returns, "Thou shalt be free" (244). Indeed, from this point on, the operative words of the play are *freedom* and *forgiveness*. Declaring that "the rarer action is in virtue than in vengeance" (28). Prospero absolves his murderous brother, Sebastian, though not before venting his full measure of self-righteous indignation. Caliban and his companions are absolved of their treachery, even though Prospero, assessing the formidable powers of Sycorax, describes her son with the same epithet Othello used for Iago, as a "demi-devil" (275). Nevertheless, like a disappointed parent saddled to an incorrigible child, Prospero must accept Caliban as his own — "this thing of darkness I/Acknowledge mine" (278–79). Indeed, "this thing of darkness" is even promised a pardon, provided he mend his ways, which Caliban, somewhat unconvincingly, thereupon promises to do ("I'll be wise hereafter/And seek for grace" [298–99]).

Prospero's last action is once again to promise Ariel, his "chick," her freedom, after she has calmed the seas and prepared an expeditious voyage for the shipwrecked Europeans. (Prospero always seems to add just one more condition to the price of Ariel's liberation.) The savage native, Caliban, has been pardoned for his crimes, not liberated. The ethereal spirit, Ariel, has fulfilled her master's final commands and earned her manumission. And Prospero, in an epilogue (many find him speaking for his author here), reveals his bonds with both his servants in *The Tempest*, not to mention all the Moors, all the Jews, all the subjugated and enslaved characters featured in the playwright's other plays. Declaring himself to be imprisoned, too, confined within his island boundaries, he seeks release through the applause of the audience, just as Ariel found release through the approval of her master: "As you from crimes would pardoned be,/Let your indulgence set me free."

It is here, in one of the last speeches Shakespeare would write, that he acknowledges the links that exist between master and slave, indeed among all of us who are creatures of dreams.[12]

6

Intelligent Design

LEAR'S ABYSS

The heavens themselves, the planets, and this centre
Observe degree, priority, and place,
Infixture, course, proportion, season, form,
Office and custom, in all line of order.
— *Troilus and Cressida, I.iii.85–88*

In his biography *Will in the World,* Stephen Greenblatt makes some controversial speculations about how John Shakespeare might have led a secret life as a Catholic while serving as a Protestant public official, further suggesting that his son, William, may have shared some of his father's covert Catholicism and overt Protestantism. Whether this is true or not, there exists in Shakespeare's belief system what Greenblatt calls a double consciousness, and Hamlet is the ultimate example: "He seems at once Catholic, Protestant, and deeply skeptical of both"; or, as Greenblatt describes the melancholy Dane in his earlier *Hamlet in Purgatory,* he is "a young man from Wittenberg, with a distinctly Protestant temperament . . . haunted by a distinctly Catholic ghost."

Put in other words, Hamlet's religion is marked less by Catholicism than by catholicity, and this seems to have been Shakespeare's broad position as well. Throughout his plays, he makes references to Catholic ritual and Protestant belief, English folklore and pagan legend, not to mention interchangeable Greek and Roman mythology, before landing in a very dark place characterized by dawning disbelief in all religions and driven by serious doubts about the existence of a benevolent God. Of course, it is always possible to argue that the religious attitudes of each play are dictated by the demands of the play itself, and do not reflect the opinions of the playwright (to use the language of legal disclaimers). I know there is no way to prove my strong suspicion that Shakespeare's religious thinking evolved from an unquestioning belief in a personal God into a quite morbid brand of Indifferentism. But it is hard to deny that, as Shakespeare's career progresses, he becomes less and less bound by dramatic convention, and sometimes lets his personal expressions of faith and faithlessness, like his other hidden feelings and agendas, seep through the fabric of the dramatic action.

If Shakespeare's youthful belief system is what today we would call Creationism or Intelligent Design, therefore, it is a system he would soon reluctantly outgrow, though not until midway through his career. Shakespeare's metaphysics seem quite conventional, even orthodox, in most of his early plays, where he subscribes to the prevailing theology of the time. (Scholars have counted more than three hundred references to the Bible in Shakespeare's work.) These Creationist beliefs can be most succinctly described through reference to the metaphysical structures of the Great Chain of Being. In that hierarchy, as described by A. O. Lovejoy in his book of the same name and by E. M. W. Tillyard in *The Elizabethan World Picture*, everything in the universe is arranged in order, according to celestial, royal, human, animal, avian, fish, insect, vegetable, and mineral kingdoms. Each of these kingdoms has a leader—God in the heavens, the monarch on earth, the father in the family, the lion in the animal kingdom, the eagle among birds, the whale among fish, and so on. And all of them represent different "planes" or "correspondences," as Tillyard calls them—"the divine and angelic, the universe or macrocosm, the commonwealth or body politic, man or the microcosm, and the lower creation." Moreover, these planes are inextricably linked—"As above, so below"—so that, for example, storms in the heavens are reflected in the passions of humankind (as the tempest on the heath rages simultaneously with the tempest in Lear's breast).

"As above, so below" gave Shakespeare and his contemporaries a powerful maxim with which to install God in his heaven and the monarch on her throne. The issue of degree, or divine order, was the sign of a well-ordered world, as Ulysses notes in *Troilus and Cressida*, in the crucial statement that I cite in the epigraph of this chapter:

> The heavens themselves, the planets, and this
> centre
> Observe degree, priority, and place,
> Infixture, course, proportion, season, form,
> Office and custom, in all line of order. (I.iii.85–88)

Ulysses seems to be describing a fixed, invincible universe. But that celestial order can become vulnerable, especially when "degree is shaked," and the "enterprise is sick."

> Take but degree away, untune that string,
> And hark what discord follows. Each thing meets
> In mere oppugnancy. The bounded waters
> Should lift their bosoms higher than the shores
> And make a sop of all this solid globe. (101, 103,
> 109–13)

In addition to the tsunamis, typhoons, hurricanes, and floods that today we attribute to global warming, the shaking of degree can cause rifts among friends, families, and nations:

Strength should be lord of imbecility,
And the rude son should strike his father dead.
Force should be right—or rather, right and wrong.
Between whose endless jar justice resides,
Should lose their names, and so should justice too.
      (114–18)

Ulysses is describing a world we have already seen operative in *King Lear*, where child turns against father, criminal against judge, might against right.[1] It is a world where everything, in Ulysses' words, includes itself in power, will, and appetite. Ulysses' degree speech is valuable both for the way it describes the given order—and for the way it hints at the dangers threatening it.

Skepticism regarding these fixed beliefs began to seep in from a number of philosophical sources, including Shakespeare's favorite philosopher, Montaigne. It darkened the realm of discourse, especially after the death of Queen Elizabeth, in a gathering storm of dismay and apprehension most eloquently described in John Donne's "The Anatomy of the World" (1611). Written upon the premature death of Elizabeth Drury, daughter of his patron, this momentous long poem was a cri de coeur about the sickness of humanity, the old age and death of the world, the breakup of hierarchy, the shaking of degree, and the shattering of the Great Chain of Being:

And now the springs and summers which we see,
Like sons of women after fifty be,
And new philosophy calls all in doubt,
The element of fire is quite put out,
The sun is lost, and th'earth, and no man's wit
Can well direct him where to look for it.
And freely men confess that this world's spent

When in the planets and the firmament
They seek so many new; they see that this
Is crumbled out again to his atomies.
'Tis all in pieces, all coherence gone,
All just supply, and all relation.

Like Ulysses' speech on degree, Donne's poem is a howl over the displacement of the traditional Ptolemaic system, with Earth at the center, by the heliocentric Copernican system. The startling discovery that Earth was not the major star in the universe, a realization endorsed by Kepler's eponymous laws of planetary motion, was the basis for "the new philosophy" that "calls all in doubt," not to mention what appears to be a growing sense of ecological disaster ("and freely men confess that this world's spent").[2] Donne's poem is also a lament for the consequent loss of man's central place in nature, the new philosophy having "deprived human life and terrestrial history of [its] unique importance and momentousness," as Lovejoy puts it.

Such a loss will seriously influence Shakespeare's metaphysical attitudes in his later life. In earlier career, however, particularly in his comedies, we find him in an essentially cheerful and curiously secular mood. When supernatural elements appear, as they do, for example, in *A Midsummer Night's Dream,* they do not seem to issue from any consistent set of religious convictions or conventions. Oberon, the king of the fairies, is a figure from Celtic legend (originally an evil dwarf), while his wife, Titania, takes her name from Ovid's *Metamorphoses,* the Roman poet's name for Diana. As for Puck, or Robin Goodfellow, he is, of course, a familiar figure of English folklore, a charming combination of pagan trickster and woodland sprite, an early sketch for an English hobbit. Indeed, Puck seems to be a close relative of Queen Mab—the folklore figure Mercutio memorializes as the "fairies' midwife" in *Romeo and Juliet,* who comes "In shape no bigger than an agate stone/On the forefinger of an alderman" (I.iv.56–57). Queen Mab is certainly prone to the same kind of mischief as is Puck, and, arises from the same unconscious world of dreams (Mercutio's "children of an idle brain" ([97]).

The dreamlike mischievousness of Puck, of course—his elusive capacity to be here, there, and everywhere all at once—is essential to the one play of Shakespeare's that has the word *dream* in its very title. But this hobgoblin out of English legend, in the company of such equally un-English characters as Oberon and Titania, appears in an action set in ancient Athens, ruled over by a legendary Greek hero (Theseus) and his Amazonian bride-to-be (Hippolyta). In *Midsummer*, Athens is a classical city, partly based on Spenser's ethereal court in *The Faerie Queene*, whose inhabitants may occasionally show some consciousness of Greek history. But they make very little reference to the Olympian gods, aside from a few scattered allusions to such mixed Greek and Roman mythological figures as Apollo, Cupid, and Aurora (Bottom as Pyramus also mangles the Greek god Phoebus Apollo into "Phibbus" and the Greek hero Leander into "Limander").

The Moon, of course, is mentioned very often, beginning with Theseus's very first speech ("But, O, methinks how slow/This old moon wanes" [I.i.3–4]). But the Moon of *Midsummer* is less a deity than a gorgeous source of luminosity that, four days after the beginning of the play, will have reached its fullness in time to illuminate the various nuptials at court. At the celebration of this triple wedding—between Theseus and Hippolyta, Lysander and Helena, and Demetrius and Hermia—the Moon will also be theatrically personified by Robin Starveling the tailor, brandishing a lanthorn and pulling a dog.

Starveling plays the Moon in that delicious "gross-palpable" play, "Pyramus and Thisbe," written by Peter Quince for the royal wedding celebration. It is a tale of lovers betrayed by death—a goofy satire on Shakespeare's earlier *Romeo and Juliet*—which questions without actually rejecting the idea that thwarted romantic passion can lead to suicide. *A Midsummer Night's Dream* may also be the first time that Shakespeare combines the habit of dreaming with the practice of playacting, though these two exercises will henceforth seem closely joined in his mind. Bottom's description of his dream begins with his calling for a cue and ends with his decision to sing that dream at the end of a play. As Theseus remarks about the cast of "Pyramus and Thisbe," "The best in this kind are but shadows, and the worst are no worse, if imagination amend them" (V.i.208–9), which is a way of saying that actors and dreamers belong to the same ephemeral, shadowy world.

In *A Midsummer Night's Dream*, Shakespeare has so bewitched us that the hodgepodge of nationalities, religious systems, and mythologies he puts forward, however concocted and confused, somehow take on a glorious unity, representing a mystical world of his own invention. At the conclusion of the play, it is fairies, not the gods, who bless the house, just as it is fairies, not the gods, who hold sway over all of his imaginary Athens.

These fairies, nonetheless, seem more at home in the polytheistic world of the Greeks and Romans than in the monotheistic Elizabethan universe. Like the Olympian Deities, Oberon and Titania resemble mortals more than they do the Judaeo-Christian God in their anger, lusts, and jealousies, and also like the Olympians, they seem to enjoy performing sexual acts with humans. Perhaps the most surprising thing in a play produced before a Christian audience is the equanimity with which Oberon accepts an extramarital affair between his wife and a presumably well-endowed donkey (Bottom transformed into an ass), an affair that he has personally arranged with Puck's assistance.

In its serene, indifferent treatment of bestiality and adultery,

A Midsummer Night's Dream is an unusual Shakespeare work. In its benevolent attitude toward supernatural spirits, it may even be unique. A large number of Shakespeare's plays are populated by considerably more demonic species of hobgoblins and ghouls and witches, and ghosts appear in at least three of his tragedies, even in one of his histories. As a matter of fact, not one but eleven of these phantasms visit Richard III in his sleep before the Battle of Bosworth, once again represented as figments of a dream, aroused by a guilty conscience, since he has murdered most of them. Richard may refuse to be bound by any of the moral strictures that govern the religious ("Conscience is but a word that cowards use" [V.vi.39]). But supernatural misgivings provoked by ghostly figures will certainly stir the consciences of Brutus, Hamlet, and Macbeth.

In Shakespeare's plays, ghosts usually materialize in order to complete some unfinished business. On the stage, they are the direct descendants of Thomas Kyd's Ghost of Andrea, who (accompanied by the spirit of Revenge) haunts *The Spanish Tragedy.* Like the Ghost of Andrea, Shakespeare's ghosts represent an important stimulus to the plot. Too incorporeal to act themselves, they appear in order to strike fear or instill purpose in the hearts of the living, whether Christian or pagan. In *Julius Caesar,* the Ghost of the murdered Caesar appears to Brutus, while he is reading, to tell him he will see him again at Philippi—a metaphorical forecast that Brutus will lose the battle. Mirroring Shakespeare's ecumenical treatment of mystical agents, Brutus (like Hamlet) cannot determine whether the Ghost is "some god, some angel, or some devil" to which great Caesar's ghost replies that it is "Thy evil spirit, Brutus" (IV.ii.330, 333).

Whether the Ghost is referring to conscience or character, this seems to suggest a Christian context. But the play is also full of classical auguries, omens, and prophecies, climaxing in the noisy storm that interrupts Caesar's sleep. Calpurnia speaks of "horrid sights seen by the watch" (II.ii.16), including yawning graves, whelping lionesses, and drizzling blood, predictive of the fate being prepared for her husband. (Brutus describes a similar convulsive condition when he describes the spiritual tumult that arises from the acting of a dreadful thing:

> The state of man,
> Like to a little kingdom, suffers then
> The nature of an insurrection. [II.i.67–69])

All of the augurers warn Caesar away from the Capitol, having been unable to find a heart within a sacrificial beast. So does the Soothsayer who urges him to "beware the Ides of March" (I.ii.20, 25). Like Hamlet, if for more self-centered reasons, Caesar defies augury. Brutus will also defy augury before the battle at Philippi, though he fully expects to meet the Ghost of Caesar there, with its promise of certain defeat ("O Julius Caesar, thou art mighty yet!/Thy spirit walks abroad . . ." [V.iii.93–94]). In *Julius Caesar*, it is safe to say, almost every prophecy is ignored and almost every prophecy comes true.

Like the Ghost of Caesar, the Ghost of Hamlet's father is a dead spirit that walks abroad, but this apparition comes from an entirely different religious precinct. The gnawing question is which. Greenblatt's observation that the play is Catholic, Protestant, and skeptical at the same time is confirmed by Hamlet's confusion over whether the Ghost comes from heaven or from hell, whether it is "a spirit of health or goblin damned" (I.iv.21). The Ghost replies that it is neither, but rather a soul out of Purgatory, doomed to walk the night and fast in daytime fires "Till the foul crimes done in my days of nature/Are burnt and purged away" (I.v.12–13). This language suggests that the Ghost is a Catholic apparition. The English church did not believe in Purgatory, agreeing on this point with Martin Luther, who considered it a "Romish Doctrine . . . a fond thing, vainly invented, and grounded upon no warranty of Scripture, but rather repugnant to the Word of God."

In his semihysterical state, Hamlet not only is oddly disrespectful of his father's spirit ("art thou there, truepenny? . . . Well said, old mole!" [152, 164]), he is also famously skeptical regarding its benevolence:

> The spirit that I have seen
> May be the devil, and the devil hath power
> T'assume a pleasing shape. . . .
> I'll have grounds
> More relative than this. (II.ii.575-81)

These doubts may be a nod to prevailing Protestant opinion, but Hamlet is not simply skeptical about Catholic dogma; he sometimes even seems to question the central precept of Christianity itself, namely whether there is any life after death. It is true that at one point Hamlet declares, "There's a divinity that shapes our ends / Rough-hew them how we will" (V.ii.10-11). But he also seems to doubt that this shaping divinity has any coherent influence on human or divine affairs. In Hamlet's mind, death is not the beginning of another life but rather the start of an extremely long nap: "To die, to sleep— / No more" (III.i.62-63). "No more": sleep is all there is and ever will be, the summation of postexistence. There may be dreams in this sleep of death, but Hamlet is not sure that those dreams suggest a hereafter. And such uncertainty "does make cowards of us all" (85).

In short, Hamlet's indecision about his religious convictions is what makes him indecisive about his path of action. He sometimes describes death like a Stoic ("The readiness is all" [v.ii.160]) and sometimes like an Agnostic ("the undiscovered country from whose bourn / No traveller returns" [III.i.81-82]), even though his own traveling father returns from that undiscovered country three times in the course of the play. It would seem that Hamlet's belief is continually colliding with his unbelief. Only after the performance of "The Mousetrap" proves Claudius a villain is Hamlet prepared to "take the ghost's word for a thousand pound" (III.ii.263–64), and embrace him as a trustworthy Christian guide.

Taking the Ghost's word for any amount of money means embracing the concept of Purgatory, and by implication the teachings of Roman Catholicism. Hamlet's belief in Christianity is more palpable when he comes upon Claudius on his knees in prayer, attempting to repent. His decision to spare his uncle during "the purging of his soul" (III.iii.85) lest he guarantee his salvation may be a rationalization for inaction, as some critics have proposed. But it is also sound orthodoxy. To kill Claudius when he is drunk, gambling, swearing, or fornicating would better ensure his damnation. In timely fashion, Hamlet actually kills the king after Claudius has plotted to kill Hamlet and has inadvertently caused the poisoning of his own queen. This should be enough to damn him. It is also enough to damn Hamlet, who has been directly and indirectly responsible for a large number of deaths.

Yet for all this, it is difficult to accept Hamlet as a true believer. His last words make no reference whatever to God or to the disposition of his immortal soul. He utters a simple four-word comment about the acoustics of the afterlife: "The rest is silence" (V.ii.300)—a silence that hardly bespeaks a firm belief in the harrowing Purgatory described by his father's ghost.

Many commentators believe that *Troilus and Cressida* was written soon after *Hamlet*, partly because the two plays share some of the same satirical cynicism. What they do not share is the same religious point of view. With its near echoes of Chaucer and distant echoes of Homer, *Troilus and Cressida* largely concentrates on the details of the Trojan War. But unlike the *Iliad,* where the gods meddled deeply in human affairs, this play makes only cursory references to the heavenly deities (the Olympian order, invoked by both the Greeks and the Trojans, is almost entirely Roman). We have already noted how Ulysses, in his speech about "degree," paid tribute to the Great Chain of Being and its concept of order and priority. But instead of being coherently organized, this world seems to be seriously unhinged, and the kind of martial heroism Shakespeare celebrated, say, in *Henry V,* has been replaced by spite, envy, laziness, cunning, and the basest human failings.

Far from being a great love match, like that of Romeo and Juliet, the relationship between Troilus and Cressida is more like a sordid love itch. It is properly compared to Menelaus's betrayal by Helen, the friction of "a whore and a cuckold" that ignited the Trojan War (II.iii.65). Indeed, one of Shakespeare's objectives in this play seems to be deflating heroic myths. Achilles may be a great warrior, but he is an even greater egotist. He will not fight the Trojans until his pride is satisfied, and when he does, he behaves like a base coward. The Trojans are driven by a sense of honor; the Greeks by cunning and stratagems. Tyrone Guthrie's 1956 production underlined the contrast between idealism and pragmatism among the competing armies by costuming the Trojans as Confederate rebels and the Greeks in Union uniforms — thus opposing southern honor to northern pragmatism. (The concept failed to explain how a war in defense of adultery was equivalent to a war in defense of slavery.) But in *Troilus,* the Greek war plan is unquestionably driven by dishonorable strategies, which helps reinforce Shakespeare's sense of humanity as suffering from serious infection.

Allow me to cite once again Hamlet's reference to an imposthume or canker, hidden in the body, "that inward breaks and shows no cause without / Why the man dies" (IV.iv.9.18–19). The notion of a foreign body poisoning a person without his knowledge is not only a strong physiological symptom (regarding cancer, for example), but a diagnosis of the moral condition of humanity. It certainly describes the condition of *Troilus and Cressida,* which is dominated by the prevalence of disease images, particularly in the speeches of Thersites. Boils, lice, scabs, scurvy, scratching and itching, these are the verbal currency of this scurrilous man, as if the plague were infesting his tongue. In the sonnets, Shakespeare suggested that the Dark Lady had infected him with venereal disease.[3] Thersites' imagery would seem to indicate that this disease was now in an advanced stage.

Thersites is the bitterest fool in Shakespeare, one genuinely revolted by mankind.[4] Patroclus thinks him devout, and it is Thersites who makes the most frequent reference to the gods. But he prays only for misfortune. He appeals to Jove, for example, the "thunder-darter of Olympus," and to Mercury, "cupbearer to the gods," but only to inflict the "Neapolitan bone-ache" on the entire camp, who "war for a placket" (8–9, 16, 17). Confronting Hector, Achilles asks Thersites "in which part of his body / Shall I destroy him—whether there, or there, or there" (IV.vii.126–27). The final "there" (the Guthrie production made this abundantly clear) is no doubt his genital area. The whole play is pervaded by a morbid sense of mortality, of sickly sexuality.[5]

And by an even more powerful sense of deception. Troilus is cuckolded by Cressida, who, almost without hesitation, flirts with the entire Greek camp. The unarmed Hector is killed not by Achilles but by his army of Myrmidons. On hearing this, the Trojans cry, "The gods forbid," but the gods have no more forbidden this treacherous act than they have prohibited or punished the other betrayals in the play. The heavens are empty and the earth is sick. *Troilus and Cressida* concludes appropriately with the ailing Pandarus bequeathing us his diseases.

Measure for Measure would seem to embody a more orthodox metaphysic, but the appearance is deceptive. The heroine of this play is a novice nun (Isabella), the hero is a duke who disguises himself as a friar (Vincentio), the villain is a Puritan who falls from grace (Angelo), and the supporting cast includes a number of characters drawn from religious orders. Furthermore, the play revolves around the issue of sin and redemption, and the testing of moral character, both familiar Christian concerns. And it contains a magnificent speech about preparation for the afterlife (the duke's "Be absolute for death") that rivals in its metaphysical depth Hamlet's "To be or not to be" (and appears in the same place in the two plays—III.i). Yet *Measure for Measure* is an odd amalgam of belief and unbelief, of orthodoxy and skepticism, of piety and license.

This is obvious from the start in the kind of permissive sexual atmosphere the duke, ignoring Vienna's "strict statutes and most biting laws" (I.iii.19), has permitted to flourish in his commonwealth for the past fourteen years. The result has been chaos, and a reversal of degree: "The baby beats the nurse, and quite athwart / Goes all decorum" (30-31). Rather than lance the hidden imposthume of corruption himself, the duke commissions Angelo ("a man of stricture and firm abstinence" [12]) to do it for him. We have looked at this decision from a political point of view in Chapter 4. Let us now examine its religious implications.

In an extremely obscure, contorted speech, the duke commends Angelo's virtue and puts him in his place as fit to judge "mortality and mercy in Vienna" (I.i.44). Unlike most political figures, the duke is not a bit interested in being a popular leader or a darling of the people ("I do not relish well / Their loud applause and aves vehement" [69-70]). Angelo, for that matter, is even less of a crowd-pleaser, since his first official act is to condemn Claudio to death for getting the unwed Juliet with child.

Angelo's judgment on the offender is harsh in the extreme; yet Vienna is sore in need of cleansing. It is a sump, a stews, a whorehouse, where the Scriptures are mockingly invoked to justify stealing and whoring. Lucio represents the lower depths of that world, and so do Mistress Overdone, Pompey, Froth, and Barnadine. Angelo, who "scarce confesses that his blood flows" (I.iii.51–52), finds this debauchery as disgusting as Malvolio does the hedonism of Sir Toby Belch or the Chief Justice the gluttony of Falstaff. Malvolio believes that because he is virtuous, "there shall be no more cakes and ale" (II.iii.104); Angelo has the same compulsion to impose his narrow moral strictures on the whole world. Lucio tells us Angelo thinks his blood is "very snow-broth," that he "never feels /The wanton stings and motions of the sense" (I.iv.57–58). Inevitably, this oblivious charlatan will attempt to seduce the virtuous Isabella, just as the Puritan Malvolio will make an unwelcomed move on the Lady Olivia.

As a play about religious hypocrisy, *Measure for Measure* centers around the Tartuffian Angelo. Yet almost all of the characters of this play are in some kind of moral extremis, even the chaste Isabella, who is willing to let her brother die rather than sacrifice her virtue. It is curious, therefore, to find Isabella, a woman on the threshold of a nunnery, arguing her brother's case to Angelo through references to a Roman god:

> Could great men thunder
> As Jove himself does, Jove would ne'er be quiet,
> For every pelting, petty officer
> Would use his heaven for thunder,
> Nothing but thunder! (II.ii.113–16)

Angelo's response to this, indeed his characteristic response whenever Isabella shows modesty and merit, is to feel repentance for his quickened appetite, to "sin in loving virtue" (187). As Lear will learn later, he is beginning to perceive the paradoxes of justice: "Thieves for their robbery have authority/When judges steal themselves" (180–81).

Poor Claudio. Everyone in authority agrees that he must die for his premarital relations with Juliet. Angelo has sentenced him to death; Isabella repeats this sentence when she begs her to save his life ("Take my defiance/Die, perish!" III.i.144–45); and the duke, in religious habit, is preparing him for execution. But although the duke's disguise is that of a Christian friar, his language more resembles that of a Roman Stoic: "Merely, thou art Death's fool. . . . The best of rest is sleep" (11–17)— yet another replay of Shakespeare's persistent theme that life is a dream, and death another form of sleep. We have heard it already in *Hamlet* and we will hear it again in *The Tempest*. Here the duke informs the idea with perhaps its most poignant phrasing:

> Thou hast nor youth nor age,
> But as it were an after-dinner's sleep
> Dreaming on both. (32–34)

As for Claudio, he occasionally makes poetry out of his fate, using a well-worked Shakespearean metaphor that conflates wedding nights and death:

> If I must die,
> I will encounter darkness as a bride,
> And hug it in mine arms. (81–83)

More often he is petrified by the prospect of oblivion—

> To lie in cold obstruction, and to rot;
> This sensible warm motion to become
> A kneaded clod

—and even more by the idea that he might, as a soul in hell, be damned to "fiery floods" or "thick-ribbèd ice" (119–23).

The duke, a universal stage manager, manages to resolve all the conflicts in the plot not just through the bed-trick device but though a reawakened compassion. The duke has learned that one can be too strict as well as too lenient, and that true godliness lies in mercy:

> He who the sword of heaven will bear
> Should be as holy as severe,
> Pattern in himself to know,
> Grace to stand, and virtue go. (481–84)

In another substitution, he plans to decapitate Barnadine in place of Claudio, but Shakespeare allows the drunken wretch a scene so engaging that he wins the audience's, and presumably the playwright's, sympathy and absolution. So the duke reprieves him, and executes the pirate Ragozine instead.

Angelo, who has been feeling a bit of remorse over Isabella and Claudio, nevertheless continues to parade his judiciary self-righteousness. But the duke, endowed by Shakespeare now with almost godlike powers, is able to "resurrect" the presumably dead Claudio, and to tie off the plot by marrying Angelo to Mariana and himself to Isabella (who, not surprisingly, says not a word about this unanticipated turn of events). Barnadine is pardoned. Lucio is wedded to a whore. And presumably the corrupted Vienna that the duke has seen "boil and bubble / Till it o'errun the stew" (V.i.312–13) will be restored to moral balance.

As the kids used to say, Not.

In *Macbeth*, the supernatural functions either as the feverish symptom of a guilty conscience (the ghost of Banquo) or as a forecast of events to come (the Three Apparitions and the Show of Eight Kings). But in a play already crammed with ghosts and apparitions, the most significant otherworldly figures are the weird sisters, also known as the three witches, who both prophesy and determine the future of the hero. In their second scene together, having earlier paid homage to their tutelary spirits, Grimalkin (a cat) and Paddock (a toad), these skinny, bearded wretches are preparing to sink the ship of a man whose wife refused their demand to share her chestnuts—a punishment woefully in excess of the crime.

Immediately after, the witches inform Macbeth that he will soon be thane of Cawdor and then king of Scotland. These words, of course, are exactly what Macbeth wants to hear, and some commentators have therefore concluded that the weird sisters are extensions of his diseased imagination. Yet these women, with their eerie capacity to vanish into thin air, are also seen by other characters, including Banquo, whose children, they tell him, will be kings. Who are these creatures? Devils or humans? Prophetic omens or wishful thoughts? Mortals or extraterrestrial beings? The latter idea is not that farfetched. Macbeth himself suggests that the witches may be aliens who "look not like th'inhabitants o'th'earth,/And yet are on't" (I.iii.39–40).

In a production I directed of this play in 1971, I was goofy enough to literally treat the weird sisters as creatures from another planet, whose spaceships had landed in Stonehenge, dolmens on which their images were projected. My fanciful notion was that ETs had put down in places like Scotland during prehistory, lying in wait to change the line of the Scottish succession and thereby alter the course of human history. (I also interpreted the mysterious Third Murderer as an extraterrestrial.) It was an idea I borrowed from Erich Von Däniken's *Chariots of the Gods* and Arthur C. Clarke's *Childhood's End,* namely that primitive humanity once was visited by intelligent beings from outer space, who then left us with memories of their coming in the form of myths. One of these myths I took to be *Macbeth*.

Although my concept was admittedly superimposed on the play, scholars agree that Shakespeare had more than one motive for putting witches in *Macbeth*. We have already noted that the play was a large floral bouquet to the recently crowned king of England, James I (written just two years after James's accession to the throne). Not only does *Macbeth* conclude with the false tyrant slain and a legitimate royal line in place that will eventually be the cornerstone of the House of Stuart. The play also fortifies the new king in his dangerous misconceptions regarding those miserable women who were in 1605 being burned at the stake, with the blessings of the crown, for practicing satanic rituals. Shakespeare seems to be confirming these misconceptions in *Macbeth*, possibly against his own better judgment, but no doubt as a way of currying favor with the new regime.

Indeed, Lady Macbeth herself sometimes acts like a member of the witches' coven that influences Macbeth. In her first appearance, she seems to be praying to the same order of tutelary creatures that includes Paddock and Grimalkin:

> Come, you spirits
> That tend on mortal thoughts, unsex me here
> And fill me from the crown to the toe top-full
> Of direst cruelty. (I.v.38–41)

She makes her appeal to the "murdering ministers" who "wait on nature's mischief" (48). And in a foretaste of her famous unsexing speech, she is already asking that her womanhood be reversed, that her milk be turned to gall. That same milk, she tells her husband at the end of act I, she would have denied the baby sucking at her breast—

> I would, while it was smiling in my face,
> Have plucked my nipple from his boneless gums
> And dashed the brains out, had I so sworn
> As you have done to this. (I.vii.56–59)

It is a speech worthy of a fourth weird sister, and it immediately strengthens the resolve of her faltering husband.

Not just Lady Macbeth but Macbeth himself at times seems to be a member of this diabolical underworld. He sees an imaginary dagger marshaling him toward his purpose, and muses on a "half-world" of wickedness and witchcraft. These are not simply the subjective ruminations of a tormented mind. Lennox and Macduff also hear heavy winds, strange screams, and the screeching of an "obscure bird" (II.iii.55), not unlike the supernatural omens preceding Caesar's murder. Later, Ross and the Old Man will testify to other unnatural events—an owl devouring a hawk, horses eating each other. It is as if Macbeth had moved from the natural world into the supernatural precincts of the weird sisters, gathering unto himself all their sinister powers.[6] In a striking reversal, it is the "milk-livered Macbeth" who grows increasingly more dedicated to the evils of the night, and his unsexed witch-wife who yields to remorse of conscience and the anguish of terrible dreams.

In act IV, the witches are accompanied by the Greek goddess Hecate, queen of ghosts and sorcery. She is a character interpolated by another playwright (possibly Middleton), though she sometimes sounds like Shakespeare's Titania in her singsong rhythms and folklore references:

> And now about the cauldron sing,
> Like elves and fairies in a ring,
> Enchanting all that you put in. (IV.i.41–43)

Hecate lightens the atmosphere considerably. But when Macbeth returns to question the witches, they are back in their noxious characters. They have the capacity not only to bring down kingdoms but also to sway churches, topple castles, blow down trees, sink ships, and (in a forward glance toward *King Lear*) tumble "nature's germens" altogether (75).

Instructed by the witches, Macbeth believes himself to be fully armored by a supernatural defense. He cannot be conquered until Birnam forest comes to Dunsinane, and then only by a man who was not born of woman. But these supernatural improbabilities have a natural explanation in this play, and after they have come to pass, Macbeth's head will be dragged in upon a pike. Before he dies, however, the tyrant is permitted an extraordinary soliloquy, one of the most depressing metaphysical testimonies ever written, with its nagging insistence on the absolute meaninglessness of life:

> Tomorrow, and tomorrow, and tomorrow
> Creeps in this petty pace from day to day
> To the last syllable of recorded time,
> And all our yesterdays have lighted fools
> The way to dusty death. Out, out, brief candle!
> Life's but a walking shadow, a poor player
> That struts and frets his hour upon the stage,
> And then is heard no more. It is a tale
> Told by an idiot, full of sound and fury,
> Signifying nothing. (V.v.18–27)

This magnificent passage, with its imagistic references to writing ("the last syllable of recorded time" "a tale told by an idiot") and to acting ("a poor player / That struts and frets his hour upon the stage"), must have reverberated in the brain of the actor-playwright William Shakespeare as resoundingly as in the mind of the mass murderer Macbeth. Its message of hopelessness and nothingness, reinforced a year later by the bleak nihilism of *King Lear,* suggests that it was inspired by something more personal and immediate than the political ambitions of a thane in medieval Scotland.

Othello is a domestic play, with few references to a Christian order or a Christian hagiography. The major exception is a figure from hell, that "demi-devil" Iago. For a moment toward the end, Othello imagines Iago to be Satan himself or one of his followers—"I look down towards his feet, but that's a fable" (V.ii.292). A devil's cloven feet may indeed be a Christian fable, but Iago not only descends from the demons of the Mystery plays, he is a full-blooded fiend in his own right. He seems to confess as much when he rebukes Brabanzio for not moving faster against Othello: "'Swounds, sir, you are one of those that will not serve God if the devil bid you" (I.i.110-11). The irony of this odd phrase is that the devil is indeed bidding Brabanzio, not to serve God but to help him fulfill his diabolical will.

Iago is also the first major Shakespearean character to consciously make a deity of nature, which is to say the first to deny the idea of immanence or transcendence. This hard-edged naturalism will later find its fullest expression, of course, in Edmund's Darwinian view of the universe in *King Lear.* Indeed, as I have already noted, Iago and Edmund are evil twins. Like Edmund, Iago is all things to all people, depending on what he wants from them. But what makes him most terrifying to us, and no doubt to Shakespeare as well, is his oddly persuasive belief that the heavens are empty, that human nature is not constrained by any universal morality or religious law. "Our bodies are our gardens," he insists, "to the which our wills are gardeners" (I.iii.317-18). No gods, no morality, only the garden of evil fertilized by the human will.

Iago is profoundly cynical. He believes there is no such thing as human goodness: "Virtue? A fig! 'Tis in ourselves that we are thus or thus" (316). Iago's horticultural metaphor about the body being a garden and the individual will the gardener puts "the power and corrigible authority" (321) over what we do entirely in our own soil-stained hands. This is, in effect, a denial of the existence of God, indeed of any power beyond the self. Iago believes that human reason holds sway over "the blood and baseness of our natures" (323–24), which is certainly true of this particularly cold-blooded villain. But such reasoning leads him to conclude that any form of unbridled emotion—"our raging motions, our carnal stings, our unbitted lusts" (325–26)—can be controlled by the will.

Iago employs the word *will* not as Shakespeare used it in the sonnets, as a quibble on his own name and on his sexual appetites. No, he uses it now in the way that certain German philosophers would later employ it (Schopenhauer in *The World as Will and Representation*, Nietzsche in *The Will to Power*), as a function in the transvaluation of values that leads to the evolution of the *Übermensch*. Indeed, Iago is an early example of Nietzsche's Superman, the individual who follows his own desires without scruples or remorse—he will reappear in such conscienceless figures as Dostoevsky's Stavrogin and Ivan Karamazov. Where he errs is in assuming everyone else shares his own faults of character. Desdemona is fickle in her desires, because she is a woman (her "very nature will . . . compel her to some second choice" [II.i.228–29]), and so is Othello, because he is black ("These Moors are changeable in their wills" [I.iii.339–40]).[7]

But this is only one of his disguises. A major faculty of the devil (also the major talent of an actor) is his capacity to change shapes. Iago fulfills that requirement, being a different person with everyone he meets. With Othello, he is the loyal, blunt plain-dealer; with Roderigo, a cynical pimp; with Cassio, an avuncular friend and counselor; with Desdemona, a witty courtier. To virtually everyone but his wife Emilia, he appears to be "full of love and honesty" (III.iii.123), playing the very opposite of himself in a familiar satanic manner. "Divinity of hell!" Iago notes.

> When devils will the blackest sins put on,
> They do suggest at first with heavenly shows,
> As I do now. (II.iii.324–27)

His very being resides in "shows," his motto being that of every transforming actor, "I am not what I am" (I.i.65). Iago is as much a histrionic masquerader as an anti-Christ.

Othello's religion is not deeply explored in the play. He makes mention of heaven and hell, particularly in relation to woman's virtue after Iago suggests it is possible to be "naked in bed" with a male friend and "not mean harm": "It is hypocrisy against the Devil," Othello responds. "They that mean virtuously, and yet do so, / The Devil their virtue tempts, and they tempt heaven" (IV.i.5–8). Henceforth, he will use the word *devil* over and over when referring to the virtuous Desdemona, most tellingly when he strikes her in front of Ludovico and his attendants. As a Moorish general in the hire of Venice, Othello is no doubt a Muslim convert to Christianity. But as we have seen, his imagery and, we are to assume, his savagery, are strongly influenced by his Moroccan origins.

He is concerned, for example, that Desdemona pray before he kills her because he does not wish to "kill thy unpreparèd spirit; / No, heavens forfend! I would not kill thy soul" (V.ii.33–34). This is the same reasoning that Hamlet used for refusing to kill Claudius at his prayers—though Hamlet actually *wanted* to kill his victim's soul—and it reveals Othello to be just as familiar as Hamlet with Christian notions of salvation. He says "amen" when Desdemona asks for mercy from the Lord. Yet Othello refers to the murder as a "sacrifice" (70), a ritual belonging more to pagan than to Christian practices. Just as he blames the proximity of the moon ("She comes more nearer earth than she was wont,/And makes men mad") when Emilia appears to report Roderigo's murder, so he expects "a huge eclipse of sun and moon" (119–20), similar to the auguries in *Julius Caesar,* after he smothers Desdemona. Even in his deepest grief and remorse, he does not speak of God, but appeals to demons: "Whip me, ye devils,/From the possession of this heavenly sight" (284–85). Nor does he ever mention heaven. Othello anticipates being blown about in winds, roasted in sulfur, washed in liquid fire. He is already in hell, his soul ensnared by the "demi-devil" Iago. In a previous chapter, I noted that his final speech, with its references to "the base Indian," to "Arabian trees," to "Aleppo" and "a malignant and a turbaned Turk," suggests that, facing death, he has spiritually returned to his home continent. It may also suggest his return to the Muslim faith into which he was born.

Written immediately after *Othello* in 1605–6, *King Lear* represents a further breakdown in Shakespeare's view of a structured cosmos, a growing loss of faith in human nature. *Lear* is the crowning achievement of Shakespeare's metaphysic, not just the greatest play ever written but also one of the most terrifying philosophical testaments ever conceived. The ancient-Britain setting locates the work in a period before the coming of Christianity. There are occasional references to Roman gods. Cursing Cordelia, Lear appeals to Hecate, goddess of the lower world (also the spirit of witchcraft and magic), a deity who had previously appeared in *Macbeth,* courtesy of Thomas Middleton. Turning on Kent when he comes to the aid of Cordelia, Lear threatens that blunt old soldier with the vengeance of an oracular Greek god ("Now, by Apollo")—to which Kent replies "Now, by Apollo, king,/Thou swear'st thy gods in vain" (I.i.159–61).

Thy gods? Is Kent suggesting that he does not believe in Lear's pre-Christian deities? Actually, he reaffirms the pagan order when, comforting Cordelia, he says, "The gods to their dear shelter take thee, maid" (183). It is only when Lear names the gods to justify his foolish rashness that Kent registers his objections. When the king banishes Kent, he swears "by Jupiter" (179) that he will never revoke the banishment. Yet there is something a little remote about the deities referred to in the play. France finds them derelict and inattentive ("Gods, gods! 't is strange that from their cold'st neglect / My love should kindle to inflamed respect" [255–56]).

For the villain Edmund, of course, there is only one god, or goddess, nature. But Edmund's nature is not that serene bucolic presence so often evoked in Shakespeare's plays as a source of woodland comfort. It suggests something not sylvan but rather sinister, brutal, coarse, and indifferent. Edmund is a bastard, conceived in "the lusty stealth of nature" (I.ii.11), therefore a "natural" child. Although Edmund asks the "gods" to stand up for bastards, the only divinity he readily acknowledges is an abstraction totally unconcerned with human existence, the natural form of life later to be described by Thomas Hobbes as solitary, poor, and nasty, and by Alfred Lord Tennyson as "red in tooth and claw." Before long, that same stern goddess nature, newly dressed in the raiment of virtue, asceticism, and respectability, will become the reigning spirit of the French Revolution, presiding over the rolling of heads.

Edmund shares Iago's ability to libel the innocent through "shows" of loyalty. And the ingenious letter he forges to turn Gloucester against his legitimate son Edgar is the product of the same cunning that Iago used with Desdemona's handkerchief to persuade Othello of his wife's infidelity. Edmund's libel on his brother Edgar immediately stimulates Gloucester's thinking, as it did Othello's before him, about astrological conjunctions ("These late eclipses in the sun and moon portend no good to us" [96–97]). Gloucester predicts human consequences from these cataclysmic portents, where "nature finds itself scourged by the sequent events" (98–99). Unlike his faithless bastard son, he begins the play as a true man of faith.

But he also knows that the best of times are over—"machinations, hollowness, treachery, and all ruinous disorders, follow us disquietly to our graves" (104–6). Edmund ridicules his father's astrological beliefs as "the excellent foppery of the world, that, when we are sick in fortune, often the surfeit of our own behavior, we make guilty of our disasters the sun, the moon, and the stars" (109–12). According to Edmund, it is genetic inheritance, not astrology—nature, not nurture—that accounts for human behavior. "Fut," he snarls, "I should have been that I am, had the maidenliest star in the firmament twinkled on my bastardizing" (120–22). Compare Iago: "'Tis in ourselves that we are thus or thus." Edmund's biological determinism comes from the same tradition.

When Edmund meets his half-brother, Edgar, he describes the evil consequences of such eclipses in phrases that mimic his superstitious father: "unnaturalness between the child and the parent; death, dearth, dissolutions of ancient amities; divisions in state, menaces and maledictions against kings and nobles; needless differences, banishment of friends, dissipation of cohorts, nuptial breaches, and I know not what" (132–36). He may be cynically assuming the role of "a sectary astronomical" (137), but, either consciously or unconsciously, he is outlining the scenario of the play that will follow, its action and its mood.

This debate over the power of sentient stars versus the indifference of insentient nature is the central metaphysical issue of the play. Indeed, it is an argument that often seems to plague Shakespeare in his later career. But though he never fully resolves that thorny question, this is the play where he explores it most thoroughly. There is a sense in *King Lear* that the Great Chain of Being has smashed into a thousand broken links. When a king loses his throne, it is as if God has also been ejected from his divine seat. Yes, Lear deposes himself, in a voluntary action, but he never expected to yield any of his authority. Lacking a good estate lawyer, he assumed he could give away all his property and revenue, abdicate from the daily business of government, even hand over his throne, and still "retain / The name, and all the additions to a king" (I.i.135–36). What he has actually done is start a juggernaut in motion that will crush him, his empire, and perhaps the whole idea of a higher moral order.

The first sign that the hierarchy is collapsing comes in Goneril's exchange with Regan in which, instead of expressing gratitude and respect to her father for a generous gift of property, she criticizes his "infirm and choleric years" (296). Regan also refers to the "infirmity of his age," and declares that "he hath ever but slenderly known himself" (291–92). Soon one of the astrological consequences predicted by Edmund—"unnaturalness between the child and the parent" (I.ii.132)—will be fulfilled both in Lear's relations with his daughters and in Gloucester's relations with his son. Lear's objective from this point forward will be to keep from going mad over the viciousness of his thankless daughters and his own vicious treatment of Cordelia. Thrust out of doors, he will be exposed to Edmund's nature in all her blind, indiscriminate ferocity. So will Gloucester, after he has lost his eyes. And, ironically, it will be the filial Edgar—not the goddess-loving Edmund—who will be identified most completely with nature, as a naked Bedlam beggar.

"Allow not nature more than nature needs," Lear advised Goneril, "Man's life's as cheap as beast's" (II.iv.261–62). That will be Lear's despair, to exist with less than nature needs, to become the equivalent of a valueless beast. It is, indeed, this very act of stripping down to the naked necessities of nature that lays bare the greatest insights of this play. Lear calls his daughters "unnatural hags" (273). A nagging question of *King Lear* is whether these hags would not be better described as "natural," since the evil characters reflect the intrinsic nature of things more accurately than the virtuous.

When Lear goes on the heath to contend with the fretful elements, Shakespeare makes us question whether there is anything left in the heavens but hail and water. In a previous chapter, I noted that what Lear asks of the storm is nothing less than total devastation of the natural world and the extermination of the human race. Lear cannot decide whether the elements are "servile ministers" (III.ii.20) in league with his daughters, or autonomous forces totally independent of humanity. Nor can we. This particular storm, as Kent tells us, is of a special fury, never before experienced, even more tumultuous than the storm preceding Caesar's death.

For Lear the storm inspires thoughts of injustice and betrayal. He invokes "the great gods," the cause of all this "pother" (47–48), to punish guilty people who have thus far successfully hidden their crimes. What will later enter his "mad" mind is the entirely lucid idea that "the great gods" are deaf, and that human authority is as corrupt as the objects it condemns. And since justice is reserved exclusively for the rich, the immunity of the privileged only increases the suffering of the perplexed. The criminal and the judge are identical in their iniquity, as are the whore and the beadle, and the king and the beggar. In his inspired madness, Lear will recognize that "unaccommodated man" (III.iv.98–99) is not just a king without a retinue. He is a creature without clothing, speech, or sanity, without "borrowings" or "lendings." Himself divested of his furred gowns, enduring the pain of exposure in "tatter'd clothes," Lear can now feel pity for the "poor naked wretches" whose torment he has been forced to share. What he has learned is the value of empathy:

> O, I have ta'en
> Too little care of this! Take physic, pomp;
> Expose thyself to feel what wretches feels,
> That thou mayst shake the superflux to them,
> And show the heavens more just. (33–37)

Lear's reference to the "superflux" brings us back to the idea of nature, and its essence obscured beneath the superfluous raiment of human beings. Lear has only slenderly known himself because, blinded by ceremony, he cannot grow into self-knowledge until he loses all his royal trappings. Just as Gloucester is able to "see" only after being blinded ("I stumbled when I saw" [IV.i.20]), so Lear will be able to understand only after he has exposed himself "to feel what wretches feel" (III.iv.35). The key term in this process is *accommodations* (after the Latin *accommodo,* meaning to adapt, to put on), the same word Lear uses to refer to his hundred knights. But Lear's accommodations are also his vestments, his language, his trappings of kingship, all those civilized "borrowings" gradually being claimed back from him by nature, including his very sanity, perhaps even his immortal soul. And when Lear, trembling on the brink of madness, prepares to tear off his clothes and face the storm as one of those poor naked wretches, he has finally reached the pitiful state of his most abject subjects.

For Lear, "poor Tom" symbolizes all those he disregarded when he was king. First, he pities his nakedness ("Why, thou wert better in thy grave than to answer with thy uncovered body this extremity of the skies" [III.iv.94–95]), and then he philosophizes about it:

> Consider him well. Thou owest the worm no silk,
> the beast no hide, the sheep no wool, the cat no
> perfume. Ha! Here's three on's are sophisticated!

Thou art the thing itself; unaccommodated man
is no more but such a poor, bare, forked animal as
thou art! Off, off, you lendings! Come unbutton
here. [*Tearing off his clothes*] (96–101)

It is one of the most extraordinary moments in literature. It is also one of the most terrifying. For the passage not only provides insights into Lear's character, it offers a profoundly radical insight into the character of Shakespeare's universe. Lear is perceiving that, rather than being a wholly different species, humans follow a continuity with the animals. Our pride and pretensions are all borrowed from nature, not intrinsic to our being. Unaccommodated man lives in a state of physical nakedness, yes, but also in a state of spiritual nakedness. All the things we value, including our sanity, are only "lendings," given us by sufferance rather than by custody.[8]

Sufferings of a similar kind make the blinded Gloucester conclude that in this world "madmen lead the blind" (IV.i.47) and that the heavens are ruled by boredom and random brutality: "As flies to wanton boys are we to the gods; / They kill us for their sport" (37–38). This awful insight presupposes a wholly indifferent universe. Edgar tries to calm his father's suicidal feelings with a dose of Stoicism:

Men must endure
Their going hence, even as their coming hither;
Ripeness is all. (V.ii.9–11)

To some, this is the Roman wisdom of Zeno and Seneca. To others, it is the creed of the defeated, the doctrine of the shrug. Hamlet proposed a similar philosophy to Horatio in act V, scene ii: "If it be now, 'tis not to come. If it be not to come, it will be now. If it be not now, yet it will come. The readiness is all" (158–60). Horatio remains silent. Gloucester, whose suffering has snuffed out his poetry, can only manage a prosaic response, "And that's true, too" (12).

Actually, Edgar does manage to restore his father's belief in life, but largely through a stratagem. He pretends his life has been saved from certain death through supernatural intervention. It is this kindly deception that restores Gloucester's belief in "the clearest gods," and converts him to Edgar's problematic Stoicism:

> Henceforth I'll bear
> Affliction till it do cry out itself
> "Enough, enough," and die. (IV.vi.75-77)

Albany's view of things is much less sanguine. He foresees a future of nature gone mad and sanguinary:

> If that the heavens do not their visible spirits
> Send quickly down to tame these vild offences,
> It will come,
> Humanity must perforce prey on itself,
> Like monsters of the deep. (IV.ii.47-51)

But the heavens send down no visible spirits in this play, only predatory monsters rising from the deep.

A monstrous humanity, then, and an indifferent nature. Is that all we are left with? It is true that some things modify this morbid view of the world. Edgar overcomes Edmund in a tourney that seems to have been lifted from the Puffin Classics *King Arthur,* and, over his dying body, affirms "the gods are just," since his father's "pleasant vices" made "instruments to plague" him (V.iii.169-70). It is true that Edmund gets his just deserts, and so do Goneril, Regan, and Cornwall. Edmund even undergoes an odd reformation just before he dies, and reveals (too late) his plot to murder Cordelia, the one person in the play said to redeem "nature from the general curse" (IV.vi.200).

But the most important act of redemption is clearly the reconciliation of Lear and Cordelia. Their reunion is a moment of
supreme love, suffused with a sense of joyousness that survives
even their capture. Lear, who once put so much store by his
"accommodations," could now, like Hamlet, be happy living in
a nutshell, if he lived there with Cordelia. In prison, he and his
daughter will sing "like birds i' the cage," and pity the "poor
rogues" who can only talk of court affairs, "Who loses and who
wins; who's in, who's out" (V.iii.9, 13, 15). This kind of *People*
magazine gossip no longer interests Lear, who, having been
stripped to his bare soul, has abandoned all interest in the trappings of ceremony or the vanities of ambition. Speaking in the
metaphors of the monastery, Lear tells Cordelia that they will
take upon themselves

> the mystery of things,
> As if we were Gods' spies; and we'll wear out,
> In a walled prison, packs and sects of great ones,
> That ebb and flow by the moon. (16–19)

It is the ultimate rejection of the worldly court life, and the
ultimate embrace of its spiritual substitute, filial love.

But then "my poor fool is hanged" (304).

The death of Cordelia, this heartbreaking climax, heaped on
all the bleak events of the play, reinforces the corrosive nihilism that permeates *King Lear*, verbally expressed through negatives that burst on the stage like a torrent of woe. The heart of
Gloucester, having recovered a beloved son, "burst smilingly"
(198). The heart of Lear, having lost a beloved daughter, bursts
despondently: "Thou'lt come no more. / Never, never, never,
never, never" (306–7). Kent alone retains his belief in "the stars"
that govern our conditions. His reasoning? That Lear produced
such different children. Pretty lame. Edmund could have used
the same argument to prove that nature governs our condition.

But despite Shakespeare's effort to temper the awful events we have witnessed, and find a higher meaning in them, we are left in a dark metaphysical shadow summed up in Donne's lament, "'Tis all in pieces, all coherence gone."[9]

Shakespeare's other tragedies, however full of misfortune, at least assume an ordered universe. *Lear* seems to take place on a cold and friendless planet revolving around a third-rate star.[10] Shakespeare hasn't lost his respect for Christian-Humanist values; he just can't seem to believe in them any more. Creation has lost both intelligence and design. The gods remain silent, and the predators prevail. Goodness flickers like a guttering candle about to be extinguished. The play is a glimpse into the depths of some monstrous abyss.

After such knowledge, what forgiveness? The remainder of Shakespeare's canon, while sometimes reflecting the fin-de-siècle sense of loss and woe that permeates *King Lear*, is not totally characterized by it. The Roman plays (*Antony and Cleopatra* and *Coriolanus*) and the Greek plays (*Timon of Athens* and perhaps *Pericles*) that follow *Lear*, like the Greek-Trojan play that preceded it (*Troilus and Cressida*), may occasionally name the gods. But supernatural beings are rarely very present or potent. The gods have no real significance in these plays.

To take just one example, compare the omen-ridden *Julius Caesar* with its relatively secular sequel, *Antony and Cleopatra*. Before Caesar's death, the earth erupts in ominous storms, auguries, and horrid sights. The most auspicious thing that happens in *Antony and Cleopatra* is a measure of underground oboe music that plays when "the god Hercules, whom Antony loved, now leaves him" (IV.iii.13–14). Compared to the virile Mars in the first speech of the play, Antony, like Mars, is now helpless in the arms of Venus (with whom Enobarbus compares Cleopatra). He has become "the bellows and the fan / To cool a gypsy's lust" (I.i.9–10). Thus Mars and Hercules are less sacred figures worthy of worship than personifications of the manhood Antony is losing in the arms of his lover. Antony also fears for his manhood—in a remark with Freudian overtones, he complains that Cleopatra robs him of his sword, adding "These strong Egyptian fetters I must break / Or lose myself in dotage" (I.ii.105–6). But he cannot free himself from this passion. The true object of his religious devotion is Cleopatra.

Enobarbus swears "by Jupiter," and Pompey makes mention of the "just gods," but *Antony and Cleopatra* is essentially a secular play about humans driven by cold self-interest (embodied in Octavius) or irresistible passion (personified by Antony). It is no accident that Antony's aide is called Eros. Brutus pleaded with four soldiers before he could find one to help him fall upon his sword. Antony asks only one, Eros, who kills himself rather than help his master die. Thus Antony must botch the job himself. And lucky he does, or we would have lost a great death scene. Significantly, when Antony expires in the arms of Cleopatra, he makes no mention of heaven or the gods, though Cleopatra does, however ironically, when she bows before Caesar:

> Sir, the gods
> Will have it thus. My master and my lord
> I must obey. (V.ii.111–13)

Cleopatra commits suicide in an effort to reunite with Antony, leaving us in no doubt that she believes in the hereafter. But it is an afterlife of pleasure and lovemaking. She fears that Iras, dying first, will be the first to meet and kiss her Antony, ruled by a strong erotic component even in her suicide. As in *Romeo and Juliet*, death almost loses its sting in the face of transcendent love.

In the late romances, with the one exception of *The Tempest*, Shakespeare is thinking more of experimenting with theatrical conventions than of exploring metaphysics. *The Winter's Tale* climaxes with a kind of resurrection, when Hermione's statue returns to life in Apollo's temple, but this is more a *coup de théâtre* than a sacramental affirmation.[11] *Cymbeline*, like *Lear*, is set in a pre-Christian Britain presided over by Roman gods, who do not seem to function at all in the play. That is, until the remarkable act V scene in which the ghosts of Posthumus's father, mother, and brothers appear to him in a dream, followed by the vision of Jupiter sitting on an eagle. This event is probably more a nod to the popular masques in fashion at the time than a tribute to the gods. And after the longest recognition scene in Shakespeare (perhaps one of the longest in the whole of dramatic literature), a Soothsayer comes to tie off the various strands of the plot. "Laud we the gods," Cymbeline intones at the end, in a speech that forms the epitaph to James Joyce's reflections on Shakespeare in *Ulysses*, "And let our crookèd smokes climb to their nostrils / From our blest altars" (V.vi.476–78).

The Tempest, regardless of whether or not it is Shakespeare's final play, is certainly his final metaphysical testament. It is an extension of the worldview he was developing so painfully in *King Lear*, which had seemed in suspension during the writing of his late romances. The Italian Christians in *The Tempest*, who come from Naples and Milan, who surely live in Renaissance Europe and go to Catholic churches, seem as preoccupied with Roman gods as the characters in *Cymbeline* or *Lear*. There are occasional liturgical references. The shipwrecked characters fall to their prayers during the storm in act I. Prospero makes mention of the divine Providence that brought him safely to his island. Gonzalo swears "By 'r lakin" (or by our Lady). And even Caliban's mother, Sycorax, "that damn'd witch," seems to be a member of that anti-Christian coven that obsessed King James.

Furthermore, Prospero promises Ferdinand and Miranda a

"holy rite" (IV.i.17), though virtually in the next breath he mentions the pagan goddess of marriage, Hymen.[12] But the white magic that Prospero practices is surely not a ritual that Christianity would tolerate, and there are absolutely no references to Jesus in the play. Instead, we have four-legged monsters that are half-fish, and "tricksy" spirits such as Ariel.

Like so many of the later romances, *The Tempest* also includes a masque, featuring a number of figures from Greek and Roman myth—Iris, Ceres, Juno, and a host of Naiads. Prospero, with the help of Ariel, is showing off his art, conjuring spirits, and meanwhile celebrating the coming marriage of Miranda and Ferdinand. There are references in this masque of fertility and plenty, to Venus and blind Cupid, to Dis (or Pluto), to Hymen, and to Mars. But in the middle of a dance between the Reapers and the Naiads, Prospero breaks off the ceremony, remembering the conspiracy of Caliban, Stephano, and Trinculo. Having paid his tribute to court fashion, in other words, Shakespeare is now obliged to return his attention to his plot.

But not before Prospero delivers his lovely, highly anthologized speech about the insubstantiality of the spirit world, and the fragility of life:

> You do look, my son, in a moved sort,
> As if you were dismayed. Be cheerful, sir.
> Our revels now are ended. These our actors,
> As I foretold you, were all spirits, and
> Are melted into air, into thin air;
> And, like the baseless fabric of this vision,
> The cloud capped towers, the gorgeous palaces,
> The solemn temples, the great globe itself,
> Yea, all which it inherit, shall dissolve
> And, like this insubstantial pageant faded,
> Leave not a rack behind. We are such stuff

As dreams are made on, and our little life
Is rounded with a sleep. (IV.i.146–58)

The speech is so well-known that it works not only as an expression of theology or philosophy but also as a form of incantation. Hearing its familiar chords, we can easily stop listening to what is actually being said, and thus fail to recognize that Shakespeare is reworking his insistent theme about the interchangeability and inseparability of theatre and life.

This is the theme that obsesses him throughout his writing career. From his early reference to "an imperfect actor on the stage, / Who with his fear is put besides his part" (sonnet 23), to Jaques' "All the world's a stage, / And all the men and women merely players" (*As You Like It*, II.vii.138–39), to Antonio's similar description of the world (in *The Merchant of Venice*) as "A stage where every man must play a part" (I.i.78), to Richard II beholding himself in a mirror like an actor surveying his makeup, to Macbeth's

poor player
That struts and frets his hour upon the stage
And then is heard no more (V.v.23–25),

and all the many other references in his works to the histrionic quality of life, there has been a constant metaphysical progression marked by a single consistent theme—that life and art are often indistinguishable, that the actor and the dreamer are one.

Waking and dreaming. Decades before the great Spanish playwright Calderón de la Barca published *La vida es sueño* (Life is a dream) in 1636, Shakespeare, living in England, had independently reached the same conclusion, that we may be sleeping, not living, our lives. Calderón's hero, Segismundo, comes to believe that life is a dream from which one awakens only at the point of death. Many of Shakespeare's characters also become convinced that humans are spun out of dreams, and that birth and death are best described as forms of sleep. Caliban, noting that "the isle is full of noises," and describing its "sounds and sweet airs," compares the experience to emerging out of a long sleep and longing to return—"that, when I waked,/I cried to dream again" (III.ii.130–31, 137–38). Hamlet, of course, makes much the same point when he equates dying with sleeping, and expresses fears about the dreams that come "when we have shuffled off this mortal coil" (III.i.69). But the question regarding what is real and what is dreamt—whether life is a collective illusion or a waking reality—is not just a question of epistemology. It has come to be the very basis of Shakespeare's metaphysic.

This metaphysic cannot easily be fixed as Christian or secular, Protestant or Catholic. It is Ariel, a pagan spirit, who will teach Prospero some Christian compassion, by remarking that she herself would have shown tenderness toward Prospero's enemies "were I human" (V.i.19). Prospero, feeling sheepish that an airy spirit can feel more mercy than a mortal, decides to show forgiveness too, noting that "the rarer action is/In virtue than in vengeance" (27–28). Commanding Ariel to release his enemies, he contrives an eclogue to "Ye elves of hills, brooks, standing lakes and groves" (33) that is nevertheless entirely pagan in its references, before abjuring his rough magic, breaking his staff, and drowning his book. In an epilogue, Prospero—many believe it is Shakespeare himself—addresses the audience directly, begging us to deliver him from his dream, as he delivered others, as we might wish to deliver ourselves.

A plea for freedom from dreams uttered by the man who dreamed our reality and transformed it forever into art.

Afterword

LANCING THE CANKER

This has been a book about a playwright's prejudices. But I hope it has also been a book about a playwright's insights, his largeness and generosity, his capacity to change his mind. In tracing six persistent issues throughout the body of Shakespeare's plays, I have tried to show that Shakespeare's prejudices are not hardened formulas frozen into place regardless of circumstances — Shakespeare's spirit is too open, too supple, for that. Nevertheless, they appear often enough and insistently enough to convince us that the poet held most of them personally, even if some eventually evolved into different forms of feeling and belief.

I realize that this will be the most controversial assumption in the book, especially since there is no conclusive way to prove it. Shakespeare has usually been regarded as one of the most elusive, personally unknowable writers who ever lived, the very embodiment of Keats's concept of "negative capability" in his capacity to remain "in uncertainties, Mysteries, doubts without any irritable reaching after fact & reason."

Matthew Arnold also famously said about Shakespeare's elusiveness:

> Others abide our question. Thou art free
> We ask and ask; thou smilest and art still,
> Out-topping knowledge.

Both remarks are true. It is also true that Shakespeare not only smiles but frowns sometimes, and that these scowl lines delineate the inner discontents of the man. Regardless of how impersonal a playwright may be, when a particular idea or character trait is repeated often enough, it suggests the possibility of a personal obsession. Chekhov, for example, is just as steeped in the negative capability as Shakespeare, and also resists our questions. But there is no doubt what he thought about vainglorious actresses and nerveless writers (in *The Seagull*), or about the deterioration of the environment (in *Uncle Vanya*), or about the destructive effect of a ruthless female termite on a noble family house (in *Three Sisters*), or about the necessity of combining beauty with utility (in *The Cherry Orchard*). Each of Chekhov's characters, like Shakespeare's, has a particular function determined by the needs of the text and the design of the action. But some of them, like Shakespeare's, also have a subtextual wormhole where the playwright's personal predilections sometimes wriggle through.

The word I have chosen to describe this compound of convictions, ideas, obsessions, attitudes, and opinions is *prejudices*. It is a strong word, suggesting strong feeling. But unlike some of the New Historicists, whose work I otherwise admire, I have tried not to impose modern judgments on older beliefs. Of course I realize that, because of my own prejudices, I have not always succeeded in this effort. As a Jew, I resent the generic villainy of Shylock. On the other hand, I am not a Jew who believes that *The Merchant of Venice* (not to mention *The Jew of Malta*) should be boycotted or banned unless the Jewish character is rehabilitated as a Holocaust victim. I also regret the pressure on black actors to refuse parts like Aaron the Moor (or the Emperor Jones) because such characters are considered insults to the race. For similar reasons, I have debated with the distinguished playwright August Wilson his demand that black actors should refuse to perform in plays written by whites, regardless of the nature of the character or the quality of the part, a prohibition that would have robbed us of some great Shakespearean performances. Actors of any race, class, or sex should be permitted to play characters of any other race, class, or sex, as long as they have the talent. The choices of theatre people as private citizens or political animals is one thing. But they also share a responsibility *as public artists* to advance a work of art, not just a moral, social, or political platform. And that is why I have tried my best to describe Shakespeare's prejudices without turning them into moral, social, or political combat zones.

Does Shakespeare evolve into our contemporary? Certainly, his sexual, racial, and political prejudices undergo varying degrees of change as his career progresses. But the biggest variation in Shakespeare's thinking is clearly in his religious beliefs. In the course of his writing life, he moves away from the orthodox values shared by most of his contemporaries toward a reluctant acceptance of the secular universe later embraced by the Enlightenment. Considering Shakespeare's darkening view of human nature, this must have been a very painful progress indeed. Evolving from unquestioning Christian piety to growing skepticism to a foreboding sense of universal injustice and indifference that sometimes borders on Manichaeism, Shakespeare ran the gamut of the religious opinion available in his day. His apparent capacity to contemplate a universe without God, without transcendence, without coherence, in such a pious time, was the act of a brave spirit, one more willing to challenge received opinion than has been assumed.

In short, Shakespeare prevails in spite of his prejudices, and sometimes because of them, since like all great artists he possessed a great soul. Dostoevsky survives for the same reason, despite his hatred of atheists and Jews, and so does Tolstoy, who despised meat-eaters and even William Shakespeare. Within the sometimes menacing world of Shakespeare's plays, there is always some room for humanity and grace. He may have shared the intolerant values of his age, but bigotry never hobbled him. And that is why it is fruitless to reject his contemporary attitudes without questioning our own, which will no doubt seem just as repellent, alien, and wrongheaded to some future generation. Only when the world is totally free of prejudices will we have the right to make fundamental judgments on Shakespeare's. Only when we have lanced our own hidden imposthumes can we perform radical surgery on his.

NOTES

Introduction

1. T. S. Eliot, "Tradition and the Individual Talent," in *The Sacred Wood* (London, 1920).
2. Lionel Trilling, "The Meaning of a Literary Idea," in *The Liberal Imagination* (New York, 1950).

1. Misogyny

1. Robert Pack, in *Willing to Choose*, even makes the interesting point that the interchangeable romantic couples in *A Midsummer Night's Dream* are not that different from the faithless quartet in Mozart's *Così fan tutte*.
2. Similarly, Elaine Showalter ("Representing Ophelia: Women, Madness, and the Responsibilities of Feminist Criticism," in *Shakespeare and the Question of Theory*, ed. Patricia Parker and Geoffrey Hartman [New York, 1985], 77–94) tries to rehabilitate Ophelia in feminist terms, treating her as a "study in sexual intimidation, a girl terrified of her father, of her lover, of life itself."
3. Garber, *Shakespeare After All*, 3–4.
4. Ibid., 588.
5. Ibid., 91.
6. Robert Greene will remember this phrase when referring to Shakespeare as a "tiger's heart wrapped in a player's hide" in *Greene's Groatsworth of Wit* (1592).
7. Garber, *Shakespeare After All*, 713.
8. James Shapiro devotes an entire book to this year in his recent *A Year in the Life of William Shakespeare: 1599.*
9. Much of this, of course, is traditional literary and religious misogyny, an inheritance from Juvenalian satire, Senecan drama (especially *Hippolytus* and *Medea*), and the Pauline strain of medieval teaching. In his sixth satire, for example, Juvenal rebukes women for their lust, ill-temper, vulgar tastes and passions, debauchery, loquacity, gaudy

apparel, painting, superstition, and treachery to their husbands. Anticipating Hamlet, Juvenal believes that only one maid in a million (and she a countrywoman) can be called pure, and that virgin is certain to be corrupted when she comes to the city. Elizabethan satirists are later to appropriate Juvenal's scathing satire as an antidote to the idealism of courtly amorists and their Platonic notions of courtly love.

10. In the same *ubi sunt* mood, Robert Rypon counseled women to keep their deaths continually in their thoughts: "If only such folk would call to mind how vile they were at the beginning, and how much viler they will be at their end, they would not boast so insanely of their . . . beauty" (quoted in Mason, "Satire on Women and Sex").

11. In Middleton's *A Mad World, My Masters* (1604), a character with the suggestive name of Sir Penitent Brothel exhorts a lecherous wife to virtue after a devil has appeared in her shape:

> What knows the lecher, when he clips his whore,
> Whether it be the devil his parts adore?
> They're both so like, that in our natural sense,
> I could discern no change nor difference.
> No marvel, then, times should so stretch and turn;
> None for religion, all for pleasure burn.
> Hot zeal into hot lust is now transformed;
> Grace into painting, charity into clothes;
> Faith into false hair, and put off as often . . . (IV.4)

12. As Robert Greene hinted about the opposite sex in his *Orlando Furioso* (c. 1591), women are "Borne to be plagues unto the thoughts of men, / Brought for eternal pestilence to the world." Virtue and constancy then, in the satiric view, were the result not of self-control but rather of absence of opportunity. As Marston wrote in *The Insatiate Countess* (c. 1609): "Faire women play: she's chaste whom none will have" (I.1).

13. In *Gargantua* (1534), Rabelais gives us a highly comic version of this sexual panic. Panurge greets a man who is carrying a three-year-old girl in front of him and a six-year-old in back. "I say," says the irrepressible Panurge, "are those girls virgins?" The man answers: "I can't vouch for the one in the back since I haven't been able to keep my eye on her. On the other hand, I've been watching the three-year-old in front since the day she was born—and I can't vouch for her either."

14. This is a typical couplet: "God bless my soul, why are poor women blamed, / Or by more faulty men so much defamed." Aemilia Lanyer

was a fierce defender of the female sex against insult and calumny, and despised those women who accepted their bad treatment without complaint.

15. It is certainly a quintessential example of sexual relations in the English court. The number of remarriages under Queen Elizabeth, and later King James, was proportionately as high as that in modern Hollywood society, so that one frequently needs the aid of a genealogical table to keep the relationships straight. To name but a few examples, Lady Hoby was successively married to Walter Devereux, Thomas Sidney, and Thomas Posthumous Hoby; Frances Walsingham was married first to Sir Philip Sidney and then to Robert Essex; Penelope Devereux was forced into marriage with Lord Rich but divorced him to marry Charles Blount; Frances Howard was married first to Robert Essex (the second earl) and then to Robert Carr; Lettice Knollys married first Essex (father of the first earl) and then Leicester. Or take Penelope Rich, who uncharacteristically remained in an unhappy marriage but for years carried on an affair with the Earl of Devonshire, bearing him five illegitimate children. In 1605 she scandalized the nation and even the court by marrying her lover while her husband was still alive. This is only a sampling of the deluge of remarriages that Elizabeth's father, Henry VIII, initiated with his own divorces, for the easier implementation of which he established the Church of England.

16. Compare sonnet 101: "Truth needs no color . . . beauty no pencil."

17. John Lyly, usually a defender of the court lady, was also an early critic of her abuse of fashion: "She is here acompted a slut that commeth not in her silkes, and she that hath not every fashion hath no man's favour" (*Euphues*, 1578).

18. Thomas Nashe complained in 1593 that women "theyr round Roseate buds immodestly lay foorth, to shew at theyr handes there is fruite to be hoped"; Stephen Gosson was repelled in 1595 by "these naked paps, the devils ginnes"; and in 1606 Barnabe Rich was still writing of women's "open breasts, their naked stomaches."

19. Moralists followed Montaigne in supposing that not just suggestive attire but clothes in general served primarily to excite desire in the opposite sex. Some, like Phillip Stubbes in his *Anatomy of Abuses* (1583), proposed a modified form of nudity as preferable to the provocative fashions then in vogue. Indeed, the fig-leaf simplicity of Adam and Eve was often invoked to remind us of a golden age before the explosion of sartorial pride and vanity.

20. *Paddling* seems to have had particularly lubricious associations for Shakespeare. Hamlet recoils from his mother because of Claudius's habit of "paddling in your neck with his damned fingers," and the image of "paddling palms and pinching fingers" poisons the mind of Leontes in *The Winter's Tale* as well.

21. Compare Jonathan Swift's scatological "The Lady's Dressing Room": "Celia, Celia, Celia . . . shits."

22. A. D. Nuttall in *Shakespeare the Thinker* suggests that Leontes' misogyny is motivated by homosexual feelings for Polixenes. (This Freudian writer also hints that Prospero's feelings for Miranda are "proprietary" or incestuous, in order to explain his aggressiveness toward Ferdinand.)

23. The fact that Shakespeare allows Mamillius to die in a play otherwise characterized by resurrections suggests that he may have still been mourning the death of his young son, Hamnet. Some critics speculate that Hamnet's death was also caused by "the dishonor of his mother."

24. The same silence greets the duke in *Measure for Measure* when he perfunctorily proposes marriage to Isabella.

25. In the modern rewriting of the myth of Hercules and Omphale by August Strindberg, *The Father,* Hercules' symbolic emasculation is reenacted once again by Adolphe in the present as it was by Antony in Roman times.

2. Effemiphobia

1. Shakespeare will follow Osric's example upon retirement and do some property speculation and rack-renting of his own.

2. Even in the Gravedigger scene, Hamlet finds occasion to comment on the flattering courtier "which could say 'Good morrow, sweet lord, how dost thou good lord?' and "lord such a one that praised my lord such a one's horse'" (V.i.76–78)

3. Hamlet's disdain for neologisms is odd, considering that Shakespeare himself added about three thousand words to the language.

4. The same sort of kinky relationship characterizes the friendship of Proteus and Valentine in *Two Gentleman of Verona*, when Proteus, to prove his love to his best friend, offers him the hand of his betrothed.

5. J. P. Wearing gives considerable space to this legend in his fictional autobiography *The Shakespeare's Diaries*.

6. Consider this exchange in *Haec-Vir*. After *Haec* criticizes the gender-

bending propensities of *Hic, Hic* retaliates by accusing *Haec* of copying female fashions both in dress—"our ruffes, our earrings, our busks ... not so much as the very Art of Painting, but you have so greedily ingrost it"—and behavior—"You have gone a world further, and even ravisht from us our speech, our actions, sports, recreations. ... Goodness leave me, if I have not heard a Man court his Mistris in the same words that *Venus* did *Adonis.*" The reference, of course, is to Shakespeare's popular narrative poem about an older goddess who seduces a younger mortal, and it reinforces the core of the rebuke about the reversal of sexual roles: women are chasing men. *Hic's* greatest criticism of *Haec* is that he has given up horsemanship, hung up his arms to rust, and glued his sword in its scabbard in order to entertain a dull, effeminate niceness, to "languish in the weak entertained sinne of womanish softnesse." This is precisely the complaint that Patroclus levels against Achilles.

Hic further argues that since *Haec* behaves like a woman, it is only natural for *Hic* to dress as a man in order to preserve those masculine qualities that he has forsaken. *Hic,* the masculine woman, generally finds *Haec,* the feminized man, at court, as do most satiric commentators of the time.

7. The anonymous pamphlet *Leicester's Commonwealth,* written in 1584, charged Elizabeth's then favorite, the earl of Leicester, with the same Machiavellian crimes.

8. And yet the Castiglione ideal had appeal only for those at court. The middle-class satirists, and presumably most citizens, were extremely skeptical, if not openly hostile, toward such a formulation. In England, unlike Italy, the courtier *as courtier* had never been a folk hero. Only when he laid down his courtly trappings and donned a helmet and buckler did he fire the popular imagination, as Patroclus suggests in his rebuke of Achilles. Nashe, for example, in *The Anatomie of Absurditie* (1588) rejects most of Castiglione's precepts as "effeminate follies," allowing "that the only adjuncts of a Courtier were schollership and courage." Indeed, the English satirists found all of Castiglione's civic virtues to be either foolish, evil, or lascivious when put into practice. Courtly conversation or "discoursing" they viewed as affected verbal games, dancing and masqueing as precursors to seduction, courtly greeting as insincere bowing and scraping, and Platonic love as a polite name for adultery.

9. Thomas Nashe (in *Pierce Pennilesse*) is only one of a number who seems to be describing Hotspur's pouncet-box lord when he writes

about such a Castilio: "All malcontent sits the greasie son of a Cloathier, & complaines (like a decaied Earle) of the ruine of ancient houses. . . . All *Italianate* is his talke, & his spade peake is as sharpe as if he had been a Pioner before the walls of *Roam*. . . . If he be challenged to fight, for his delatorye excuses, he objects that it is not the custome of the Spaniard or the Germaine, to look back to every dog that barks." He might be describing Falstaff or Pistol or Parolles or any braggart soldier pretending to a valor he does not possess. In *Christs Teares Over Jerusalem* (1593), Nashe found it "scandalous and shamefull" that the true nobility, having wasted their substance on gorgeous attire, should lose their stately palaces to upstarts who imported foreign fashions for the express purpose of ruining the aristocracy.

10. Although English court speech had become extremely artificial, it was hardly accurate to put the entire blame on Castiglione. John Lyly alone had done more than any Italian to change the speaking style of the courtier through his invention of "Euphuism"—a style Shakespeare was hardly reluctant to exploit in such plays as *Love's Labor's Lost*. In the ornamental symmetry of his writing, and his overuse of antitheses, rhetorical questions, alliteration, and repetition, Lyly had exercised an enormous influence on both conversational and literary endeavor around the court.

11. Even the normally tolerant John Donne was highly critical of that mode of speech called courtly complement, as illustrated in this 1593 satire on a foppish courtier:

> Yet I must be content
> With his tongue, in his tongue call'd complement:
> In which he can win widdoes, and pay scores,
> Make men speak treason, cosen subtlest whores,
> Out-flatter favorites, or outlie either
> Jovius, or Surius, or both together.

12. It was also becoming known for James's attraction to younger men, such as the earl of Somerset, Robert Carr, and the duke of Buckingham, George Villiers. In a 1606 letter to Sir John Harington, Elizabeth's godson, Sir Thomas Howard writes that Harington should not bother to come to court unless he is willing to flatter Carr, then the current favorite: "Robert Carr is now most likely to win the King's affection. The young man doth study much art and device; he hath changed his tailors and tiremen many times, and all to please the

Prince. . . . The King is nicely heedful of such points and dwelleth on good looks and handsome acoutrements. . . . I will advise one thing: the Roan jennet whereon the Kind rideth every day, must not be forgotten to be praised. . . . Will you say the moon shineth all summer? That the starrs are bright jewels for Carr's ears? That the Roan jennet surpasseth Bucephalus, and is worthy to be ridden by Alexander? That his eyes are fire, his tail is Berenices locks, and a few such fancies worth your noticing?" In describing James, he might be describing the Dauphin in *Henry V,* who demands that nobles praise his armor and his horse — an animal he also has difficulty distinguishing from his mistress.

13. Ben Jonson, in *Sejanus* (1603), adapted Latin sources to modern satiric opinion in describing two Machiavellian dissemblers who employ flattery for their baser purposes:

> These can lye,
> Flatter, and sweare, forsweare, deprave, informe,
> Smile, and betray. . . .
> Laugh, when their patron laughs, sweat, when he
>   sweates;
> Be hot and cold with him; change every moode
> . . . ready to praise
> His lordship, if he spit, or but pisse faire.

Or, as Hamlet more succinctly put it, thinking of Claudius, a man "may smile and smile and be a villain" (I.v.109). John Marston (partly Italian himself) seems to be describing the same such dissembler when he writes about

> a courteous-minded man
> . . . a damn'd Machiavellian
> Holds candle to the devil for a while,
> That he better may the world beguile,
> That's fed with shows.

Possessed with the knowledge that the court is attracted only to "shows" or appearances, this kind of courtier hides his true design behind a false seeming.

14. Joseph Hall cited the same thing in his *Collected Poems* (1597): "A French head joined to necke Italian; Thy thighs from Germanie, and brest from Spaine: An Englishman in none, a foole in all."

15. Once again, this habit of overdressing suggested a reversal of degree

and confusion, not just of classes but of sexes. Barnabe Rich wrote in 1581 of walking down the Strand one day and encountering a person riding a "Footcloth nagge, apparelled in a French ruffe, a French cloake, a French hose, and in his hand a great fanne of Feathers, bearing them up (verie womanly) against the side of his face," and of mistaking this shameless hussy for a woman—until seeing his beard. A few years later, in 1592, Robert Greene was accusing the Italianate courtier of having imported from Italy women's trinkets and clothes for the use of men. In his *Farewell to Folly* (1591) he reminds his contemporaries at court that "Sardanapalus was thrust from his empire, for that he was a little effeminate, and we strive to be counted womanish, by keeping of beautie, by curling the haire, by wearing plumes of feathers in our hands, which in warres our ancestors wore on their heads, they feared of men, we to be favored of women."

16. As G. Rattray Taylor has observed in *Sex in History*, the fear of homosexuality was historically the greatest source of panic in northern countries dominated by the Puritan ethos—the masculine-driven culture that Taylor calls "patrist." By contrast, according to Taylor, the greatest fear in southern Catholic, or "matrist," countries, which idealized the mother (and worshiped the Virgin Mother), was the idea of incest.

17. I am thinking particularly of a 1953 production of *Midsummer* at Theatre on the Green in Wellesley, where the erotic relationships between Oberon, Titania, and their various wards were made quite explicit.

18.   What, though Jove dallied,
         During thy wars, in fair Alcmena's bed,
         Yet Hercules, true born, that imbecility
         Of corrupt nature . . .
         [Did] vow himself a slave to Omphale
         Puling "Aye me!" O valour's obloquy!
         He that the inmost nooks of hell did know
         Whose ne'er-crazed prowess all did overthrow,
         Lies streaking brawny limbs in weak'ning bed;
         Perfumed, smooth-kembed, new glazed, fair surphuled.

19. The obvious biblical parallel is with Samson and Delilah.

20. Why did Elizabethans, in marked contrast, say, with American antiwar protestors, prefer the iron blasts of war over the modest stillness of peace? One reason is that too much leisure was assumed to lead directly to vice. Edward Guilpin in his *Skialetheia* (1598) satirized "My

Lord" for his lounging, for his uselessness, and for his luxury, naming
him Gnatho after the parasite in Terence's *Eunuchus:*

> My Lord most court-like lyes in bed till noone
> Then all high-stomackt riseth to his dinner,
> Falls straight to Dice, before his meete be downe,
> Or to disgest, walks to some female sinner.

By awakening at night and going to sleep at dawn, such courtiers
were believed to have reversed the normal pattern of life, thus breaking the laws of Nature and the laws of God.

21. See, for example, Philip Stubbes in *The Anatomy of Abuses* (1583).

22. A few years after *Hamlet* and *Othello* were first staged, the plain-
dealing Sir John Harington, writing in 1606 to Mr. Secretary Bar-
low of a visit of the Danish king to James's court, might have been
describing a debauch at Elsinore: "I think the Dane hath strangely
wrought on our good English nobles, for those, whom I never could
get to taste liquor, now follow the fashion and wallow in beastly
delights. The Ladies abandon their sobriety, and are seen to roll about
in intoxication. . . . I do often say (but not aloud) that the Danes have
again conquered the Britains, for I see no man, or woman either, that
can command himself or herself. I wish I was at home." And lest we
conclude that inebriation was purely a vice of the later Jacobean aristocracy, John Florio, writing in 1591 (in *Second Fruites*) of the Elizabethan period, reported that the excess of drunkenness was likely to
"kill more men in England than any infirmitie else."

23. The harshness of the satirists toward the courtly amorist was the
result of a prejudice at once moralistic and skeptical. The idealism
implicit in the conventions of courtly or chivalric love—popular in
England since the fourteenth century—never took root among the
middle classes of England as it did in France and Italy. Even Edmund
Spenser, despite his theoretical approval of Platonic love, always
deplored what he perceived to be the gap between the ways love was
practiced among chaste and innocent shepherds and by seducers
at the profligate court: "For with lewd speeches, and licentious
deeds,/[Love's] mightie mysteries they do prophane." For Spenser,
lovemaking at the court was merely a refined form of seduction, the
itchings of a lecher for a coy wanton.

24. Today, half a century after seeing Katharine Hepburn on stage as
Rosalind in *As You Like It*, I can still smell that burning campfire and
hear those twittering birds. It was one of the few indoor productions

of the play that tried to reproduce the wholesome environment of the countryside.

25. Sir Andrew also has linguistic affectations, along with considerable cowardice, befitting one "on carpet consideration" (IV.iii).

3. Machismo

1. Sir John Harington, whom I liberally quote throughout this book, is perhaps the best example I know of the old-fashioned Elizabethan plain-dealer. Jaundiced letters to and from him and other courtiers are collected in a miscellany called *Nugae Antiquae.*

2. A few decades later, Nicholas Breton, in *The Court and the Country* (1618), is still mounting this familiar attack on the courtier, through the mouth of a plain-dealing rustic who charges him with all the familiar failings. The countryman reminds the courtier that he has laid waste his father's land through his own extravagance. In contrast to the courtier's love of "rich Apparell, precious Jewells . . . Princely coaches, stately horses, royall Buildings, and rare Architecture," Breton praises the virtues of the country, where "wee exercise the body in plaine dealing, and not the braine in subtile device." He continues: "For kissing of the hand, as if hee were licking of his fingers, bending downe his head, as if his neck were out of joynt; or scratching by the foote, as if he were a Corne-cutter; or leering aside, like a wench after her sweet-hearte . . . for swearing and braving, scoffing and stabbing, with such tricks of the divels teaching, we allow none of that learning here."

3. Middle-class city dwellers themselves, the English satirists assumed the role of "rusticall and naked Sylvanes" (William Rankins), sometimes even pretending to live in the woods or in the scholar's cave, composing their satires in seclusion and melancholy. Rankins, in the induction to his *Seven Satires* (1599), for example, writes of leaving the quiet of the country in order to view the human condition: "My shaggy Satyres doe forsake the woods. . . . To view the manner of this humane strife."

4. In that gold mine of contemporary reference the anonymous *Parnassus Plays* (1598–1601), the reader finds scholars expressing familiar complaints against the inequity and effeminacy of court life: "Schollers unregarded walke / Like threed bare impecunious animals / While servinge men doe swagger it in silke." As a result, the hero, Philomusus (whose name means lover of the Muse) appears in

London wearing a "blacke frise coat," highlighting with his modest attire the extravagance of upstarts. Amoretto, on the other hand, makes his living off upstart courtiers, writing love poems in the manner of *Venus and Adonis*—which earns him, along with his model, Shakespeare, a reputation for lewdness. For his part, Amoretto dismisses the scholar, using the courtier's contemptuous arguments: "He is one that cannot make a good legge, one that cannot eate a messe of broth cleanly, one that cannot ride a horse without spur-galling, one that cannot salute a woman, and look on her directly." These negative comments are, of course, among the highest compliments a plain-dealer can receive.

5. In one of these letters, written in 1603, the crookback Robert Cecil, formerly the queen's faithful minister, observes the disappearance of honest plain-dealing counselors from court with a mixture of astonishment and disgust. Writing to Harington, now aging and infirm, Cecil says: "Farewel, good knight; but never come neare London till I call you. Too much crowdinge doth not well for a cripple, and the Kynge doth find scante room to sit himself, he hath so many friends as they chuse to be called, and Heaven prove they lye not in the ende."

When Harington found his way back to the new English court that year, he confirmed Cecil's anxieties in a letter of his own to Lord Thomas Howard: "Manie have been the mad caps rejoicing at oure newe Kynges cominge, and who in good trothe darede not have set for the their good affection to him a monthe or two agoe; but alas! What availeth truthe, where profite is in queste? . . . A new Kynge will have soldiers, and God knowethe what men they will be. One saith he will serve him by daie, another by nighte; the women who love to talke as they lyke are for servynge him bothe daye and nyghte. . . . But I am a cripple, and not made for sportes in new Courtes."

Harington proceeds to talk, in his wry mordant way, about the king's new favorite, Sir Robert Carr, who may also have been James's homosexual lover: "St. Paul hath saide, that the race is not alwaie givene to the swifte. I doubte Sir Robert will give the Sainte the lie, for he is like to get both race and prize, and, as fame goeth, creepeth not a little into favoure." Harington's disaffection reminds us of Hamlet's grumbling about the rise of men like Osric at the court of Claudius, and of Kent's preparing to trip up Oswald by the heels.

6. Chapman's eponymous hero Bussy D'Ambois, Beaumont and Fletcher's Mardonius (in *A King and No King*) and Melantius (in *The*

Maid's Tragedy), Webster's Bosola (in *The Duchess of Malfi*), among others, are typical of the military truth tellers who wear the satirist's angry mantle.

7. Polonius's full account of his acting career is this: "I did enact Julius Caesar: I was killed i' the Capitol; Brutus killed me" (III.ii.93–94). Shakespeare is not only looking backward to a recent play of his, he is looking forward to Hamlet's killing of Polonius "i' the Capitol" of Denmark.

8. Indeed, in Ingmar Bergman's 1988 production, Fortinbras bids his jackbooted soldiers shoot Horatio, and everyone else left alive in the court, throwing the bodies in a pit, and ending the play with a deafening volley of machine-gun fire. It is a terrifying forecast of modern totalitarianism.

9. An earlier example of the Iago type is Cassius in *Julius Caesar.* Apart from pretending to be a blunt, honest man, one who plays on the gullible Brutus in the same way that Iago manipulates Othello, Cassius shares the conviction of Iago that human actions are hardly guided by transcendent powers: "The fault, dear Brutus, is not in our stars / But in ourselves, that we are underlings" (I.ii.141–42). Later, in *King Lear,* Edmund will come to similar conclusions about the irrelevancy of the stars in relation to behavior.

10. One of the few places where I find myself in disagreement with Marjorie Garber's excellent analysis of *Othello* is in her assertion that Iago doesn't believe in external reputation. That is all this dissembler does seem to believe in.

11. In sonnet 121, oddly enough, Shakespeare seems to endorse this Machiavellian notion when he writes: "'Tis better to be vile than vile esteemed." This is strange coming from the poet who always seems to prefer reality over appearances.

12. In the 2004 Jonathan Miller production of the play, starring Christopher Plummer as Lear, Cordelia was played as if she were Cinderella, and Goneril and Regan as if they were her evil stepsisters. This approach emphasized the fairy tale roots of a play that Miller has always oddly viewed as a comedy: his ideal Lear, he has often said, would have been Jack Lemmon!

13. This remark puts Volumnia in a class with Shakespeare's other masculine women who depreciate the manliness of their menfolk: Lady Macbeth, Goneril, etc.

4. Elitism and Mobocracy

1. *The War of the Roses* was Peter Hall's name for this tetralogy when he produced it at the Royal Shakespeare Company in 1963. When his son Edward staged it forty years later with the Chicago Shakespeare Company, he called it *Rose Rage.*

2. Meeting Sir John Harington, James was interested mainly in enlisting the knight's support for his opinions about witchcraft. The king asked Sir John, for example, why Satan preferred ancient women in his employ. Harington replied, with a trace of the wryness for which he was famous, that Scripture had taught the Devil to walk in dry places.

3. When their efforts were thwarted in England following the Restoration of Charles II, they came to America in 1660 and later helped establish democracy here.

4. The prevalence of this sort of thing led Frank Harris to describe Shakespeare (inaccurately) as a "snob."

5. Actually, Barack Obama began on a similar principle before repudiating the use of public funds.

6. Three centuries later, Henrik Ibsen will make this phrase, "An Enemy of the People," the title of his own satire on representative democracy and inauthentic idealism.

7. L. C. Knights, "How Many Children Had Lady Macbeth?" in *Explorations: Essays in Criticism, Mainly on the Literature of the Seventeenth Century* (New York: New York University Press, 1964), 15–54.

8. Compare the separation of Alonso and Ferdinand in this play, as a result of Prospero's manufactured tempest, with that of Viola and Sebastian in *Twelfth Night* and Pericles and Marina in *Pericles.* There is also a significant tempest in *Othello* that sinks the entire Turkish fleet. It is possible that Shakespeare may have suffered some sort of family loss at sea since he harps so much on this theme.

9. Actually, Shakespeare stole the speech almost intact from Montaigne's account of the New World, where the French philosopher offered a vision of an ideal nation, one "That no kind of traffic, no knowledge of letters, no intelligence of numbers, no name of magistrate, not of political superiority, no use of service, of riches, or of poverty; no contracts, no successions, no partitions, no occupation but idle; no respect for kindred but common, no apparel but natural, no manuring of lands, no use of wine, corn, or metal." In short, Gonzalo's Utopia.

5. Racialism

1. Shakespeare remembered this character even as late as *The Tempest*. In his slavish loyalty to Barabas, Ithamore sounds sometimes like Caliban fawning on Stephano ("Oh brave, master, I worship your nose for this"). He also resembles Caliban when right before his death he expresses his desire to his executioners "to torment you with my bitter tongue."

2.   Sweet Helen, make me immortal with a kiss
           Her lips suck forth my soul; see where it flies!—
           Come, Helen, come, give me my soul again.
           Here will I dwell, for Heaven is in these lips.
                   (*Doctor Faustus,* scene XIII)

3. Hamlet also makes invidious comparisons between the fair and the dark when he inveighs against Gertrude for supplanting his father with his uncle, "Could you on this fair mountain leave to feed, / And batten on this moor!" (III.iv.65–66) The comparison is topographical (mountain and moor) but the double entendre (moor and Moor) suggests a contrast in color as well.

4. Barabas is obviously named after the criminal in Scripture (Barabbas) whom the Jews asked Pilate to pardon instead of Jesus.

5. In 2006 F. Murray Abraham played Shylock and Barabas back to back in productions by the Theatre for a New Audience that demonstrated the villainous and comic kinship between these two characters.

6. Some centuries later, Strindberg, in *The Father,* will quote this speech in its entirety, substituting the word *man* for *Jew,* in his effort to demonstrate that, under feminism, the new oppressed minority was the male of the species.

7. The only modern actors I know, aside from F. Murray Abraham and Will Lebow, who didn't go for easy sympathy in the role of Shylock were George C. Scott in a rasping performance at Joseph Papp's Shakespeare Theatre in Central Park in the sixties, and Ron Leibman giving us a snarling Shylock thirty years later in the same venue.

8. Oscar Wilde must have been hearing these words in his head when, in "The Ballad of Reading Gaol," he wrote that "each man kills the thing he loves."

9. Compare Rufio in Shaw's *Caesar and Cleopatra,* who, although a general in his army, is also Caesar's slave, a role that brings him much more satisfaction.

10. Sycorax would seem to be another attempt to indulge King James's belief in witchcraft.

11. In describing Miranda to Stefano, he again harps on her procreative capacities: "She will become thy bed, I warrant, / And bring thee forth brave brood" (III.ii.99–100).

12. *Henry VIII* is now generally assumed to be Shakespeare's last play, written in collaboration with John Fletcher. But there is no reason to doubt that *The Tempest* was partly intended to be his spoken farewell to the stage. In Prospero's celebrated speech abjuring his magic, he speaks like a writer giving up his pen: "And deeper than did ever plummet sound / I'll drown my book" (V.i.56–57). Curiously enough, Alonso uses pretty much the same phrase ("I'll seek him deeper than e'er plummet sounded" [III.iii.101]) in describing his search for Ferdinand.

6. Intelligent Design

1. It can also be seen in the roils shaking the houses of York and Lancaster in *Henry VI,* where father and son meet in battle and kill each other.

2. The same doubts, compounded by Darwinism, led to the invention of such concepts as Creationism and Intelligent Design.

3. He often hints to her about such things as "A fever, longing still for that which nurseth the disease."

4. In the Tyrone Guthrie production, he was a photographer on the battlefield, which is to say a reporter nauseated by battle.

5. Therisites expands on these images in act V, scene i, in a veritable glossary of infection: "Now the rotten diseases of the south, the guts-griping, ruptures, loads o' gravel in the back, lethargies, cold palsies, raw eyes, dirt-rotten livers, wheezing lungs, bladders full of impostume, sciaticas, lime-kilns i'th' palm, incurable bone-ache, and the rivelled fee-simple of the tetter, take and take again such preposterous discoveries" (19.1–8). The association with venereal disease is palpable.

6. In his intriguing book *Willing to Choose,* Robert Pack correctly contrasts this reflective nature in *Macbeth* with its impersonal and indifferent function in *Lear.*

7. We have already seen that, in his act II exchange with Desdemona awaiting Othello's return, Iago plays the part of a traditional Shakespearean courtier-wit, trading barbs with Desdemona on the sub-

ject of womankind. Iago is often convivial in the company of other characters, but this is the one time he comes off to the reader and the spectator as a genuinely entertaining wag, paradoxically while playing the part of a misogynistic "carping critic."

8. No wonder Lear calls mad Tom "a learned Theban," a "philosopher." (III.iv.145). The mad are wiser than the sane.

9. The painfulness of this play accounts for the fact that *Lear* was performed for 150 years with an "improved" happy ending written by the seventeenth-century playwright Nahum Tate, in which Lear returns to life and Cordelia survives to marry Edgar. For most of its history, the play has proved too tough for audiences to take.

10. John Marston's view in *The Malcontent* is even grimmer; there he calls earth "a very muck-heap on which the sub-lunary orbs cast their excrement."

11. It should be noted, however, how fond Shakespeare seems to have been of the resurrection device, of bringing back to life putatively dead wives and daughters—Hermione and Perdita in *The Winter's Tale,* Thaisa and Marina in *Pericles,* and Imogen in *Cymbeline,* among others.

12. Hymen also presides over the marriages of all the lovers in *As You Like It.* In Andrei Belgrader's ART production, she descended from on high wearing multiple pairs of breasts and a headdress composed of phalluses, as a kind of floating embodiment of the marriage night.

Selected Bibliography

All citations of the works of Shakespeare are from *The Norton Shakespeare,* 2nd ed., ed. Stephen Greenblatt (New York: Norton, 2008).

Ackroyd, Peter. *Shakespeare: The Biography.* New York, 2005.

Akrigg, G. P. V. *Shakespeare and the Earl of Southampton.* London, 1968.

Allen, Don Cameron. "The Degeneration of Man and Renaissance Pessimism." *Studies in Philology* 35 (1938), 202–27.

Allen, Morse. *The Satire of John Martson.* Columbus, Ohio, 1920.

Alvis, John, and Thomas G. West, eds. *Shakespeare as Political Thinker.* Durham, N.C., 1981.

Armstrong, W. A. "The Elizabethan Conception of the Tyrant." *Review of English Studies* 22 (1946), 161–81.

———. "The Influence of Seneca and Machiavelli on the Elizabethan Tyrant." *Review of English Studies* 24 (1948), 19–35.

Babb, Lawrence. *The Elizabethan Malady: A Study of Melancholia in English Literature from 1580 to 1642.* East Lansing, Mich., 1951.

Barnes, Barnabe. *The Devil's Charter.* 1607; London, 1913.

Beaumont, Francis, and John Fletcher. *The Works of Francis Beaumont and John Fletcher.* Ed. Arnold Glover and A. R. Waller, 10 vols. Cambridge, 1905–12.

Birch, Thomas. *The Court and Times of James the First.* 2 vols. London, 1848.

Black, J. B. *The Reign of Elizabeth, 1558–1603.* Oxford, 1937.

Bloom, Allan, with Harry V. Jaffa. *Shakespeare's Politics.* Chicago, 1964.

Bloom, Harold. *Shakespeare: The Invention of the Human.* New Haven, 1998.

Bogard, Travis. *The Tragic Satire of John Webster.* Berkeley, 1955.

Bowers, Fredson Thayer. "The Audience and the Revenger of Elizabethan Tragedy." *Studies in Philology* 31 (1934), 160–75.

———. *Elizabethan Revenge Tragedy, 1587–1643.* Princeton, 1940.

Boyer, Clarence V. *The Villain as Hero in Elizabethan Tragedy.* London, 1914.

Bradbrook, M. C. *Themes and Conventions of Elizabethan Tragedy.* Cambridge, 1952.

Braithwaite, Richard. *The English Gentleman.* London, 1613.

———. *The English Gentlewoman.* London, 1631.

Breton, Nicholas. *No Whippinge, nor Trippinge; but a kinde friendly Snippinge.* Ed. Charles Edmonds. 1601; London, 1895.

———. *The Courtier and the Countryman.* In *Unedited Tracts,* ed. W. C. Hazlitt. 1618; London, 1868.

Brustein, Robert. "Italianate Court Satire and the Plays of John Marston." Ph.D. diss., Columbia University, 1957.

Burton, Robert. *The Anatomy of Melancholy.* London, 1867.

Calvin, John. *Institutes of the Christian Religion.* Trans. Henry Beveridge, 3 vols. Edinburgh, 1845.

Camden, Carroll. *The Elizabethan Woman.* New York, 1952.

Campbell, Oscar James. *Comicall Satyre and Shakespeare's Troilus and Cressida.* San Marino, Calif., 1938.

———. *Shakespeare's Satire.* New York, 1943.

———. *The Living Shakespeare: Twenty-two Plays and the Sonnets.* New York, 1949.

Cartwright, Julia. *The Perfect Courtier: Baldassare Castiglione, 1478–1529.* 2 vols. New York, 1927.

Castiglione, Baldassare. *The Book of the Courtier.* Trans. Thomas Hoby (1561). London, 1900.

Chamberlain, John. *The Letters of John Chamberlain.* Ed. Norman Egbert McClure, 2 vols. Philadelphia, 1939.

Charney, Maurice. *Shakespeare on Love and Lust.* New York, 2000.

Coke, Roger. *A Detection of the Court and State During the Last Four Reignes and the Inter-regnum.* London, 1696.

Cyvile and Uncyvile Life; or, The English Courtier, and the Cuntrey-Gentleman. In *Inedited Tracts,* ed. William Hazlitt. 1579; London 1868.

Dalrymple, Theodore. *In Praise of Prejudice: The Necessity of Preconceived Ideas.* London 2007.

Donne, John. *Paradoxes and Problems.* Ed. Geoffrey Keynes. London, 1923.

———. *The Poems.* Ed. Herbert J. Grierson. London, 1929.

———. *The Courtier's Library; or, Catalogus Librorum Aulicorum.* Ed. Evelyn Mary Simpson. London, 1930.

Duncan-Jones, Katherine. *Ungentle Shakespeare: Scenes from His Life.* London, 2001.

Eastman, A. M., and G. B. Harrison, eds. *Shakespeare's Critics: From Jonson to Auden, a Medley of Judgments.* Ann Arbor, Mich., 1964.

Einstein, Lewis. *The Italian Renaissance in England.* New York, 1902.

Eliot, T. S. *Elizabethan Essays.* London, 1934.

Ellis-Fermor, U. M. *The Jacobean Drama: An Interpretation.* London, 1936.

Farnham, Willard. *Shakespeare's Tragic Frontier: The World of His Final Tragedies.* Berkeley, 1950.

File, N., and C. Power. *Black Settlers in Britain, 1555–1958.* London, 1981.

Fryer, P. *Staying Power: The History of Black People in Britain.* London, 1984.

Garber, Marjorie. *Vested Interests: Cross-Dressing and Cultural Anxiety.* New York, 1997.

———. *Shakespeare After All.* New York, 2004.

Gardiner, Samuel Rawson. *History of England from the Accession of James I to the Disgrace of Chief Justice Coke, 1603–1616.* 2 vols. London, 1863.

Gentillet, Innocent. *A Discourse upon the Meanes of Wel Governing and Maintaining in Good Peace, a Kingdome, or other principalite, Against Nicholas Machiavel the Florentine.* Trans. Simon Patericke (1577). London, 1602.

Gosson, Stephen. *Pleasant Quippes for Upstart Newfangled Gentlewomen; or, A Glasse to Viewe the Pride of Vaineglorious Women.* 1595; London, 1841.

Greenblatt, Stephen. *Hamlet in Purgatory.* Princeton, 2001.

———. *Will in the World: How Shakespeare Became Shakespeare.* New York, 2004.

———. "Shakespeare and the Uses of Power." *New York Review of Books,* April 12, 2007, pp. 75–82.

Greene, Robert. *A Quip for an Upstart Courtier.* In *The Old Book Collector's Miscellany,* vol. 1. 1592; London 1871.

Greer, Germaine. *Shakespeare's Wife.* New York 2008.

Guilpin, Everard. *Skialetheia; or, a Shadowe of Truth.* 1598; London, 1931.

Haec-Vir; or, The Womanish Man: Being an Answere to a late Booke intituled Hic-Mulier. London, 1620.

Hake, Edward. *News out of Powles Churchyarde.* (Ed. Charles Edmonds. 1579; London, 1872.

Hall, Joseph. *The Collected Poems.* Ed. A. Davenport. Liverpool, 1949.

Harington, Sir John. *Nugae Antiquae.* 2 vols. London 1769–75.

———. *The Letters and Epigrams.* Ed. Norman Egbert McClure. Philadelphia, 1930.

Harvey, Gabriel. *Three Proper and Wittie Familiar Letters*. In *Works*, ed. Alexander B. Grosart, 3 vols. 1580; London, 1884-85, 1: 29-150.

Hic-Mulier; or, The Man-Woman: *Being a Medecine to cure the Coltish Disease of the Staggers in the Masculine-Feminines of Our Times*. London, 1620.

Hunt, Marvin W. *Looking for Hamlet*. New York, 2007.

Jonson, Ben. *Ben Jonson*. Ed. C. H. Herford and Percy Simpson, 11 vols. Oxford, 1925-50.

Juvenal. *Juvenal and Persius*. Ed. M. Madan, 2 vols. Oxford, 1839.

Kelso, Ruth. *The Doctrine of the English Gentleman in the Sixteenth Century*. Urbana, Ill., 1929.

Knights, L. C. *Drama and Society in the Age of Jonson*. London, 1937.

Knox, John. *The First Blast of the Trumpet Agaist the Monstruous Regiment of Women*. In *The Works of John Knox*, ed. David Laing, 6 vols. 1558; Edinburgh, 1864, 4: 351-422.

Kujoory, Parvin. Shakespeare and Minorities: *An Annotated Bibliography, 1970-2000*. Lanham, Md., 2001.

Landa, M. J. *The Jew in Drama*. London, 1926.

Leishman, J. B., ed. *The Three Parnassus Plays, 1598-1601*. London, 1949.

Leycesters Commonwealth. Ed. Frank J. Burgoyne. 1584; London, 1904.

Lovejoy, Arthur O. *The Great Chain of Being: A Study of the History of an Idea*. Harvard, 1936.

Lyly, John. *The Complete Works of John Lyly*. Ed. R. Warwick Bond, 3 vols. Oxford, 1902.

Machiavelli, Niccolo. *Works*, including *The Art of War*, trans. Peter Whitehorne (1560); *The Prince*, trans. Ed Davies (1640); and *The Florentine Historie*, trans. Thomas Beddingfeld (1595). Ed. W. E. Henley. 2 vols. London, 1905.

Marlowe, Christopher. *The Works of Christopher Marlowe*. Ed. C. F. Tucker Brooke. Oxford, 1953.

Marston, John. *The Scourge of Villainie*. Ed. G. B. Harrison. 1599; London, 1925.

———. *The Works of John Marston*. Ed. A. H. Bullen, 3 vols. Boston, 1887.

———. *The Plays of John Marston*. Ed H. Harvey Wood, 3 vols., London, 1934.

Mason, Eudo C. "Satire on Women and Sex in Elizabethan Tragedy." *English Studies* 31 (1950), 1-10.

Middleton, Thomas, and Thomas Dekker. *The Roaring Girl; or, Moll Cutpurse*, ed. Coppélia Kahn. Pp. 721-78 in *Thomas Middleton: The Collected Works*, ed. Gary Taylor and John Lavagnino. Oxford, 2007.

Montaigne, Michel de. *Essayes*. Trans. John Florio (1603), 3 vols. London, 1910.

Nashe, Thomas. *The Works*. Ed. R. B. McKerrow, 5 vols. London, 1904–10.

Nisbet, Robert. *Prejudices: A Philosophical Dictionary*. Cambridge, Mass., 1982.

Nuttall, A. D. *Shakespeare the Thinker*. New Haven, 2007.

Osborne, Francis. *Historical Memoires on the Reigns of Queen Elizabeth and King James*. London, 1658.

Pack, Robert. *Willing to Choose: Volition and Storytelling in Shakespeare's Major Plays*. Sandpoint, Idaho, 2007.

Peyton, Sir Edward. *The Divine Catastrophe of the Kingly Family of the House of Stuarts*. London, 1652.

Rankins, William. *Seven Satires*. Ed. A. Davenport. 1598; London, 1948.

Rich, Barnabe. *Faultes Faults, and Nothing Else but Faultes*. London, 1606.

———. *Rich His Farewell to Militarie Profession*. London, 1606.

Rosenbaum, Ron. *The Shakespeare Wars*. New York, 2000.

Shakespeare, William. *The Norton Shakespeare*. Ed. Stephen Greenblatt, Wallace Cohen, Jean E. Howard, and Katharine Eisaman Maus. New York, 1997.

Shapiro, James. *Shakespeare and the Jews*. New York, 1996.

———. *A Year in the Life of William Shakespeare: 1599*. London, 2005.

Sidney, Sir Philip. "Dispraise of a Courtly Life." In *A Poetical Rhapsody, 1602–1621*, ed. Hyder Rollins. Cambridge, Mass., 1931, 9–12.

Simonds d'Ewes, Sir. *The Secret History of the Reign of King James I*. In *The Autobiography and Correspondence of Sir Simonds D'Ewes*, ed. J. O. Halliwell-Phillips, 2 vols. London, 1845, 1: 319–411.

Spencer, Theodore. "John Marston," *Criterion* 13 (1934), 581–99.

———. *Death and Elizabethan Tragedy: A Study of Conventions and Opinions in the Elizabethan Drama*. Cambridge, Mass., 1936.

Stoll, Elmer Edgar. "Shakspere, Marston, and the Malcontent Type," *Modern Philology* 3 (1906), 281–303.

Taylor, Gordon Rattray. *Sex in History*. New York, 1954.

Tillyard. E. M. W. *The Elizabethan World Picture*. New York, 1960.

Tourneur, Cyril. *The Plays and Poems of Cyril Tourneur*. Ed. John Churton Collins, 2 vols. London, 1878.

Vendler, Helen. *The Art of Shakespeare's Sonnets*. Cambridge, Mass., 1999.

Waith, Eugene. *The Pattern of Tragicomedy in Beaumont and Fletcher*. New Haven, 1952.

Wearing, J. P. *The Shakespeare Diaries: A Fictional Autobiography*. Santa Monica, Calif., 2007.

Webster, John. *The Complete Works.* Ed. F. L. Lucas, 4 vols. London, 1927.

Weldon, Sir Anthony, *The Court and Character of King James.* London, 1650.

Whitmore, Charles Edward. *The Supernatural in Tragedy.* Cambridge, Mass., 1915.

Wilson, Arthur. *The History of Great Britain: Being the Life and Reign of King James I.* London, 1653.

Wilson, Violet A. *Society Women of Shakespeare's Times.* London, 1924.

ACKNOWLEDGMENTS

I wish to thank all those who have contributed to the research and preparation for this book—especially the authors cited in the bibliography, and Columbia's Low Library, the Harvard Libraries, the New York Public Library, the Bodleian Library, and the British Museum. My gratitude also to my students and research assistants, Miriam Weisfeld and Sarah Wallace, to Tali Gai and Ariane Barbanell in the ART office, and to Keith Condon, William Frucht, and Dan Heaton at Yale University Press. I have also received generous support from the Clark Fund at Harvard.

INDEX